Masculinity and Syrian Fiction

Masculinity and Syrian Fiction

Gender, Society and the Female Gaze

Lovisa Berg

I.B.TAURIS
LONDON • NEW YORK • OXFORD • NEW DELHI • SYDNEY

I.B. TAURIS
Bloomsbury Publishing Plc
50 Bedford Square, London, WC1B 3DP, UK
1385 Broadway, New York, NY 10018, USA
29 Earlsfort Terrace, Dublin 2, Ireland

BLOOMSBURY, I.B. TAURIS and the I.B. Tauris logo are trademarks of Bloomsbury Publishing Plc

First published in Great Britain 2022
This paperback edition published 2022

Series design by Adriana Brioso
Cover image: Damascus, Syria. (© CJ Clarke/Panos Pictures)

A catalogue record for this book is available from the British Library.

A catalog record for this book is available from the Library of Congress.

ISBN: HB: 978-0-7556-3762-1
PB: 978-0-7556-3766-9
ePDF: 978-0-7556-3763-8
eBook: 978-0-7556-3764-5

Early and Medieval Islamic World

Typeset by RefineCatch Limited, Bungay, Suffolk

To find out more about our authors and books visit www.bloomsbury.com and sign up for our newsletters.

Contents

Acknowledgements		vi
Note on Transliteration		vii
List of Novels Discussed		viii
Introduction		1
1	Dream Masculinity – or the Male as a Vehicle for Self-Realisation	19
2	Politcally and Ideologically Influenced Masculinities	51
3	Changing Masculinity – a Transformation from Solution to Problem	75
4	Masculinity – a Demanding Role to Play	95
5	Female Masculinity and Male Femininity – the Exploration of Gender Formulation	127
Conclusion		159
Notes		167
Bibliography		187
Bibliographical Appendix		205
Index		209

Acknowledgements

This book is an edited and revised version of my PhD thesis submitted in 2017 at the University of Edinburgh. I am grateful to my supervisors, Dr Nacim Pak-Shiraz and Dr Thomas Pierret for their guidance during the work with my thesis and to my examiners Professor Paul Starkey and Professor Jaakko Hameen-Anttila for their insightful comments on my work.

The completion of my PhD and later this book would not have been possible without the constant support of my parents, Lis and Nils Gustav, and my sister Clara, who always believed there would be a book.

Note on Transliteration and Translation

I have followed the system of the *International Journal of Middle East Studies* (IJMES) for the transliteration of Arabic, including the omission of the initial hamza', hence *ukht* (أُخْت) instead of *'ukht*. When the name of an Arabic author, critic or character is first mentioned it is transliterated. After the initial mentioning either an English version of their names Klīr (Claire) or a transliterated version without diacritical marks, for example Maysūn (Maysun) will be used. For writers and critics who publish in English I have used their preferred way of spelling their names. Contrary to IJMES, I have transliterated titles of books and articles and names of organisations. In the case of place names, the common English spelling is used, unless the name is part of a book title. For the titles of the novels discussed I give the original titles in transliteration the first time the work is mentioned and then the English translation is used for ease of reference. All translations from Arabic and Swedish into English are my own, unless otherwise stated.

List of Novels Discussed

1959, *Ayyām ma'ahu* (*Days with Him*) by Kūlīt Khūrī.

1961, *Layla wāḥida* (*One Night*) by Kūlīt Khūrī.

1961, *Thulūj taḥta al-shams* (*Snow under the Sun*) by Laylā al-Yāfī.

1963, *al-Ḥubb wa al-waḥl* (*Love and Mud*) by In'ām al-Musālima.

1965, *'Aynān min ishbīliya* (*Sevillan Eyes*) by Salmā al-Ḥaffār al-Kuzbarī.

1968, *al-Riwāya al-mal'ūna* (*The Cursed Novel*) by Amal Jarrāḥ.

1973, *Arṣifat al-sa'm* (*Sidewalks of Tedium*) by Hiyām Nuwaylātī and Umm 'Isām.

1975, *Bayrūt 75* (*Beirut 75*) by Ghāda al-Sammān.

1976, *Kawābīs Bayrūt* (*Beirut Nightmares*) by Ghāda al-Sammān.

1977, *Bustān al-karaz* (*The Cherry Orchard*) by Qamar Kilānī.

1979, *al-Waṭan fī al-'aynayn* (*The Homeland in a Pair of Eyes*) by Ḥamīda Na'na'.

1980, *Dimashq yā basmat al-ḥuzn* (*Damascus, O Smile of Sadness*) by Ulfat al-Idlibī.

1983, *al-Dawwāma* (*The Whirlwind*) by Qamar Kilānī.

1984, *Khaṭawāt fī al-ḍabāb* (*Steps in the Fog*) by Malāḥa al-Khānī.

1985, *Imra'a fī dā'irat al-khawf* (*Woman in a Circle of Fear*) by Ḍiyā' Qaṣabjī.

1986, *Shams khalfa al-ḍabāb* (*A Sun Behind the Fog*) by Nawāl Taqī al-Dīn.

1989, *Man yajru' 'alā al-shawq* (*Who Dares to Long*) by Ḥamīda Na'na'.

1990, *Ḥikāyat jaddī* (*My Grandfather's Tale*) by Ulfat al-Idlibī.

1993, *Harwala fawqa ṣaqī' tūlīdū* (*Hurrying over the Frost of Toledo*) by Mārī Rashū.

1994, *Yawmiyyāt muṭalliqa* (*Diaries of a Divorcing Woman*) by Haifā' Bīṭār.

1995, *Qabw al-'abbāsīn,* (*The Abbaseen Basement*) by Haifā' Bīṭār.

1995, *Ḥubb fī bilād al-shām* (*Love in the Levant*) by Nādyā Khūst.

1997, *al-Na'na' al-barrī* (*Wild Mint*) by Anīsa 'Abbūd.

1997, *al-Tawq* (*Longing*) by Umayma al-Khush.

1997, *al-Riwāya al-mustaḥīla: fusayfusā' dimashqiyya* (*The Impossible Novel: A Damascene Mosaic*) by Ghāda al-Sammān.

1998, *al-Ẓahr al-'ārī* (*The Naked Back*) by Hanrīyit 'Abbūdī.

1998, *Afrāḥ ṣaghīra afrāḥ akhīra* (*Small Joys, Final Joys*) by Haifā' Bīṭār.

1998, *Banāt ḥāratina* (*The Girls of Our Neighbourhood*) by Malāḥa al-Khānī.

1998, *A'āṣīr fī bilād al-shām* (*Cyclones in the Levant*) by Nadya Khūst.

1998, *Furāt* (*Euphrates*) by Mayya al-Raḥbī.

1999, *Nasr bi-janāḥ waḥīd* (*A One-Winged Eagle*) by Haifā' Bīṭār.

2000, *Shajarat al-ḥubb – ghābat al-aḥzān* (*Tree of Love – Forest of Sadness*) by Usayma Darwīsh.

2000, *Shuhadā´ wa 'ushshāq fī bilād al-shām* (*Martyrs and Lovers in the Levant*) by Nadya Khūst.

2000, *Ṣabāḥ Imra'a* (*A Woman's Morning*) by Ghāliya Qabbānī.

Introduction

المرأةُ يا بناتي، هي التي تصنع الرجال.[1]

Woman, my girls, is the one who makes men.

The above quote is part of a lecture given to a group of female students in the novel *Dimashq yā basmat al-ḥuzn* (*Damascus, O Smile of Sadness, 1980*) by Ulfat al-Idlibī. In the context of the novel, the statement can be read as a reflection on the students' future roles as mothers and teachers but, in a wider context, it can be taken to emphasise the collective formulation of gender roles. On yet another level, it is an example of how fictional characters can be used as ways of engaging with society, here through the authority of the male teacher and the message he delivers to his students. The quote further describes exactly what the female authors discussed in this book have done, they have 'made men'. Although fictional, they have created men who are loved, hated, looked up to, despised, respected, feared and humiliated. Men who are presented as lifebuoys for the female characters and men who are seen as their biggest obstacles in the search for a happy life.

The various male characters appearing in the novels analysed here do not at first sight present a unified performance of masculinity; their attempts at carrying out masculinity are also evaluated differently depending on their individual circumstances. This disparity in the performance of masculinity is part of what this book will explore, namely the creation and usage of literary masculinities in Syrian female authors' work during the second half of the twentieth century. The masculinities that exist in the novels will be examined on the same premises as the quote above, ie as examples of how, in this case fictional, societies form gender and how fiction relates to society. Through the analyses of various novels, the book looks at how literary masculinities are formulated in relation to both the masculine ideals and the female characters of each fictional society. Moreover, it analyses the function of masculinity creation in women's texts. Is masculinity defined as the monstrous side of man hindering women from developing themselves? Or is masculinity rather a definition of the best possible characteristics to be found in a man? Or maybe there is no such thing as a unified idea of what and how masculinity appears and is used in the novels examined?

Masculinity Studies and Arabic Literature

The use of literature as a basis for research on gender formation is not a new topic in the study of Arab women's fiction. However, most of the existing research has focused on the development and formation of female characters whilst the male characters, by and large, are seen as 'walk-ons' or extras. They are necessary for the plot, but not interesting for analytical purposes or as part of a theoretically informed discussion. This characterisation of the academic literature is not intended as a critique of previous academic work, much of which this book is indebted to, but rather a suggestion that there is a gap in the research – that of how women's novels depict the male characters' development and their negotiations with patriarchy and gender roles. A gap which, if addressed, not only informs about the treatment and formation of male characters but also expands the knowledge of the female characters as participants in a gender matrix, rather than being seen as separate and independent. Whereas masculinity studies have not been applied exclusively to Arab women's fiction before, there are previous studies of literary formulations of masculinity in the Arab world, most notably Samira Aghacy's seminal work *Masculine Identity in the Fiction of the Arab East since 1967* and Hoda Elsadda's *Gender, Nation and the Arabic Novel: Egypt 1892–2008*. With regard to Syria, Maysūn al-Jurf published *Binā' ṣūrat al-shakhṣiyya al-dhukūriyya fī al-riwāya al-'arabiyya al-sūriyya* (*Building the Image of the Masculine Character in the Arabic Syrian Novel*) in 2014, in which she examined the image of the male in Syrian fiction from the 1990s.

Taking the cue from the above-mentioned studies, this book aims to examine the formulation of masculinity in the novels studied, highlight the gender relations within the novels and show the relativity between masculinity and femininity. The book further accentuates the way female and male characters are used by the authors to create the novels' gender regimes. In an article on literature and masculinity, Alex Hobbs identifies the phenomenon of male exclusion from the analysis of gender as a 'partial blindness' where '[m]en become invisible due to being overly visible'.[2] However, masculinity studies in general, and this book in particular, is not a way to rectify this 'partial blindness' by excluding females or femininity from the analyses, or retaining a patriarchal domination by linking masculinity to power and thereby, as a result, negating any chances of women ever gaining power, as some critics have suggested,[3] nor is it a way of finding acceptance for what are seen as negative performances of masculinity.[4] Instead, masculinity studies, as used in this book, are an investigation into how masculinities are formulated, how they relate to male and female characters, and how they change between novels and over time. Sarah Frantz and Katharina Rennhak write in their introduction to *Women Constructing Men* that '[i]n fact, the male characters of female novelists represent the authors' negotiations with the ideologies of gender, class, and sexuality as much as their female characters'.[5] Taking this further, especially if one chooses to see gender as constructed through interaction with others, it becomes important to acknowledge that all characters are vital to the understanding of a novel's gender dynamics. In order to examine the gender dynamics of the novels and their bearing on masculinity, tools formulated by female narratology are used, particularly in relation to focalisation and character formation.

Literary masculinity studies has its origin in men's studies which, in turn, builds on and owes many of the theoretical models used to feminist research.[6] This has led to multiple ways of approaching masculinity in literature. In this book, I will build on the work of, among others, Raewyn Connell, Michael Kimmel and Keith Pringle, who argue that the theory of men's studies is an engagement with the system of patriarchy and its impact on males and their relations with each other. The initial motivator for this group of researchers was to negate the singularity of masculinity and instead, as Henry Brod and Michael Kaufman state: '[e]mphasize the plurality and diversity of men's experiences, attitudes, beliefs, situations, practices and institutions [. . .]'.[7] This strand of masculinity studies is closely connected to Judith Butler's work on the performativity of gender.[8] Connell, for example, states that gender is: '[t]he structure of social relations that centres on the reproductive arena, and the set of practices that bring reproductive distinctions between bodies into social processes'.[9] As such, masculinity is considered a socially constructed phenomena and a role that can be performed more or less well.

To bring the concept of masculinity studies to the analysis of novels means that the novels are seen as separate spheres that present an idea of male and female gender. It further means that the books use textual evidence and close reading, in conversation with the theory of masculinity studies, in order to discuss the formulation of gender and the practice of masculinity. The viewpoint adopted for the close reading is borrowed from aspects of feminist narratology as developed by, among others, Robyn Warhol, Susan Lanser and Ruth Page.[10] By choosing this starting point, the focus of the analysis will try to answer the question: '[H]ow does this text construct masculinity or femininity in and for its reader?'[11] It will not concern itself with the author of the text in the examination of the masculinities formed and the way(s) they can be interpreted and function in the texts. The focus on how gender is presented will build up to a discussion of hegemonic masculinity and variations thereof in the novels, as seen through the characters' actions. This, in turn, means that the book will look at '[h]ow gender is produced through narrative processes, not prior to them',[12] as Sally Robinson explains feminist narratology. In contrast to classical narratology, which does not concern itself with how gender, sex and sexuality play a role in the construction and interpretation of narrative texts, feminist narratology argues that these three aspects are central to the understanding of a narrative.[13]

The analysis of masculinities in the novels will rest on the following assumptions: (a) male and female characters jointly construct masculinity in the (fictional) societies discussed; (b) the perception of masculinity varies according to, among other things, context and place; and (c) The approval of others rather than the actions of an individual determine the value of a performance of masculinity. The content of the novels and the literary masculinities are examined using a version of RW Connell's theory of hegemonic masculinity developed in her seminal book *Masculinities.*[14] The theory of hegemonic masculinity presents a model where emphasis is put on the plurality of masculinities and their internal negotiations for power, in addition to relations between men and women. Connell modelled her theory on Gramsci's explanation of hegemony, arguing that the power certain performances of masculinity generate are shaped through others' acceptance and acknowledgment of it, rather than out of fear.[15] As a starting point, Connell argues that hegemonic masculinity is:

> [t]he configuration of gender practice which embodies the currently accepted answer to the problem of the legitimacy of patriarchy, which guarantees (or is taken to guarantee) the dominant position of men and the subordination of women.[16]

Connell further stresses the binary opposition between femininity and masculinity. This is of particular interest to this book since, in a majority of the novels, the voices of female characters filter the understanding of the masculinities presented. It is through the female characters' perception that masculinity is understood and, to some extent, evaluated.

To use masculinity studies and Connell's theory of hegemonic masculinity as a framework for analysis of Syrian novels requires some adaption. The theory was developed in the West, more precisely in Australia, and will here be used in an Eastern setting. As has been shown by, among others, Lila Abu-Lughod in connection with feminism and the Middle East, to impose theories developed in one part of the world on others with different cultural ideas, can be seen as problematic and might lead to imprecise results, especially in studies where cultural understanding is a major part.[17] Since Connell's structure rests on the assumption that hegemonic masculinity differs from time to time and place to place I believe that the framework of masculinity studies is adaptable enough to allow for these cultural differences. The theoretical framework, in itself, does not suppose any particular characteristics in hegemonic masculinity. On the contrary, Connell states that:

> [h]egemonic masculinity is not a fixed character type, always and everywhere the same. It is rather the masculinity that occupies the hegemonic position in a given pattern of gender relations, a position always contestable.[18]

The hegemonic masculinity that was dominant in 1950s society might very well be seen and treated as a subordinate masculinity in the same society in 2021. It further means that in a country where the segregation between city and countryside is substantial, there are varying hegemonies of masculinity depending on where one lives. Thus, even though the outer structure of the theory and the dynamic relations between levels of masculinity can be applied to various ages, places and cultures, what defines each masculinity and distinguishes it, is unique to the individual setting. Connell's theory is modelled on a patriarchal society where male relations uphold and create power, a scenario that is repeatedly seen in analytical work on the Middle East and Syria and a structure that is also clear in the novels analysed.

When literary masculinity studies first emerged, the focus was on male authors' fictional works but has then moved on to cover both men and women. An example of this with regard to Arabic novels is Jūrj Ṭarābīshī's (George Tarabishi) *Sharq gharb rujūla unūtha* (East West Masculinity Femininity) from 1977, where he analyses how Arab (male) writers relate to Western cities and countries in their novels and explores that in relation to male identity politics. I have chosen instead to focus on women writers in order to examine the portrayal of 'the other's other' as Naomi Schor has characterised women's creative constructions of men.[19] I have done this because women's construction of male characters and masculinity offers an opportunity to both support and subvert existing gender patterns, in addition to formulating new ways of performing masculinity. As Stefan Horlacher points out, the fictional masculinities of films and literature are normative and influence what a certain culture sees as masculine behaviour.[20] Although this often means a reinforcement of already accepted ideals and norms, it potentially gives literature and visual media an enormous power to introduce a versatility of masculinities. In an article on female literary criticism in Syria, Samar al-Duyūb, for example, argues that the novel is the one place where women can overthrow the power of the virile man and re-organise society,[21] a possibility less likely in other, non-fictional, situations. Similarly, Peter F Murphy maintains that literature can both reinforce assumptions about masculinity and, at the same time, offer 'other images, other roles, other options for men and masculinity'.[22] Taking this as a starting point, this book will look at how the novels examined have served as an arena in which women writers can explore concepts of masculinity and the impact they could have on women, children and society.

Though literary and hence already 'created' the book focuses on how the characters, male and female, together create and/or undermine the novels' hegemonic masculinity. The complexity of gender construction and how class, education and regional backgrounds, among other factors, play a part in how certain masculinities are received and formulated, is shown by analysing the novels as units. In order to avoid adding external values to the novels analysed, with the exception of masculinity studies from the area, I argue that the rules and norms of these fictional societies must be the scaffolding on which the characters are discussed. The term 'fictional societies' is borrowed from Samar Rūḥī al-Fayṣal,[23] who uses the term to separate the political ideas of real life from those that appear in the novels he analyses. Fictional societies can thus be situated within real cities and, through the social realism used, can be seen as images of reality. Nevertheless, in order not to claim that truth is fiction and fiction is truth, real society and the fictional society are dealt with separately. By considering the novels as fictional societies, the analyses can be concentrated on how masculinity is constructed within a specific novel. At the same time, the novels' shared connection to Syrian society can be used for comparisons throughout the analysis.

Whereas the male fictional characters cannot be taken as a statement of truth about masculinity, it is at the same time not possible to argue that there is a firm division between literature and the society it is written in. As Evelyn Accad points out, an author offers an image of their society, which builds on a tension between individual and collective imagination and adds complexities and subtleties not found in more scientific documents.[24] Like media stories and films, novels both represent and, at the same time, participate in, the shaping of ideas and reactions to various phenomena. Stefan Horlacher elaborates on this and states that fictional masculinities have a '[p]erformative function, allowing for new subject positions, since novels function as machines of cultural reproduction'.[25] In his book on masculinities in American film, Brian Baker tackles the same question but through an analysis of the relationship between American movies and American society. His conclusion is that:

> [t]hese popular fictions and films negotiate, or more properly renegotiate, forms of masculinity that express something about the cultural, social and political formations of their period of production and taken together form a kind of loose history of both representations of masculinity in Anglo-American texts and in the postwar period as a whole.[26]

Correspondingly, the masculinities constructed in the selection of novels discussed in this book can be seen as the individual views of the specific writers. At the same time, when read together, they give an idea of values and ideals during specific periods and they further show how these ideals are shaped and negotiated.

Though acknowledging that a homosocial environment, as put forward by Michael Kimmel,[27] is an important factor in the shaping of gender identities, especially in societies where gender segregation is practiced, I agree with, among others, Marie Nordberg[28] and Farah Ghannam,[29] who have shown that women through their roles as mothers, sisters, grandmothers, wives, friends and girlfriends exert great influence over the formation of masculinity. In the novels discussed in this book, the majority of the male characters are described as formulating their masculinity in contrast to, or together with, a female character. The changing representation of masculinity that appears in the analysis is therefore both created by women and reflected through and shaped by female characters.

Writing in a Gender Regime

Although all the novels examined are written by female writers, it does not mean that all the authors will bring the same values and ideas to their texts. Except for being identified as women there might not be many similarities between them. Class, education, religion and political views, among other things, will play a part in how these women see the world and choose to present it in their novels. However, apart from these diversities, the authors discussed all live and write (or lived and wrote) in a patriarchal society and they are/were active in a region where religion plays a formative part in society and where it is possible to talk about a 'gender regime'. This term is borrowed from Chris Haywood and Martin Mac an Ghail and used to refer to the institutionally dominant arrangement of gender relations where laws and social structures enforce a difference in gender roles.[30] A gender regime does not necessarily favour men over women, or women over men, it merely outlines differences in obligations and rights between the sexes. However, when the gender regime is built on patriarchal value systems, it solidifies men's dominant position over women. The 'patriarchal gender regime' thus creates a subordinated position for women and the viewpoint their novels are studied from is hence the subordinate's view of the subordinator. This initial positioning in relation to power makes it interesting to see how women construct masculinity. Whether the female characters feel hindered or supported by the patriarchal gender regime, they must work either within it or around it. The different masculinities formulated by the female writers reflect how certain types of gendered behaviour are promoted or demoted. They further function as an engagement with varieties of masculinities and their impact on the female characters' lives.

The analysis of masculinities and their usage in the novels demonstrate women writers' roles in the maintenance, or possibly undermining, of certain ways of performing masculinity. In their book *Kvinnorna gör mannen* (*Women Make the Man*) on the female construction of masculinity in literature, art and film, Kristina Fjelkestam, Helena Hill and David Tjeder argue that:

> [w]omen's views on and constructions of men and masculinity have had an impact on many different fields. In a considerable way they enlighten how patriarchal structures have been reproduced, reformulated and undermined. They contribute to research on women's active re-creation of their own subordination and, at the same time, the research on how women have challenged patriarchal structures, and through that challenge contributed, with sharp critique on men and masculinity, to re-shape the existing power structures in society in the long run.[31]

In their novels, women writers have the possibility to form and promote masculinities they appreciate, but they also have the power to 'punish' masculinities they do not champion. The fact that hegemonic masculinity works like a role model for how men could (and should) act makes literary attempts at formulating and engaging with masculinity an invaluable platform for experimental and alternative masculinities.

Women's construction of masculinity is, however, not always seen as unproblematic. In her ground-breaking study on British female writers, Elaine Showalter shows how pioneering women writers were often critiqued for their unrealistic heroes, who were either considered too good or too bad to be true.[32] Showalter reports that this was explained by male critics and, in some cases, by the writers themselves, as a result of their lack of life experience, in addition to an inability to understand the male psyche.[33] Correspondingly, Ḥusām al-Khaṭīb argues in relation to Syrian writers that, whereas women [only] can be understood in men's fiction, women are unable to construct realistic male protagonists.[34] Maysun al-Jurf voices similar criticism and argues that women writers in Syria produce either brutes or feminised male characters and cannot formulate deep psychological portraits of men.[35] Muḥammad Qarānayā raises the same point in a critical essay on the Syrian writer Nadya Khūst's characters, where he points out that the main male character comes across as a fantasy rather than a real man.[36] For the purpose of this book, I am not interested in examining the level of truthfulness, or closeness to reality, regarding the male characters presented. On the contrary, I hold the view that even though literature is a reflection *on* the society it is written in, it is not necessarily a reflection *of* it. Regardless of whether the male characters presented in the novels have 'real' counterparts, they still represent the masculinities hoped for, critiqued and created by Syrian female writers and, as such, offer their perspectives on both gender relations and society. The fact that critics disagree with the formulations of masculinity found in the novels strengthens the argument that some of the characters created transgress the expected gendered behaviour and, as such, provide ideas on new ways of performing masculinity.

The Syrian Literary Scene

In studies on the Middle East there is always the choice of working with the whole region or parts of it. If one limits the discussion to literature, there are valid arguments for both choices. Arabic literature is often treated as one whole entity, both in Western and Arab literary studies, due to the many shared characteristics in the development of the genre. It is impossible to overlook the fact that literary magazines,[37] collective movements (such as pan-Arabism) and major political events (like the war in 1967) have influenced the general trends of literature in the Arab world. At the same time, it is as difficult to disregard that political and cultural factors such as the Lebanese civil war, the Algerian war for independence, the oil wealth in the Gulf countries, the different religious establishments, views on women's rights and state socialism have distinctly shaped the national literatures of the different Arab countries. In a discussion on the relationship between fictional texts and their origins, Yumnā al-ʻĪd argues that as early as 1916, after the Sykes-Picot agreement, the 'new' countries' literatures started to take shape and individual factors became more important than the shared literary heritage.[38] Since this book is concerned with the performance of masculinity, which is closely connected to customs, traditions and social changes,[39] the choice of one country rather than many has been made.

The choice of one country, though not necessarily representing a homogenous masculinity, still presents masculinities constructed within a national framework. This choice finds support in a study by Hartmut Fähndrich, in which he shows variations between the Arab East and the Arab West in men's autobiographical work and their approaches to family issues.[40] He means that the outer political and regional changes affect how internal family relations are perceived and described in fiction. A similar trend is noted by al-Khatib, who demonstrates that in the novels produced before 1976, when his article was published, Syrian female writers were less open in their description of sexual encounters and less outspoken in their social critique in comparison with their Lebanese and Egyptian colleagues.[41] This leads me to believe that masculinities in Syrian female-authored fiction also differed, at least in this period.

Though relatively unknown outside the borders of Syria, with the exception of the works of a few writers, the literary milieu inside the country has seen a growing number of novelists, short story writers, dramatists and poets, in addition to literary critics, during the last half of the twentieth century. Literary journals and the literary supplements of the daily newspapers bear witness to a vivid and active literary scene, well in tune with contemporary international literary issues, whilst at the same time engaged in national literary production. Since Syria's independence in 1946, literature has played an important part in the project of nation formation, both through state-controlled initiatives[42] and on an individual level. The state, which recognises the power of literature, runs journals, pays stipends to writers and publishes literary works. However, this involvement also results in a strict control of what is published, by whom and where, in an arbitrary way.[43] Despite the state's involvement, or maybe because of it, individual writers and poets have seen and used literature as a way of engaging with social and political issues, with varying degrees of openness. This trend is not specific to Syria, but can be seen in the whole of the Levant, as noted by Samira Aghacy.[44]

She further states that writers and critics engage with their societies through written texts and thus, in a subversive way, challenge or support their different social establishments.[45] Thus, the general literary atmosphere in Syria since the 1950s and through the final part of the twentieth century, can be summarised as 'writing for a cause' whether political or social.[46]

Another reason to engage with the Syrian literary scene is that it has, to some extent, been its own closed universe. 'Adnān bin Dhurayl describes how, at an early stage, Syrian writers made a point of using the local environment in their novels,[47] making cultural and political references national rather than international, hence contributing to the idea of a nationally committed literature. As the critic Fayṣal Summāq concludes, this means that is difficult to use the term 'realism', in its wider meaning, to describe Syrian writing, since it is so formed by its own cultural and political life that it bears no resemblance to 'realism' in other countries.[48] An analysis of Syrian literature might, therefore, offer new insights into the cultural and literary scene of the country. These are, of course, valid for male as well as female writers. As discussed above, the choice of female writers is connected to their position in society and the fact that the Ba'th party, since it came into power in 1963, has engaged in a rhetoric of equality and women's participation in society.[49] Changing gender roles has thus been a state policy and women's interaction with this policy, through literature, gives another dimension to historical events.

In the 1950s, Syria saw the formation of the Syrian Writers' Collective, later to be transformed into the Arab Writers' Union, and literature began to be treated as an important foundation for cultural and political change. The novel, though previously attempted by male and female writers, became increasingly popular during this period.[50] Concentrating only on women's novels, the Syrian Ministry of Culture states that the number of novels published by women writers between 1959 and 2000 was 95, with an increase from two novels in the 1950s to 42 in the 1990s.[51] These figures have to be considered estimates since not all novels seem to be counted in this statistical overview, but regardless, the numbers provide evidence of the growing popularity of the novel among women writers in Syria after a somewhat hesitant beginning. Many of these novels are of a political and social nature. In a study on the development of the Syrian novel from 1985, al-Faysal states that:

> The traditional Arabic novel has [. . .] taken on a social and political function in Arab life. Because of that, Arab writers have been attached to, and stay attached to, this form, since they see it as useful for their societies and nations.[52]

This does not mean that the Syrian novel has not changed or developed during the twentieth century. On the contrary, in his study, al-Faysal points at new methods of character composition and other technical changes, but he means that the Core issues examined in the novels remain political and educational, despite structural changes. Among the writers included in this study, this political and educational desire can be seen, for example, in *Thulūj taḥta al-shams* (*Snow under the Sun*, 1961) by Laylā al-Yāfī. The heroine of the novel, who is on holiday in Cairo with her adoptive parents, suddenly finds herself in the midst of the Suez crisis, takes up arms and fights side-by-side with the Egyptians. The novel's main theme, the education and fostering of a young woman, is disrupted for a few pages to give an example of a political sacrifice. However, after this section, the novel does not touch upon the topic again and the main character does not seem to have gained anything from her experience, thus making the whole section seem more of a political stand from the author than a clear part of the plot. Another political event which had a great impact on Syria is the Lebanese civil war, which has most famously been dealt with by Ghāda al-Sammān in her novel *Kawābīs Bayrūt* (*Beirut Nightmares*, 1976) where the fragmented style of narration, and the daily struggles of the narrator living in Beirut, give a vivid description of the atrocities of the civil war. Other writers, such as Qamar Kilānī, have also written on the subject. In *Bustān al-karaz* (*The Cherry Orchard*, 1977), the Syrian army, though not at the centre of the narration, is portrayed as a liberator by the main character, in what must be seen as an obvious political statement. Ḥamīda Naʿnaʿ has instead dealt with the question of Palestine and freedom fighters in her two novels *al-Waṭan fī al-ʿaynayn* (*The Homeland in a Pair of Eyes*, 1979) and *Man yajru' ʿalā al-shawq* (*Who Dares to Long*, 1989). In both her novels she examines the relationship between these fighters and their countries on one hand, and the greater pan-Arabic struggles on the other; it becomes clear that the line between celebrated hero and political migrant is very fine. These examples show that Syrian women writers are and were engaged with political history at both a national and regional level during the 1960s and 1970s. Later examples of engagement with political and social issues include Ghāliya Qabbānī's novel *Ṣabāḥ Imraʾa* (*A Woman's Morning*, 2000) on the Iraqi invasion of Kuwait and Nadya Khust's trilogy about Syria at the beginning of the twentieth century. The trilogy was published at the turn of the twenty-first century with the double aim of explaining the area's history and working for the preservation of the older parts of Damascus.[53] Many have written about the topics of social inequality and women's rights, for example Kūlīt Khūrī (Colette Khory), Haifaʾ Biṭār and Ulfat al-Idlibi. The writers' engagement can be guessed at from the topics of their novels, but is strengthened through interviews and their other work, where they state that writing is their way of making women's voices heard in society.[54] Gender relations, a fundamental part of the construction of a society, shown in the division of labour, opportunities for education and religious obligations, are naturally reflected in the texts and give an insight to how these women see, and would like to see, the organisation of their societies.

The Syrian novel's close connection to the political movements in the country is further asserted in *The Experimental Arabic Novel*.[55] This is also something the critic Nabīl Sulaymān has shown, together with co-author Bū Ali Yāsīn, in the study *al-Adab wa al-idiūlūjiyya fī sūriyā* (Literature and ideology in Syria).[56] Sulayman and Yasin categorise novelists into different political constituents depending on the topics and styles of their novels. The authors seem to be strongly in favour of Marxist and socialist ideas and novels that they deem to be in this category receive greater praise than others. This categorisation is not unique to their study nor is their bias towards this type of novel which, for most of the second half of the twentieth century, has been seen as the model style in Syria, by critics and writers alike. Marxist, and later Ba'athist, socialist ideas have favoured social realism as a genre and this was the dominant literary style in Syria from the 1950s until the late 1990s.[57] Novels by male writers Ḥannā Mīna and Hānī al-Rāhib, masters of social realism, were, and still are, seen as the ideal style of writing.[58] However, a realism that dealt with the broader aspects of social change was preferred. Kamal Abu Deeb argues in *Jamāliyyāt al-tajāwur aw tashābuk al-faḍā'āt al-ibdā'iyya* (*The Aesthetics of Contiguity or the Interlacing of Creative Spaces*) that, until the end of the twentieth century, the prevailing themes in Arabic fiction were generally political while the private sphere and the individual voice were shunned.[59] This idea is developed by Alexa Firat, who demonstrates how literature was seen to be a field for political engagement and should hence concern itself with the 'problems of the masses' over individual development.[60] To diverge from this type of writing could be interpreted as a political stand against nationalism and socialism. Samira Aghacy maintains, for example, that towards the end of the 1960s, it was seen as unpatriotic and unmanly not to engage in politics while writing literary texts.[61] Abu Deeb further states that personal reflections and individual development were considered topics of the 'bourgeoisie' during the second half of the twentieth century,[62] a label authors concerned with social realism did not want.

'Bourgeoisie' is exactly what Nabil Sulayman calls the novels by the female writers Colette Khury, Hiyām Nuwaylātī and Salmā al-Ḥaffār al-Kuzbarī in his 1978 book *Ḥiwāriyyat al-wāqi' wa al-khiṭāb al-riwā'ī* (*The Conversational Nature of Reality and the Discourse of the Novel*). Though women writers themselves, as pointed out above, often see their work as socially committed and grounded in questions of equality and the distribution of power, their plots were (and are) often read as the individual life stories of the main female character. This, in turn, leads to the novels being interpreted as descriptions of the personal development of a single character, rather than offering a view on, for example, poverty in general. This might, to some extent, explain the secondary position of much of women's fiction within literary circles in Syria. Their work is not deemed to fit what is seen as the acceptable 'standard' for a novel and are therefore excluded from many critical works on Syrian literature.[63] This view is verified, for example, by the Syrian critics Husam al-Khatib and Aḥmad Jamīl al-Ḥasan, who see Syrian women's fiction as largely self-biographical, self-centred and far from the ideological debates. al-Khatib argues in three articles published in the 1970s that it is difficult to distinguish the author's own voice from the fiction she is producing, which in turn leads to what he sees as a lack of quality.[64] Thirty-six years later, al-Hasan makes the same claim about women's literature in Syria, stating that it is very rare that a female writer's main character does not borrow traits from her own personal life.[65]

Through comparisons between plots and the writers' personal lives, it is indisputable that some of the female-authored novels indeed borrow from reality.[66] That being said, the use of the personal does not need to be interpreted as a wish to ignore the greater political landscape. Critics such as Buthaina Shaaban and 'Āṭifa Fayṣal argue, instead, that it is precisely by using personal stories, rather than general movements, that Syrian women's fiction deals with the political. They assert that female writers analyse relationships between men and women and between society and individuals, in their fiction,[67] an argument that this book further develops in its analyses of the individual novels. The critic Imān al-Qāḍī, moreover, demonstrates how major events such as the October war in 1967 and the Lebanese civil war have influenced a number of Syrian female writers.[68] The personal and intimate narratives, which have been interpreted as a lack of skill and ability in women's writing, can instead be seen as a way of contesting the hegemony of male writing. In an article on ideology and literature, Abu Deeb concludes that the connection between dominant political thought and central trends in literature is clear. At the same time, he demonstrates how it is the fiction which does not conform, and which offers the literary scene new voices, which stands for the force of change.[69] In this light, the female-authored novels can be read as alternative voices, both stylistically and based on the content. The amalgamation between personal and general, private and political, in addition to the wish for provoking a change, makes the creation of masculinity in these female writers' novels a reflection of society through the looking glass of their characters.

Even though one genre, that of realism, has been the dominant influence since the 1950s, this does not mean that other styles and genres have been non-existent. In her article on Syrian writers, Firat shows that although the hegemony of social realism was strong during the twentieth century, other voices with different interpretations were not stifled. She provides further examples of critical debates within the genre and about its foundations, in addition to comparisons with other styles and genres.[70] Despite not conforming to the prevalent form, women writers were thus not excluded from the literary scene and female critics and writers were active in the ongoing debates. This is demonstrated by the critic and writer Widād Sakākīnī, herself a pioneering novelist and short story writer, who disputed the first of the three articles by al-Khatib on women's writing in a later issue of the same journal. She argued that he, along with other critics, had overlooked the literary aspects of the female-authored novel and treated it as a personal diary.[71] Her reply illustrates both a different view on women's writing and the participation of women in the literary debate.

Many female writers have been active within more than one field of literature; the short story is a popular genre for women writers in Syria. However, this book only examines the creation of masculinity in novels. Many writers state that they move between genres depending on the topic on which they are writing. In a study of the status of women, Roger Allen notes that the short story, from its beginning, has explored the particular, while alluding to the wider implications of a theme often developed in the novel.[72] Two Syrian writers, who have written both short stories and novels, say the following on the difference between the genres. Salma al-Haffar al-Kuzbari:

> There is a huge difference between the two. While the first [the short story] pictures a specific happening or a specific psychological state in a limited artistic frame the second [the novel] comprises a wide phase, like a phase in life.[73]

Colette Khury makes a similar comment when she says that the short story is equivalent to a snapshot, whereas the novel is equivalent to life.[74] These comments agree not only with the two writers' own literary production, but also with women's writing in general in Syria, as well as Allen's comment quoted above. Whereas the performance of masculinity indeed can be both personal and particular and explored in a short story, the focus of this book is on the formation of masculinity, thus concentrating on novels permits the characters to develop, change and interact to a greater extent than what is possible in a short story. The engagement with political and social developments exemplified above, though evident in other literary forms, is also especially prominent in the novel. This is demonstrated in detail by Jābir 'Usfūr in his book *Zaman al-riwāya* (*The Time of the Novel*),[75] in which he argues that the novel has now become the most significant literary form in the Arab world. Atifa Faysal further claims that in Syria, women's engagement for equal rights and women's emancipation, were particularly evident in the genre of the novel,[76] which makes this genre interesting with regard to masculinity creation and a fictional gender matrix.

The choice of individual authors and novels is closely connected to the period chosen for examination. Having defined the beginning and the end of the period, the selection of novels and novelists between 1959 and 2000 is based on several criteria. One condition has been appearance in the Syrian press and in Arab literary publications. The three literary journals *al-Mawqif al-adabī*,[77] *Fuṣūl*[78] and *al-Ma'rifa*[79] have been examined to see which writers have made an impact on Syrian and Arab literary life during the period studied. Through reviews, interviews, articles and the participation of authors in critical debates, these journals have offered a good view of the female authors considered influential during the second half of the twentieth century. The journals have, moreover, shown how female authors have been received in the literary world, both inside and outside Syria. The number of novels published by each author has not been considered a marker of their importance. Some writers, like Ulfat al- Idlibi and Hamida Na'na', made their names in other genres before publishing their novels, and, despite only publishing two novels each, are prominent figures in Syrian cultural life. Iman al-Qadi further notes that most Syrian female writers do not tend to publish more than one or two novels,[80] therefore writers like Qamar Kilani and Haifa Bitar, who have both published an extensive number of novels, are the exception rather than the rule. In the case of a writer such as Ghada al-Samman, who has published during the whole period covered, several novels have been chosen since they are seen to represent different eras of her writing or focus on a specific theme. Although gender formation as a social practice can be said to appear in all novels, some forefront gender issues or masculinity formation more than others; these novels have naturally been chosen for analysis. The selection process resulted in a list of 34 novels, written between 1959 and 2000, by 26 different authors.

The timeline, from what is seen as the first attempt at fiction writing by women in Syria until the present, is often separated into three sections. Rūla

Ḥassan divides the period with focus on the writers and calls them 'the Pioneers' (1940–1960) 'the Second Wave' (1960–1980) and 'the Third Wave' (1980–2010).[81] This division is then adapted to serve various purposes: Atifa Faysal renames the periods as 'Traditional Female Discourse', 'Romantic and Rebellious Female Discourse' and 'New Female Discourse'.[82] Focusing on the creation of masculinity in these periods, the division used here will be the 'Dream Man' for the first period between 1959 and 1970, the second period between 1970 and 1980 will be named 'the Political Man' and the third period, between 1980 and 2000, will be labelled 'Problematic Masculinity'.

Although I have just divided the masculinities into three categories I find it more fruitful to borrow Kamal Abu Deeb's concept of literary waves,[83] rather than talking of clear-cut periods, hence the years above should be seen as tentative markers for beginnings and ends rather than full stops. The advantage of a literary wave is that it allows trends to co-exist before a change takes place, which happens frequently in the novels analysed. It also shows the organic nature of fiction as a continuous development and a constant dialogue with the ideological climate in which the literature is produced, which for Syrian literature, often stated to be both realistic and politically committed, seems crucial. Furthermore, as Kifah Hanna points out, women writers from the Levant distinguish themselves through a continuation and linkage between the generations, which creates an innovative revolutionary literary heritage.[84] In the novels examined in this book, this plays out in a reusage of previously explored masculinities or novels that can be read as commentaries of previous generations' struggles with ideas on gender. For this reason, Chapters 1, 2 and 3 follow a chronological order where Chapter 1 explores the masculinities created by the pioneering writers in the 1950s and 1960s, Chapter 2 discusses the novels of the 1970s and Chapter 3 outlines the new themes and topics of the 1980s and 1990s, themes that are then followed up in Chapters 4 and 5.

Chapter 1 analyses how the writers use particular masculinities as ways of opening new possibilities for their main female characters, thus working for a change from within the patriarchal system. Chapter 2 examines novels from the 1970s and how women writers during this period created ideologically and politically coloured masculinities as ways of engaging with social changes in society. Chapter 3 deals with the time period after the 1980s and discusses the burdens of masculinity and how women writers have chosen to depict not the privileges certain masculinities entertain, but rather the strains connected with the role of hegemonic masculinity. Chapter 4 engages with the same time period but focuses on how women writers have investigated the formation of gender roles, both as created through the upbringing of children and through male and female characters who exhibit traits of gender fluidity. Chapter 5 looks at the father figure as a symbol for the change masculinity formation has undergone during the period studied and examines how portrayals of aggressive and oppressing masculinity can be seen as a third form of masculinity formulation after the 1980s.

1

Dream Masculinity – or the Male as a Vehicle for Self-Realisation

حلمتُ بحبيبٍ يمنحني كلَّ ما حرَمتْني الأيامُ[1]

I dreamt of a lover who would grant me all that life [the days] had denied me.

The first female-authored novel in the Arab world is said to be *Ḥusn al-ʿawāqib: Ghāda al-zahrā'* (*Good Consequences: Ghada the Radiant*) by Zaynab al-Fawwāz, published in 1899.[2] At the time, Lebanon and Syria were combined in Greater Syria and this could therefore be seen as the first Syrian female-authored novel. With that said, as stated in the introduction, it was only after the formation of the Syrian state in 1946 that literature and culture began to play an integral part in the formation of national identity. Therefore, only works produced after this date have been considered for inclusion in this book. After 1946, the first female-authored novels were written by Widād Sakākīnī and Salma al-Ḥaffār al-Kuzbarī.[3] Following these initial novels, published in a short time span, it took eight years until the next female-authored novel was published. It is this novel, Colette Khoury's *Ayyām maʿahu* (*Days with Him*) published in 1959, that begins the period studied in this book.

The choice to start with this novel is based on several reasons. According to Ḥusām al-Khatib, it was received very differently and much more favourably than previous female-authored novels.[4] This might be due to the fact that Sakakini's and al-Kuzbari's novels were, to some extent, seen as didactic and preaching in their tone. Khoury's novel can instead be seen as an exploration of a personal relationship. The publication of Khoury's novel, in addition to the Lebanese Laylā Baʿlabakkī's *Ana aḥyā* (*I Live*) published in 1958, meant a new style of writing and the beginning of a strong 'I' formulation in Arab women's fiction.[5] Correspondingly, Khalīl al-Mūsā argues that, in contrast to the few women writing novels before her, Khoury was the first Syrian woman writer to 'free herself from the male language'[6] and formulate a new, female, voice in her fiction. The voice that appears in the novel not only describes, but clearly states, what it wants regarding life in general and relationships in particular. Subhi Hadidi further defines the late 1950s as the time when women's literary production began to seriously take shape in Syria and he states that this period includes a 'qualitative leap' in women's writing.[7] Without taking a stand on the question of quality, the decision to start with Khoury means that the first novel to be discussed in this chapter was, to some extent, considered, and treated by its contemporaries as a novel in its own right and thus also paved the way for other novels written by women.[8]

The novels analysed in this chapter are from the 1950s and 1960s and are written by middle- or upper-class women. The plots are situated in different places of the world and the main characters go on holiday to Lebanon, Egypt and Paris or the setting of the novel is Spain. Whereas the places of narration are somewhat exotic and some of the novels include historical events of the era, at the core of the novels analysed in this period is the story of one woman's development and her personal exploration of what she wants from life. *Days with Him* (1959) tells the story of Rīm, a well-to-do Damascene girl, who lost her mother at a young age and then later also her father. Rather than moving in with her uncle, which is what she is expected to do by society, she decides to stay with her sister and their maid in the family home. Although she does not need the money, she looks for a job to have something to do. Rim is engaged to her cousin Alfrīd, but neither of them is particularly excited about the engagement, and when she meets Ziyād she embarks on a relationship with him instead. Rim feels trapped in her life and she believes that Ziyad will be her saviour, the one who can grant her the life of art, music and freedom she longs for. In *Layla wāḥida* (*One Night*, 1961) by the same author, the novel takes the form of a letter from Rashā to her husband Salīm. For a long time, Rasha refused all the suitors presented to her by her family, hoping that she would be allowed to study instead of marrying, but in the end, she gave in and agreed to marry Salim. While he is an exemplary husband, in terms of position and wealth, according to the hegemonic norms of the fictional society they live in, Rasha is not content with her life. The couple are childless and Rasha is made to believe that it is her fault. During a trip to Europe, she takes the train by herself to yet another appointment with a doctor. On the train she meets Kāmil. They talk and laugh during the train ride and later end up spending a night together in a hotel. After their night together, Rasha tragically dies in an accident. In *Thulūj taḥta al-shams* (*Snow Under the Sun*, 1961) by Laylā al-Yāfī, the main female character, Rīma, is an orphan who is adopted by a judge and his wife who have no children of their own. Her adoptive father insists that Rima should receive a complete education and, when she is old enough, he takes time off work so the family can travel together to different Arab countries, to allow Rima to get to know the region. During the trip, Rima falls in love with an unsuitable person but, rather than punishing her for this, her father talks to her and shows her why her choice is inappropriate. Despite Rima's mistake, her father later argues that she should be allowed to choose her husband. This time she chooses her cousin, a decision approved by both her parents. *al-Ḥubb wa al-waḥl* (*Love and Mud*, 1963) by In'ām al-Musālima is another novel from this era featuring a father who has progressive ideas on education for his daughter, Inās. However, the father dies relatively early, and the main male character of the novel is instead Aḥmad. As in *One Night*, this novel is told in the form of a long letter, in which Ahmad, who has fallen in love with Inas, explains to a friend what has happened to him. Inas is accustomed to being seen as someone different because she has chosen education and work over marriage and family life. When Ahmad approaches her, she falls in love with him since he is different from other men she has met. However, due to previous relationships she has had, she cannot allow herself to believe that he will continue to love her and hence she refuses to marry him. *'Aynān min ishbīliya* (*Sevillan Eyes*, 1965) by Salma al-Haffar al-Kuzbari, also describes the relationship between a father and his daughter Carmen and how he tries to bring her up without her mother. However, in this novel, the actions of her evil stepmother force Carmen to leave her house and find work in another city. When Carmen leaves the house, her father breaks off all contact, seeing her as a fallen woman. Through hard work and luck Carmen marries well and manages to reconnect with her maternal uncle whom everyone thought was dead. Happily married and now also rich due to her uncle's fortune that she will inherit, Carmen is reunited with her father who accepts her back as his daughter. In *al-Riwāya al-mal'ūna* (*The Cursed Novel*, 1968) by Amal Jarrāḥ, the relationship between father and daughter takes a slightly different turn. Although it begins, as in the previous novels, with a motherless daughter and a father who is forced to step in and assume the role of both educator and companion, the novel continues with Ḥanān falling in love with her father. She begins to make plans to take her late mother's place as love interest of the father. The father, who is seen by Hanan's friends as an ideal man because he takes an interest in her studies, encourages her to make something of herself in the future and gives her the freedom to make her own decisions, slowly falls for Hanan's plan of seduction. But before anything too scandalous happens, Hanan is taken ill and requires hospital treatment abroad. Hanan's illness means that the relationship reverts back to that of a caring father and his daughter. The final novel to be discussed in the chapter, *Arṣifat al-sa'm* (*Sidewalks of Tedium*, 1973) by Hiyām Nuwaylātī and Umm 'Isām, returns to the topic of lovers and tells the story of Mārīā who is unhappy in her marriage, mainly because her husband cannot fulfil what she holds as ideal masculinity. When her husband travels abroad, Maria begins to search for ways to change her life. At work she meets Ḥabīb, a younger man who falls in love with her. Maria is flattered by the attention and the fact that he is interested in her thoughts and opinions and he becomes her lover. The relationship develops and Habib begins to make demands on a future together but in the end, the secrecy and her fear of being found out, kill Maria's feelings and she leaves him.

The men in these novels function as role models and facilitators for women's emancipation and development. Whereas new performances of masculinity are suggested, the criticism of previous performances of masculinity are not developed, even when it is mentioned in passing. The novels echo the social reality of a well-to-do upper and middle class as seen at the time of creation, and key aspects of all the novels are men's encouraging views on education and women's role in society. However, the last novel included in the chapter, *Sidewalks of Tedium*, published ten years into the reign of the Ba'thist government, shows that these ideals are beginning to change and that women are expected to work and contribute to society,[9] something that the ideal masculinities in the earlier novels had proposed but did not expect.

As mentioned above, these early novels introduced a new voice and perspective to the Syrian novelistic scene, but they also introduced a new gaze, the female gaze, piercing through relationships and traditional mind-sets and focusing on the questions 'Who sees?' and 'What does that person see?' The term 'Focalization' is used in narratology to draw attention to the relation between that which is focalised (characters, objects, actions) and the focaliser, the agent who determines how the focalised person or item is perceived in the text.[10] I will make use of Mieke Bal's development of Gerard Genette's original term of focalisation, which includes the relationship between the focalised and the focaliser. The connection here is particularly telling in the case of masculinities because it forefronts how masculinity is a constantly changing concept, depending on others' actions and reactions to it; depending on 'who' sees the action, it may be condoned or condemned. Bal points out that in the discussion of focalisation, there are three important questions: What is the focalization aimed at, with what attitude is the focalization done, and whose focalized object is it?[11] The answers to the three questions are informative not only about the focalised item or person, but about the viewpoint from which these events are presented. In the novels analysed in this book, the analysis of the focaliser offers clues to the understanding of the masculinities presented and the characters' acceptance or rejection of them.

The focalised 'object' in these novels is a man, a father or a lover, who is looked upon with an admiring attitude for most of the time. The main characters in all these novels are a man and a woman, and large parts of the novels are conversations between them, or individual thoughts developed through letters, diaries, or dreams. These choices make the novels appeal to the readers as some sort of truth, camouflaged as fiction. Colette Koury goes further. She begins both her novels with letters to her reader, where she writes that she hopes that the novels will be of use and add new perspectives to the life of women and men. In *Days with Him*, an additional introduction by an older Rim to a younger Rim, makes clear that the novel will teach important life skills.

The novels make use of secondary characters – friends, aunts, mothers and uncles – but these characters are never developed into anything more than bearers of a message, either in support of the main female character, or with more traditional views. The one novel that stands out from the others is *Love and Mud*, where the focaliser is Ahmad. However, much of the narrative is focused on him so it is possible to argue that he is both the focaliser and the focalised in large parts of the novel. In *Sidewalks of Tedium*, almost 30 pages are devoted to the diary of Habib, Maria's lover, before the narration returns to Maria's perspective. The usage of this narrative tool, the male focaliser, which will be discussed in more detail in later chapters, has implications for the understanding and formation of masculinity since the focaliser has power over the text's presentation. Through the male focaliser, the text forefronts the experience of the male character and his way of handling expectations around masculinity which, in turn, is situated in contrast to femininity.

The new female gaze introduced by the writers in this period is to be seen as an addition to the existing male gaze rather than as a complete break with tradition. As Shaaban points out, these writers did not so much work to break the existing structure, as to find a place for women inside it.[12] In the novels written during this period, the female characters are still created around a male centre and described as being in need of male support. The male characters fulfil the function of championing female emancipation and demonstrating its advantages and, as such, the masculinities they performed were often seen as educational. al-Musalima, for example, seems to have made a point about creating an alternative masculinity for her main male character in *Love and Mud*, resulting in Ahmad being considered a 'woman's male character'[13] in the sense that he, according to the critics, behaves and thinks like a woman. However, within the fictional society he is situated in, though aware that he sports different views from other men, he is not treated as being strange. On the contrary, he is the model for a new type of masculinity and thus an example of subversion from within. This shows that although the novels adhere to a social structure built on marriage, where the woman is looked after by the man, the female authors are not content just to describe society as they see it before them and thus maintain the status quo. In fact they do quite the opposite, creating instead masculinities as fathers and potential husbands who are described as being different, progressive and understanding of the need of women. These seemingly simple stories of women's love affairs or relations with their fathers are, read with different glasses, a reformulation of masculinity that was still being used by writers towards the end of the twentieth century.

Dream Masculinity as an Attempt to Influence Hegemonic Masculinity

According to Connell, hegemonic masculinity can be seen as the foundation for patriarchal, social structures, whether they help to form complete societies or informal groups. The performer of hegemonic masculinity is made out to be the leader, the father figure and the only one who can guarantee the group's security and prosperity.[14] Both males and females are seen to support and uphold the patriarchal structure through their reliance on, and acceptance of, the concept of a superior male. In the novels discussed in this chapter, the writers have chosen to locate their novels within the patriarchal structure and have created variations of the father figure as a way to authenticate their formulated masculinities. The idea of a patriarch appears even in those novels where a lover is the main male character. In *Days with Him*, Rim compares the emotional protection and guidance Ziyad offers to that of her late father and she states that she sees him as a father figure.[15] She also connects the loss of her father at an early age to her additional need for male protection. However, she does not turn to her uncles for support, but instead imagines a future husband who will be able to look after her the way she needs.

The descriptions of ideal masculinity in the above novels differ in several ways from what is presented as the fictional societies' hegemonic masculinity. Instead, each novel describes what can be seen as a dream for a better world through a new performance of masculinity. The chapter's usage of 'dream masculinity' refers to a masculinity formulated by the female protagonists to meet their wishes for a model masculinity. The dream masculinity is their imagination of how an ideal future partner or husband, with all the traits they wish for, would behave. In addition and, more importantly, the performer of dream masculinity has the ability to grant the protagonists a better life. He can transform their lives in a positive way, whether that is the ability to study, more personal freedom, protection or something else that the protagonist sees as necessary. Whereas the dream masculinity is formulated in contrast to how life would be for the main character without his presence, the focus in these novels is on the portrayal of ideal men and the good influence they have, instead of focusing on the negative aspects of oppressive masculinities. Dream masculinity in this context does not mean a rich husband, a tall husband or a husband who likes children, but is instead offers a chance of self-fulfilment for the female characters through the behaviour of a close male figure .

The dream masculinity thus mirrors the protagonist's hopes for the future and how she thinks she wants to live her life. The performer of this masculinity is seen as a guarantee of this transformation. As such, dream masculinity forms an alternative to the hegemonic masculinity of the fictional society and, at the same time, for the female characters, it creates a new standard, specific to the protagonist, against which she measures masculinity. The protagonist, therefore, often finds herself caught between her own, personal ideals and those of society and must relate to the social power structures that might not support the man and masculinity she favours, and instead work to uphold the prevalent hegemonic masculinity. In Helena Eriksson's study of American female-authored fiction, the masculinity of lovers and dream lovers appears as instrumental to the female protagonists' search for freedom.[16] This agrees, to a certain extent, with the novels examined in this period, in particular, with the main character Rim in *Days with Him,* who searches for a man who can help her to become free. But whereas the opposition in Eriksson's study stands between the masculinity of husbands and that of lovers and dream lovers, the opposition in *Days with Him*, and the other novels discussed in this chapter, rests between a masculinity represented by society in general and a dream masculinity which is what the main female characters prefer. Disregarding the cultural differences between the American novels in Eriksson's study and the Syrian novels under discussion in this book, the search for an ideal masculinity as a way for the protagonists to achieve their dreams is similar. Eriksson notes that the masculinity of the dream lovers is often based on a mixture of the protagonist's own constructions of desirable masculinity and conventions idolised in popular culture.[17] It is hence not solely an individual desire stemming from the protagonist, but a combination of influences. The same can be seen in the Syrian novels discussed here: the protagonists look for the traditional male characteristics in agreement with the hegemonic masculinity they have grown up with, but they also have other requirements that make up their dream masculinity. The breaking point between individual hopes and general expectations is what formulates an alternative to, or a variety of, hegemonic masculinity.

The constant reformulation of hegemonic masculinity, which Connell argues is vital to the theory,[18] is here exemplified both through the writers' formulation of alternative masculinities and the protagonists' desires which develop during the novels due to changing financial, educational, and personal circumstances. There is no specific set of characteristics that makes up dream masculinity, which, as Eriksson shows, makes dream masculinity ambiguous and difficult to characterise.[19] What is similar is the belief that the man in question can save the protagonist. Although the novels discussed in this chapter, as well as those discussed in Eriksson's study, can be read as individual creative expressions, together they create a selection of masculinities that differ radically from the hegemonic norms of the fictional societies in which they operate. If this gap between ideal and hegemony is put into conversation with the notion of 'writing for change' and the time period of state formation and social change the novels were written in, I find it possible to read them as engaging with gender roles on a social rather than individual level and proposing, through examples, new ways of performing masculinity.

At the same time, the dream masculinities described in the novels are often presented as saviours of the individual characters. The idea of 'being saved' and hence the meaning of it, is based on individual needs stemming from the backgrounds of the female protagonists. In *Snow under the Sun* Rima is saved from being sent to an orphanage by her adoptive father and it is the upbringing she receives from him that shapes her expectations regarding her future husband. For Rim, in *Days with Him*, it is a feeling of being hindered by the structures of society and a need to find a way to freedom that shapes her idea of dream masculinity. In *Sevillan Eyes* it is Roberto's ability to provide social and physical protection for Carmen that makes her feel saved. In *Love and Mud*, it is a combination of Ahmad's world view, in which men and women are equal, and the idea that he, as a man, should be strong and protective and look after Inas.

The idea of masculinity as something desirable appears in almost all the novels of the period although none actually defines the meaning of the word 'rujūla'.[20] In *The Cursed Novel,* Hanan says that a masculine smell[21] emanates from her dad and it is clear that she finds it appealing. In *Days with Him*, Rim enjoys Ziyad's masculine voice over the phone[22] and in *Sevillan Eyes* it is stated that:

كان أكثر ما أحبته كارمن في روبيرتو لباقته ورجولته وبساطته.[23]

> The things Carmen liked most about Roberto was his cleverness, his masculinity and his simplicity.

The use of 'rujūla', as a noun or adjective in theses novels is used to signify the difference between these and other men, if it was something everyone possessed it would not be worth mentioning. It also allows the female characters to position themselves as feminine women in relation to the masculine men. I further argue that a reason for emphasising how masculine these men are, is to balance the view of their critics as being 'women's characters' and showing that, despite their views on women's rights, they have not lost any of their manliness.

The view of what dream masculinity really contains changes as the protagonists develop. In *Sidewalks of Tedium*, Maria, the main character, is from a poor background, so as a young girl, a future free of financial problems is high on her list of demands. However, growing up and marrying a wealthy man she finds that her husband's world is just as restrictive as that of her childhood. Her idea of what she wants from a man then changes and she begins to think that she wants respect, companionship and equality instead. The individually expressed needs, and the changes over times, are important ways of re-negotiating hegemonic masculinity, but of higher importance is that the female characters project their needs onto male characters and thus see men as vehicles through which to realise their hopes and dreams. However, the dream masculinity is not only formulated for the benefit of women – some of the novels, like *Snow under the Sun* and *Love and Mud* make it very clear that this dream masculinity is something which the male characters also benefit from. In *Snow under the Sun* the main female character refuses to marry her cousin until he has changed his behaviour and become more like her understanding and progressive adoptive father, which he himself then acknowledges is a better way for a man. In *Love and Mud,* Ahmad, the main male character, offers an alternative masculinity, appreciative of women's problems, supportive and understanding and, at the same time, ready to look after and protect his beloved. In his letter to his friend, Ahmad describes himself as having woken up and is now able to see women as they really are.[24] Having freed himself from his previously, as he now sees them, misogynist ideas, he no longer has any problem in knowing how to perform masculinity.

Bargaining to Get a Share of the Patriarchal Dividend

Regardless of these male characters' understanding of the importance of new male gender roles, the fictional societies they live in still uphold the rule of female subordination. This can be seen in the described relationships between the characters, the way decisions are made or negotiated and the possibilities offered to the characters based on their sex. This, in turn, means that all the male characters automatically receive privileges denied to women, simply by being male, a part of hegemonic masculinity termed 'the patriarchal dividend'.[25] In the context of the novels analysed in this book, this is of great importance since it is one of the factors that distinguishes men from women in the patriarchal systems described. The characters, male and female, have to position themselves in relation to this knowledge, hence the idea of the patriarchal dividend is immensely important for understanding the masculinities constructed. Especially since the patriarchal dividend can be used by male characters to the benefit of the family and those dependent on them, while at the same time it can be used to exert power over female relatives, wives and children in all areas of life. The patriarchal dividend is also the foundation on which the female characters in this chapter formulate their dream masculinity, or rather they create ways to profit from the patriarchal dividend by finding someone who is willing to share it with them.

This paradoxical situation of a woman using a certain way of doing masculinity to escape another performance of masculinity can be seen as a variation of the patriarchal bargain as described by Deniz Kandiyoti.[26] Kandiyoti's formulation of the patriarchal bargain can, in a simplified way, be described as a young woman's acceptance of men's privilege in order to be able to profit from the power of her own, male children. The woman hence accepts patriarchy, even though it is a system that restricts her ability to act, in order to benefit from the same system at an older age in the position as mother or mother-in-law. The female protagonists discussed in this chapter are not organising their lives around a waiting period in order to assume power through conceiving male children and thus obtaining a position as powerful mothers-in-law in their old age. Instead, they are concerned with obtaining power over their own lives to begin with. However, they too accept the patriarchal structures of their societies and the dream masculinity becomes a way of managing the system from within. It is therefore both a support for, and a challenge to, hegemonic masculinity. It is supportive in the sense that the dream masculinity builds on popularly accepted ideas of masculinity, thus strengthening the hegemonic image of masculinity. At the same time, it challenges this hegemony, since all the dream masculinities described in the novels acknowledge a woman's role in society, her right to education and later to work and her ability to make her own decisions. By embedding the new traits within the old structure, they are presented in a way that is more easily integrated into their fictional societies.

Though paradoxical, as described above, the exchange of one masculinity for another is, in many cases, the only way the female protagonists can have influence over their own lives. The fictional societies described are very close to the middle- and upper-class Syrian society of the time, and even towards the end of the twentieth century, single households were rare.[27] Both men and women tended to live with their family until they married, and marriage was the most likely way for a girl to leave her family home. This structure is found in the novels where, for example Maria in *Sidewalks of Tedium,* and Rasha in *One Night,* find themselves accepting arranged marriages because that is what is expected of them. Maria, who is brought up being told that men are monsters of whom she needs to be scared[28] has never really contemplated marriage. However, when she finds out that her mother's, and society's, way of protecting her from 'the monsters' is to marry her off to one of them,[29] she accepts the idea and begins to project her dreams and hopes for a better future onto her husband-to-be.

In *Days with Him,* Rim decides to get married to her cousin, despite having stated several times that she is against the idea of marriage, because she thinks he is going to be her way to a better life.

> [...] وحين طلب مني أن أتزوجه، قبلتُ فوراً، مع أنني كنتُ دائماً أكره الزواج، إلا أنني إِعتقدتُ أن زواجي به هو الوسيلة الوحيدة التي تجعلني أحقق آمالي، فأكمل دراستي، وأغذي ميولي الفنية، وأكوّن شخصيتي بحرية.[30]

> And when he asked me to marry him I agreed immediately, despite the fact that I hated marriage, because I assumed that my marriage to him was the one way I could realise my dreams, complete my studies, feed my artistic inclinations and build my personality in freedom.

When they later conclude that they are not meant for each other, they make an agreement to stay engaged for a year, which will give each of them a chance to behave freely under the cover of being seen as engaged. In interviews with Damascene women conducted at the beginning of the twenty-first century, Sally K Gallagher shows that marriage is still seen by many as the natural choice for a girl, and that unmarried girls, even if it is an active choice on their part, are pitied.[31] To be married is not so much of a choice as a social expectation, and a husband becomes a bridge to another kind of life; that as a grown-up with the responsibility for a family and the respect the institution of marriage carries with it. However, a future husband is not only the father of a woman's children and a life partner; he is also responsible for the female's wellbeing in the eyes of the law and society.[32] The husband further holds the threat of divorce, which gives him the ultimate tool to exercise his will over the family concerning both small and big decisions, if he chooses to use it. To choose a husband is hence not only an emotional decision, but one that is life changing. In *One Night,* this is poignantly described by Rasha who almost faints when she sees her husband for the first time.[33] Not because he is the first man to ever touch her hand, the reason her family finds for her rection, but because in this older, slightly fat man, she sees all her hopes and aspirations for her future crushed.[34] The descriptions of future, and present, husbands in the novels are not just examples of romantic ideas, easily dismissed as some sort of feel-good-literature, but negotiations for the basis of a future life.

To navigate within the patriarchal system in the way the novels' protagonists do, has the consequence that there is no outright rejection of a specific type of masculinity, or patriarchy, in the characters' thoughts or comments. Even in the cases where the father figure is seen to perform, in the eyes of the protagonist, an old-fashioned masculinity, he is excused, if not immediately, at least after the protagonist has left the family home and moved in with her husband. The dream masculinity is not a sign of rebellion towards the patriarchal structure, but an attempt to renegotiate its content. It shows, as Eriksson proves in her study on dream masculinity, the difficulties involved in moving beyond familiar cultural models of desire, even when they are deemed insufficient to realise the protagonists' hopes.[35]

The marriages the protagonists hope for are not meant to lead to lives as housewives and mothers but to give them opportunities to develop their interests and talents. The characters were created during the 1950s and 1960s and operate in fictional societies where the gender regime dictates that there must be a man to hold responsible for a woman's actions. The importance of marriage is not only to create a family, but also to be able to influence the possibilities one will have in life such as an opportunity to work or study. This could explain the paternal uncle's rage at Rim's father in *Days with Him* for allowing his daughter to choose her husband herself. By granting her this power, her father is allowing her to shape her future. Her uncle, who seems to feel that the more freedom she is given the less power he is seen to have, fears that she will make choices that will have an impact on him and his family too. The question of having a say in one's marriage is part of all the novels examined, for the ideal father figures described, as well as Ahmad in *Love and Mud*, it is clear that the girl herself should be the one who decides whom to marry. In *Snow Under the Sun,* the father leaves the decision of whether to accept a marriage proposal to his daughter, rather than taking the decision himself; the same stance is taken by Hanan's father in *The Cursed Novel* when he and Hanan discuss her future husband. However, neither of the fathers contemplate the idea that their daughters might decide not to marry. By creating male characters who advocate this idea without any apparent loss of power or manliness, the writers present a model for a behaviour that differs from the traditional way of doing things in the novels. They further deviate from the stereotypical patriarchal male character who often is described as refusing to give any consideration to a female's point of view.

In addition to choosing one's spouse, the female characters are looking for men who value education and will allow them to continue their studies. At the beginning of *Days with Him,* Rim is told by her father that she is not allowed to attend university. Rim, who has just finished high school and is full of hopes for the future is devastated. After long discussions, she is allowed to study by correspondence. A mixed-university environment is not seen as a possibility for a young girl. In *One Night,* Rasha dreams of studying to become a doctor but she is told by her parents that she does not even have to study for the final exam of secondary school since they have found her a husband. In *Sidewalks of Tedium,* Maria has high expectations of her life with her husband, but he quickly forbids her from both studying and working, confining her to their home instead. When he later leaves the country, she enrols in university and later finds a job at one of the ministries. The ideal fathers of *Snow Under the Sun* and *Love and Mud* both stress the importance of education for their daughters. In *Love and Mud,* the father of the main female character makes a point of bringing her up in the same way he would have brought up a son to give her the same opportunities a boy would have had. This results in Inas becoming a doctor, excelling both at university and in her job. She is described as self-reliant, intelligent and logical. The novel shows that women are a result of their upbringing whilst, at the same time, it confirms the stereotypical picture of the male mind, which Inas, through her father's planning, now can enjoy. She is depicted in the novel as performing female masculinity, which creates problems for her when she comes into contact with the male characters. The complete acceptance that these male characters show for the female characters' desires and wishes, without losing their own power or position, makes them models of ideal men suitable for the discourse of female emancipation. The clearest example of this can be seen in *The Cursed Novel* by Amal Jarrah, where the father is described as being extremely proud of his daughter's success at university, her future as a teacher and also the prospect of her publishing poetry and becoming famous, all things described as enraging the hegemonic masculinity of the time.[36]

Society and Hegemonic Norms

The fictional societies described in the novels are often very strict, and through the narratives in the different novels it becomes clear that the characters, male and female, blame these social structures more than individual characters for the way they have to organise their lives. In *Love and Mud*, Ahmad says that Inas' problems stem from social pressure in an oppressive society.[37] In addition to general rules, these societies are preoccupied with categorising people according to gender. In all the novels, it is important to adhere to, and correctly perform, the expected gendered behaviour. The concept of hegemonic masculinity becomes vital, since it is the tool used to measure a man's performance. It further indicates that if anyone deviates from this expected behaviour it creates instability and becomes a threat to others' performance of gender. At the same time, by locating the problems of the novels within the social structure, the authors acknowledge that a possible solution could be a change of these norms. In *Diaries of a Divorcing Woman* by Haifa Bitar, although from a later period, it is even spelled out in a conversation between a mother and her daughter.

ومَن سيغيّر هذه التقاليد والمفاهيم البالية، يا أمي؟
الناس يا ابنتي
كل الناس؟
لا- بعضهم، الجريئون، المغامرون، المؤمنون بمبادئ جديدة.

> Who will change these worn-out understandings and traditions, mother?
> The people, my girl
> All the people?
> No, some of them, the brave ones, the adventurous and those who believe in new ideas.[38]

After this exchange, the daughter suggests that they should be the brave people and advocate change, but the mother immediately stops her by saying that society is not kind and forgiving towards those who dare to break the norms. Hence, for the created characters, it is important to adhere to the norms of their fictional societies. For the female writers, it is also important that neither the plot nor the structure deviates since, as Susan Lanser notes, '[n]on-hegemonic writers and narrators may need to strike a delicate balance in accommodating and subverting dominant rhetorical practices', in order for their novels or short stories to be deemed credible.[39] To create characters that are too far from social norms and who stand for a clear break with the past is perhaps not a viable solution; instead, the dream masculinities are influenced by the society the female characters belong to and are embedded in the prevailing hegemonic masculinity. The conflict this creates is demonstrated in the novels. Rim in *Days with Him* is caught between her wishes and reality. Her choice of Ziyad, and the fact that she openly goes out with him, causes controversy among her relatives and friends. Concurrently, the fact that she wants an open, non-sexual, pre-marital relationship confuses Ziyad, who, like the fictional society, seems to think that a relationship is either all or nothing. Rim's dream for a performance of masculinity that respects her in a traditional way but spends time with her in what she sees as a modern way, is hence difficult for both society and Ziyad to grasp. In *Sidewalks of Tedium*, Maria lives through a similar dilemma. She sees how her neighbour has a stream of different women visiting him in his flat without anyone commenting on his behaviour. She also expresses that she thinks that her relationship with Habib is a real relationship, whereas her marriage was more or less forced upon her. Despite the happiness she feels with Habib and the dreams she has for their future, the pressure of these social norms are too strong; she breaks up the relationship, only to be left devastated when she finds out that Habib has got engaged to someone else.

In *Love and Mud*, Ahmad describes himself as an ideal, thoughtful, patient and caring future husband. This is also how the novel's women see him. The wife of Ahmad's friend is so enchanted by him that she tries to marry him off to her sister and Inas' mother cannot understand why her daughter does not accept to marry him. The importance of the ideal masculinity Ahmad performs is exaggerated by these positive reactions from the female characters and it appears that the character fulfils a somewhat didactic role. Whilst not abandoning the idea of himself as the provider and protector of the female, he advocates her right to work and study and proposes that she is an equal rather than a servant. What he sees as a 'modern' performance of masculinity does not entail any major changes in his own performance but has a distinctly different attitude towards femininity than other male characters in the novel. The female perspective in this novel functions as a blessing for a specific performance of masculinity and through this new performance Ahmad gains popularity and influence over women. Despite this, Inas does not trust him to actually love her. She is afraid that he, like others before him, will not be able to forget that she once loved another man, and consequently leaves him. Even though Ahmad promises that he is different, Inas is not able to see that his values and views could be different than those of other men in her society. His change into a 'woman's man' does not help him to get the love of his life, even though the novel positions him as a new and modern man.

In *Love and Mud,* society's views are presented through comments on Inas' behaviour more than on Ahmad's actions. Ahmad is made out to be the ideal male and, as such, he only meets with approval from the other characters, both male and female, but he is not described contemplating his own conduct concerning what other men do. However, by comparing other men and their behaviour, the hegemonic view on masculinity and femininity in the society described in the novel does not agree with Ahmad's performance of masculinity. At the same time, the hegemony described is not one that is supported by the narrative, and the other male characters are not favourably depicted. Set against this background, Ahmad stands out as different because of his acceptance of women's work and his respect for their choices and beliefs. Throughout the text, Ahmad advertises himself as a model man. He is given textual space to eloquently discuss his feelings, hopes and fears and his wish to live in an equal relationship, while at the same time supporting and helping Inas. The novel explains that he wants to be a model man because he has met Inas; she has opened his eyes to women's abilities and he, accordingly, changes his behaviour. The text describes Ahmad's awareness of the change he has gone through, and that an educated woman is the reason for this, something that emphasises the novel's point that gender is relational and that women have a role in the formation of masculinity. At the same time, Ahmad is the one who has changed. Instead of accepting one of the marriage proposals he is offered, he visits Inas, talks to her, and tries to come to an agreement with her. He himself is described to be surprised at the patience he shows when he could just marry any girl. However, the new masculinity he is described to perform wants a woman of his choice who also wants him, not just any woman to start a family.

As such, the novel formulates a strong critique against the hegemonic masculinity of the novel, which forms the shadow to Ahmad's 'new masculinity' and which has shaped Inas' image of men. This looks down on women, does not allow them a personal life and wants to separate them from the public sphere. This is not followed by Inas' father, nor by Ahmad, but is seen and quoted as the dominant view in society. Ahmad presents a masculinity that he believes to be what Inas, or any woman, would want. He is portrayed as an educated, well-travelled man, therefore he seems sure that others will follow suit. He is also convinced that Inas will change her mind and marry him. Although she does not, both the father in *Love and Mud* and especially Ahmad, can be read as important contributions to the gender debate at the time of the novel's publication, as a content and satisfied divergent masculinity. As such, the novel, like other novels of the time, supports women's freedom but with the help of men rather than as a reaction against them. The fact that the novel makes use of a male focaliser further changes the perspective and reinforces the idea that this type of behaviour is not only for the sake of women but also a natural position for an educated man. A similar attitude can be seen in the other novels, although these are mostly presented through the female characters or an all-knowing narrator's voice.

In *The Cursed Novel*, Hanan invites her friends over to see how she has rearranged her flat. She asks her father to be present and meet them. The girls are all described as being very taken with Hanan's father who jokes with them and treats them as grown-up women. He has also bought them different types of sweets and cigarettes in case they feel like smoking. Hanan has previously been smoking behind his back, and his gesture is both an acknowledgement that he knows that she smokes and does not care and a sign of his open-mindedness in front of her friends. His interest in them and his care for them and his daughter, is seen by the friends as something rare and strange but at the same time very desirable, and something they would like their own fathers to emulate. One of the braver girls even asks Hanan's father if he would agree to be the model for a painting she wants to do, which she is planning to call 'hope'. She explains the theme of the painting as follows:

أقصد أنني سأرسم رجلا أضع فيه كل الصفات التي تحلم بها الفتاة.

I mean that I will paint a man and give him all the traits a girl dreams of.[40]

The father's behaviour is thus not seen as the normal way of behaving in the fictional society, but he holds 'all the traits a girl dreams of'. His deviant masculinity is praised by the girls and described as something one would hope for in a future husband. The fact that the novel, like *Love and Mud*, turns to secondary characters to support the main male character's different masculinity works both to show not only the hegemony of the society but also that the behaviour is a welcome change, a possible new way of behaving.

Thus far, the focus of the dream masculinity has been on acceptance of the female characters' life choices and the contrast between this and the prevailing hegemonic view that the man should make all the decisions. Another angle of hegemonic masculinity as seen in the novels of this era is the need to be able to provide for one's future wife. As mentioned above, money is not an issue for Rim in *Days with Him,* but in the eyes of society, Ziyad's career, despite being a successful and famous musician, is not stable enough for him to be described as desirable marriage material. Although he works as a teacher on top of his position in an office, these career choices do not grant status in the fictional society described. Rim, who is more interested in their emotional and intellectual relationship, is not bothered by Ziyad's occupation, but the comments made by family and friends, and their comparisons between Ziyad and Alfrid, her fiancé, make her consider the subject. Alfrid, on the other hand, is seen as the ideal man by both relatives and friends. He is educated and well off, so his ability to provide for her cannot be doubted. He has no known love affairs and he is from within the family. Rim's initial excitement about Alfrid, which disappears when she feels no love for him, is slowly reignited when he returns a second time to Damascus. Through her relationship with Ziyad, Rim's expectations have changed and she finds herself drawn more to Alfrid's calm and steady way of behaving than Ziyad's emotional changes. Through experience, and because of comments from friends and family, her image and her expectations have changed and she admits that the dream masculinity she projected on Ziyad did not work.

A further aspect taken into consideration in the novel are how the male and female characters react to breaking specific social rules. For example, Rim has from a young age written poetry that she now has begun to publish. This enrages her uncle who believes that she brings shame on the family by publishing poetry with her name and picture.

The fictional societies that the novels describe are relatively similar. As an example, the narrative of *Love and Mud* is situated in a society where, according to the characters, most men consider women as incapable dolls. Inas' father has only one child, and he wants the best for her. To do this, he decides to bring her up as a boy, acknowledging that within their society, boys have more opportunities and possibilities to shape their own lives. Through the narrative and dialogue, the father's decision is described as surprising. Neighbours and relatives expect Inas to marry and have children rather than to study. They are worried that no man will agree to marry her since she will have a better education than he will; the fact that Inas might not want to marry or that there are men who see education as an asset is not something they consider. Rasha's mother in *One Night* is described in a similar way when she firmly explains to Rasha that the society they live in is not ready for girls who study and educate themselves. She then threatens her daughter that if she chooses the path of education she will be the talk of the town, no one will agree to marry her and she will also ruin the reputation of her sisters.[41] Rasha, who is described as very obedient, agrees to marry whoever the family decides on and accepts her fate; she does not actively try to look for someone other than the candidate presented by her family.

The Ideal Father-Figure

It is not only lovers or potential husbands that can personate dream masculinity, another common character who performs this role is the father of the main character. The choice of the father as an example of an ideal masculinity is logical given the importance of the father figure in Syrian society – by making the father perform ideal masculinity the writers give additional authorisation to their creations. The masculinity performed by these fathers is almost didactic in its idealness, as seen in the description of Hanan's father above, and it is shown in the novels that it is looked up to by both men and women. In her study of masculinity in Syrian fiction in the 1990s, Maysun al-Jurf criticizes the masculinities formed by women writers as 'not performing true masculinity',[42] since she means that the focus is on violent and oppressive men only. The traits that she lists as missing from the later novels could just as well be a list of characteristics of the father figures of this earlier period, someone who is described as brave, honourable, just, generous, strong and protective, while at the same time connected to his inner feelings. The adoptive father in Layla al-Yafi's novel *Snow Under the Sun* encourages his daughter to study, he then takes time off work in order to take her and her mother on a trip around the Arab countries so that she can learn about their culture. He does all of this in agreement with his wife, but he is clearly the one who makes decisions in the household.

The masculinity this father presents is not seen as 'common' and performed by all men. On the contrary, he is singled out as a positive example as he is changing the life of the main female character. The masculinity he performs becomes the role model for his nephew, who fails in his early, aggressive attempts to win the hand of the main character. When he changes, due to the reaction of his beloved and later acknowledges the validity of her adoptive father's masculinity, she accepts him as her husband. In its presentation of the ideal father, and the daughter's wish to re-create his masculinity – one that is wise, careful, protective and never loses control and becomes aggressive – in her future husband is formulated and portrayed as successful and rewarding for both the male and female characters . In *Sevillan Eyes*, the father is left in charge of the upbringing of his daughter after the death of her mother. Like the adoptive father previously described, he does everything possible to give his daughter a good start in life, despite his poverty. He is hard working, trustworthy and generous despite his limited financial means. He instils high morals and the importance of correct conduct in his daughter, in addition to encouraging her to study. Although Carmen's father loses faith in her when she leaves home, they are reunited at the end of the novel. This leads to a similar conclusion as the one made in al-Yafi's novel, namely that a thoughtful and caring, while at the same time strong and decisive masculinity, is both sought after and required by the female characters. A masculinity which allows for, and accounts for, her needs of education, work and freedom but which is ever present as a security if something goes wrong. As in al-Yafi's novel, both the male characters performing this masculinity and the female characters supporting it are rewarded with happiness and wealth at the end of the novel.

A novel which can be read both as the ultimate example of the ideal father figure, and as a strong critique of it, is Amal Jarrah's award-winning book, *The Cursed Novel*. It begins, in line with the other novels, with a father who encourages his daughter to live her life as she wants to, but it soon moves on to describing the slow beginnings of an incestuous relationship between father and daughter. Before the relationship becomes serious, the daughter falls ill and is diagnosed with a dangerous heart disease. The tension built up around a potential relationship between father and daughter is removed, and the father returns to his role as the able guardian. However, despite taking her to Europe for treatment he is not able to save his daughter. Her idolisation of her father, to the point where she sees no problem in breaching social conventions and imagining embarking on a relationship with him, is, in contrast to the other novels, shown to be fruitless. Read like this, the benign patriarch's ability to run the world is questioned, as is the female character's blind trust in him. It is further telling that heart disease kills Hanan, since her whole life circled around her love for her father. Jarrah was not sure how the novel would be received and, having sent it to a literary competition and won, she decided to not publish it, hence it did not have a chance to make an impact on the reading public at the time, except those on the literary prize committee.[43]

The Protector as Part of Masculinity Performance

The construction of dream masculinity reuses traits from the hegemonic masculinity of the fictional society but in a new way. Rim objects to her father's way of protecting her by not letting her go to university and to her uncle who wants her to live in his house so that he can look after her. She reads these actions as control, whereas the men see them as ways of protecting her, and themselves, from things that might happen to Rim. When it comes to her dream masculinity, she wants to be protected and looked after, but only so that she can do what she wants. She does not want to be locked up in the house so that people do not talk about her, but rather to be taken out by a man who will then protect her from gossip. Hence, the same trait that is rejected in the hegemonic masculinity of the fictional society is repeated in the dream masculinity, although in a different form. The father in *Snow Under the Sun* protects his wife and daughters from various types of danger, even physical fights, when they are travelling. When Rima grows up, this is one of the things she expects her future husband to do. In her eyes, and in the fictional society in which she lives, protection is part of what a man is supposed to do – how he is supposed to do it varies from understanding to understanding. In *Days with Him*, it is Layla, Rim's best friend who articulates this expectation of protection most clearly when she claims that for a woman to love a man, she needs to feel that he can protect her.[44] What she means, as is clear from the context of the novel, is nothing more than that the man should take responsibility for everyday problems whereas the dream masculinity, as articulated in the different novels, includes protecting the main female character so that she can life her life as she prefers to, regardless of society's views or the opinions of her relatives. Nadya, the wife of Rim's maternal uncle, disagrees with Layla, and argues that protection has nothing to do with love. Nadya, who voices ideas of female liberation throughout the novel, argues instead that the wish for protection has its roots in the psyche of women and says:

> لأنّها كسلى لا تتجرأ بمفردها على شقّ طريقها في الحياة. . . نعم إنّها كسلى! إنها تمشي وراء الرجل تتستر بظله للتهرّب من مجابهة مشاكل الحياة بمفردها.[45]

> Because she [the eastern woman] is lazy and does not dare to pursue her own path in life . . . yes she is lazy! She walks behind the man, hiding in his shadow to avoid facing the problems of life by herself.

Nadya's statement, despite negating the wish to be protected, confirms the notion that, in general in these novels, men protect and women are protected. Whereas Layla sees being protected as something desirable, Nadya sees it as something that consciously or unconsciously hinders women from creating their own lives. Rim declares that being protected is highly desirable when she formulates her dream masculinity and projects it onto Ziyad. She wants him to protect her physically, like he did one time when they went to the cinema.

مدّ ذراعه بصورة طبيعيّة، وأحاط كتفيّ وظهري ليحميني، أوّلاً من الجموع المحتشدة ثمّ من ظلام الممرّ. وددتُ لو يبقى دائماً هكذا كبيراً. . .جدياً. . .قوياً، يشعر بضعفي فيحميني.[46]

He stretched his arm in a natural way around my shoulders and back to protect me, first from the gathered crowd and then from the darkness of the corridor. I wished that he would always stay like this; big ... serious ... strong, feeling my weakness and protecting me.

In addition to this physical type of protection, Rim in *Days with Him,* wants to be protected in an emotional sense. She wants to have someone who decides for her and tells her what to do, urges her on and takes responsibility for her decisions, such as to continue to study, publish her poetry and be less traditional in her behaviour. She does not feel that she herself is able to do these things unless she has protection and support. Rim reads Ziyad's protectiveness as love and care. In another scene, she compares his way of protecting her with, as she feels it, Alfrid's way of taking her for granted and assuming that she will tag along like his male friends.[47] Nevertheless, her wish to be protected is not specifically connected to Ziyad, even if he currently performs the role, rather she says that she has always yearned for masculine men and to be engulfed in their protection. Ziyad's behaviour becomes a testimony that he is impersonating the dream masculinity she has always wanted.

كنتُ دائماً أتلهّف إلى رجلٍ يحيطني برجولته، وبأسه وحبه [. . .] كنتُ عطشى إلى الشعور بحماية رجلٍ.[48]

I always yearned for a man to surround me with his masculinity, his power and his love ... I was thirsty for the feeling of a man's protection.

In one scene, he cooks for her and reassures her that he is there to look after her and make sure she is well fed and taken care of.[49] This caring way becomes an ultimate sign of his protectiveness and confirms her feelings that he indeed performs a role that she needs. He further worries when she is sick, and orders her to stay in bed and dress well. Small actions, that for Rim, indicate that he indeed is the man who will look after her for the rest of her life and make sure that it will unfold as she wants it to.

The idea of man as the protector remains even when the male character is not present. In *One Night,* Rasha rushes through the heavy Paris traffic but, as the novel states, she has forgotten that her lover Kamil is not there to look out for her[50] and, after a few steps, she is hit by a car and taken to hospital. Reading the novel only through this sentence would lead to the conclusion that a woman is constantly in need of male protection and is incapable of even walking down a street without a man by her side. However, in the larger perspective of the novel, it is firstly interesting to note that it is Kamil's presence that she misses, not that of her husband of ten years whom she has left behind to go to Paris alone. Secondly, her accident happens after she realises that it will be impossible to have a relationship with Kamil, a man she found supportive and helpful who was willing to discuss things with her as an equal, all things she missed with her husband. It is also unclear if the accident is an accident, although it is described as such, or a suicide attempt, since Rasha states that she sees no point in living when, as she says, her real life was one night only.[51] Regardless, I argue that the character is looking for the protection of an understanding masculinity rather than the physical protection from traffic suggested above.

In *Sevillan Eyes*, the father does his best to protect Carmen from harm. One of the things he does, with the best interests of his daughter in mind, is to remarry. However, the woman he chooses is not just unkind to Carmen, she also sees another man during the days when Carmen's father is at work. When the stepmother's lover becomes interested in Carmen, she is unable to tell her father since she does not want to burden him with his wife's infidelity and instead decides to escape. When she later meets Roberto, one of the things that attracts her to him is the fact that he can look after her. Maria, in *Sidewalks of Tedium*, hopes that her husband will be able to protect her but is disappointed to discover that he is not interested in a such a role. However, when he later leaves the country, she appreciates the status of having a husband's protection in the eyes of society as she can act freely since he is abroad. This is a similar situation to that of Rim in *Days with Him* who enjoys the protection of being engaged while knowing that Alfrid is in France and will not interfere with her life. Both women use the absent man to achieve their own goals and the protection of a formal alliance to save their reputation in the eyes of society. However, both women use their freedom to look for another man, a man who not only gives them formal protection through marriage but who can also fulfil other dreams.

Hegemonic Femininity

In the novels discussed in this chapter there seems to be a fear that the male characters will be perceived as 'female masculinities'; the male characters are therefore clearly juxtaposed with the female ones to create a contrast. Similarly, Connell argues that hegemonic masculinity is always relational to hegemonic femininity. She defines hegemonic femininity as the accepted way of performing femininity, giving a woman status within a group of women and acceptance by men.[52] Sarah Frantz and Katharina Rennhak further note that women's texts about men give clues to '[t]he underlying mutually constitutive ideals and stereotypes of femininity and masculinity with which every era must struggle'.[53] In Ghada al-Samman's novel *Kawābīs Bayrūt* (*Beirut Nightmares*, 1976), Connell's claim that masculinity always is relational to femininity is supported by both the male character Amīn and the female narrator. They are described as measuring Amīn's masculinity in relation to the narrator's behaviour. What he, as the male, is supposed to do in comparison to the female character seems to define not only the masculinity of his character but also the assumed hegemonic masculinity in the fictional society in which the characters live.

This theme is also prominent in *Days with Him*, where Rim feels that she has become a woman through meeting Ziyad,[54] and she describes how he has awoken her inner female. Rim, who is at an age when she tries to find out what type of person she wants to be, uses Ziyad as a model man. This means that the opposite behaviour to his should be performed by a model woman, which she strives to be. Her constant search for ideal behaviour leads her to scrutinise every action performed by herself or Ziyad in order to determine if it was up to her standards. The dream masculinity she projects on him is instrumental not only in reaching her outer goals, such as studying, but also her inner goals and the formation of her own self. He has to be strong so that she can be weak; he has to be rational so that she can be emotional. Her way of performing femininity is closely linked to his way, or her expectations of his way, of performing masculinity. When he does not do what she expects him to do, she feels lost. Not only because their relationship is breaking apart, but also because she can no longer see herself through his eyes. When the dream masculinity fails, her dream of herself fails too.

Maria, in *Sidewalks of Tedium*, is looking for similar reassurance from her lover Habib. She wants to be seen as a woman and needs confirmation that her behaviour is correct. Her husband, who has not turned out to be able to perform masculinity in the way she hoped, is not available and she does not see him as someone on whom she can model her own behaviour. However, at the beginning of their relationship, Habib does make her feel that she is a woman again, not only because of the sexual attraction but also because he looks out for her in a way in which her husband does not. Despite being older and having more experience than her lover, she looks for certain traits in a man to justify and find support for her own behaviour. In *Snow Under the Sun* and *The Cursed Novel* the situation is slightly different as they portray relationships between fathers and daughters, where part of the relationship is expected to be a correction of the child's behaviour. Nevertheless, the girls still try to behave in what they see as feminine ways with regards to clothing, activities, and appearance to please their fathers and underline the importance of being model girls for their model fathers. The importance of looks and clothing is accentuated by Rim who initially does not pay attention to the way she looks or dresses,[55] and whose favourite pastime activity is to eat.[56] When she begins to fall in love with Ziyad, she says to herself that he has awoken the woman within her, and it suddenly becomes imperative for her to define herself in relation to him. His opinion becomes important as, for example, when he points out to her that looking after her hair in a better way would be desirable.[57] She shrugs off his comment at the time but then duly starts to comb her hair and put it up in order to look feminine. She dresses to look womanly[58] and thinks about how she behaves and talks in order to perform femininity correctly. She navigates between the traditional expectations of her society and what she thinks Ziyad wants. Her will to adapt means that she thinks a man has the right to put conditions on her appearance and that femininity – in opposition to masculinity – includes being neat, quiet and well behaved, whereas these points are not mentioned in the descriptions of the male characters. Rim is delighted when Ziyad describes her hand, which she finds very normal, as feminine,[59] whereas she herself dreams of his strong, masculine hands.

Rim wants Ziyad to be free and open minded, so she tries to find a female reaction to this behaviour that is accepting, but not too free. When Ziyad accuses her of not being a woman since she does not want to be intimate with him, she is devastated.[60] Devastated because he does not see her as a woman and more so because her performer of dream masculinity is not meant to see women as commodities in the way Ziyad seems to do. Having imagined that the performer of dream masculinity would see her in a pure and asexual way before marriage, she is shocked when he demands a kiss. This not only tells her about his behaviour, but it also changes her view of herself. Through Ziyad's demand, she sees herself as a woman who could be intimate with a man before marriage.[61] Rim accepts Ziyad's definitions of her both as not being a woman, as he says, and as being an easy woman, as she interprets his demand for a kiss. Having no other way of defining herself, she is lost in the way he defines her. The way Rim adopts Ziyad's perception of femininity and masculinity demonstrates how the male gaze is incorporated in her understanding of gender roles. Even though she portrays herself as a free-thinking young woman, she reifies the male values of the society in which she lives. In *Love and Mud*, it is Inas' lack of femininity that is considered her problem, her father's good intentions have made her behave more like a male than a female, which makes it difficult for her to participate in gendered relations at work, for example.

At the beginning of their relationship, Rim is worried that Ziyad, as a musician, will be emotional and she is relieved when she finds him to be very rational.[62] This strengthens her view of her own femininity as emotional and that he then stands for the opposite. Towards the end of their love story, when Ziyad becomes more and more emotional and vocal about his feelings, she finds him overbearing. As a man, she wants him to stand for reason and leave it to her to base her decisions on feelings. The dream masculinity she wants is therefore partly built on what she thinks she is not capable, or willing, to do. She sees herself as emotional and looks for someone to balance that; stability and rationality therefore become part of her dream masculinity. Rasha, in *One Night*, similarly searches for opposites and is pleased when Kamal offers to carry her bag and she notes that she, as the weak women, is spoilt by him, the strong man.[63]

The fact that Ziyad is a lot older than Rim adds to the feeling of opposites. He tells her that she is very young and does not understand. She agrees and accepts this distinction and looks to him to be taught and guided. The age difference and his experiences are, in her mind, changed into a gender difference where he, the man, teaches her, the woman, what to think and do. In another scene, she describes how she positions herself in relation to him.

> تكوّمت عند قدميه كقطة صغيرة أليفة. ورفعتُ الطرف، أتأمل في هذا الوجه الذي انطبع في عيوني فأصبحتُ أرى الدينا من خلاله.[64]

> I curled up by his feet like a small friendly cat. I looked up and contemplated this face which had been imprinted in my eyes and through which I have come to see the world.

Again, it is clear how Rim sees, and formulates, the power distribution within the relationship. She seats Ziyad in the armchair and places herself on the floor next to him. She makes the performer of her dream masculinity occupy the position of a small God who will save her and sort out her life. Later, when they are on the verge of breaking up, she feels a sudden urge to see Ziyad to tell him that she loves him, but also, to yet again, feel small and childlike in his arms.[65] He still upholds the position of the powerful masculinity, able to sort everything out in an instant and make her feel good again by offering the support she cannot give to herself. She does not blame him for making her feel miserable but looks to him for the cure.

When the relationship turns from wonderful to bad, Rim begins to wonder if Ziyad really is the right performer of her dream masculinity. She is not willing to give up easily and decides to be patient to see what is going to happen. She is still sure that Ziyad embodies the answers to how she can become happy.

وصبرتُ، آملة أن يجدُ زياد نفسه، فأجد حينذاك نفسي.[66]

> I was patient, hoping that Ziyad would find himself so that I, at that time, would find myself.

Seeing masculinity and femininity as two sides of a coin, she needs him to be in balance for herself to be in balance. When he performs masculinity the way it should be done according to her, she knows how to perform femininity. She cannot, at this point, see herself independently from him but can only find herself through him.

Continued Dreams – A Reoccurring Masculinity

The novels discussed thus far are all from the period labelled 'The pioneers' or 'Dream masculinity,' between the 1950s and the early 1970s. However, although other formulations of masculinity begin to take over from the middle of the 1970s, male characters who perform variations of dream masculinity return in later novels. In *Shuhadā´ wa 'ushshāq fī bilād al-shām* (*Martyrs and Lovers in the Levant*) by Nadya Khūst, written in 2000, ideal or dream masculinities are used to symbolise correct political views. The characters who are nationalistic are also for women's emancipation and they support strong women, whereas the characters who exhibit what the novel sees as incorrect political views are described as brutes. In Khust's novel, dream masculinity becomes a part of the characterisation of the male protagonists as well as a comment on the difference it would make if masculinity was not interpreted as a tactic for men to remain in power, but as a possibility to use one's position to help one's wife and family and, in the long run, society as well. Another more recent novel that makes use of the idea of a dream masculinity is *Shajarat al-ḥubb - ghābat al-aḥzān* (Tree of Love – Forest of Sadness) by Usayma Darwīsh written in 2000, where Madā is trying to find an escape from her dictatorial father. Initially, Madā is not reacting against the patriarchal gender regime; on the contrary, she uses it for her benefit. Madā has no say in choosing her husband 'Abdu-lah (Abdallah), but when she gets to know him, she considers herself lucky because he has all that it takes to 'save' her from the life she is leading. During their long engagement, she projects her hopes for the future onto Abdallah's character and feels sure that he will give her a better future. Her idea of a better future includes a life full of travels, freedom and a loving family home,[67] all things that she has missed while growing up. When her father cancels the marriage, she is so sure that her husband-to-be is the right man for her that she elopes with him, not willing to let her dream of a better future become a mere mirage. She, too, sees marriage as the only way of achieving the future of her dreams. By choosing the person who will be in charge of her, she has participated in shaping her life, even though she has only chosen the one who will choose for her. Rather than feeling protected by her strong father, Mada, in *Tree of Love,* is terrified of him and describes his voice as a thunderstorm.[68] Her need for protection is both physical and emotional. When Abdallah offers to elope with her and then suggests they travel out of the country she agrees. When he later, as she sees it, becomes overprotective and does not want her to go out alone,[69] she feels captured, not secure. At this point, one of the characteristics she first fell for becomes a reason for her to look for someone else. When she feels that she can no longer live with Abdallah, whom she thinks has turned into a despotic tyrant, her mother and sisters do their best to make her change her mind. They see what Abdallah does from an outsider's perspective and, as such, he seems perfect. He fulfils all the aspects of what they believe is hegemonic masculinity and, more importantly, he is all that Mada ever dreamt of. They therefore cannot understand that whereas Abdallah indeed *was* the answer to Mada's dreams, Mada herself has changed. What she wanted as a young girl, and what her sisters still look for, is no longer enough for her.

Is a Dream just a Dream?

The novels in this chapter have dealt with dream masculinities through prospective husbands, fathers and lovers. However, in novels that anchor the plot in societies built on marriage it is interesting to note that, even though as discussed above, the characters act and plan according to these premises, it is only in two of the novels, *Snow under the Sun* and *Sevillan Eyes* that marriage is presented as the sought-after happy ending. In the other novels, the characters later make other choices, distorting the social order. In *Sidewalks of Tedium* and *One Night* the main female characters embark on extra-marital affairs, in *Days with Him* and *Love and Mud* the female characters decide not to marry and in *The Cursed Novel* the main female character dies. These five novels thus acknowledge social structures and portray how the female characters see the role of masculinity as a power factor that they need to take into account, then present desirable masculinities that support the female characters but finally avoid adhering to the social expectations by not making matrimony the answer to the female characters' search for freedom. The novels can thus be said to be doublevoiced,[70] meaning that they serve two opposing, or at least different, agendas, but where both are as strong as each other. The first is that of describing an ideal masculinity and the second that of women's independence. In *Sidewalks of Tedium* and *Days with Him*, the two novels dealing in most detail with dream lovers, these two levels are most apparent. At first, Maria first has high hopes that her husband will change her life, but when he turns out to care more for his friends and their wellbeing, she understands that he is never going to perform the dream masculinity she had hoped for as a girl. Instead, she pins her hopes on Habib and starts an affair with him, although the initial infatuation quickly fades when she realises that he is too worried about her husband to be able to protect her. The clash between the reality that the male characters present and her dream picture forces her to rely on herself rather than to project her dream of protection onto a third man after her husband and Habib. For Rim, although it seems that as soon as the dream masculinity has been projected onto a specific male it is difficult to reapply it to someone else, it takes a bit longer to overcome her infatuation, but she does eventually. Leaving Ziyad, after what she knows is their last meeting, she feels empty. However, she soon realises that for the first time in her life, emptiness feels good. She tells herself that she will fill the emptiness with things she likes and decides to travel with her aunt and uncle to Europe to see new things and meet new people.[71] The dream femininity she lost when Ziyad was not able to perform her expected dream masculinity is no longer important to her; she herself will fill her own life and reinvent herself.

For both characters it seems that trying the dreams against reality tells the protagonists that they cannot rely on someone else to sort out their lives for them. This is also the conclusion Rim reaches at the end of *Days with Him*. Having looked for protection and not found it, she decides to depend on herself and take responsibility for her own decisions. At the same time, without the experiences with Ziyad and Habib, the female characters would never have reached this conclusion. In this respect, the failure of dream masculinity to save them has, ironically, saved them and made them aware that they, themselves, must formulate the life they want to live. The critique of the hegemonic masculinity in these two novels is hence double. First, by painting a picture of a perfect male in contrast to other, less agreeable versions and then secondly, by showing that no one of the protagonists finds true happiness living through her dream masculinity. At the same time, none of the novels propose a fundamental change of society but sees what happens to the characters as personal failures, which they now have to clear up themselves. In these two novels the dream masculinity can hence be said to be only a dream, or a hope for something, that did not really work out. The same conclusion can be made in *Love and Mud* and *The Cursed Novel*. Inas, although she has a good job and position, does not find happiness with Ahmad, the ideal man, despite her father's good intentions and the fact that he stands for everything that she wants in society. In *The Cursed Novel*, Hanan dies from heart failure without her idolised dad being able to save her. Hence these dreams did not work out, even if they can still be read as reformulations of masculinity in their fictional societies. Although formulated for different reasons, the novels discussed portray a dream masculinity created to save the female protagonist and change her life. The most important quality they see in the masculinities is thus the agency to promote change. With this initial expectation, the female characters subscribe to the stereotypical division of masculinity as being equal to activity and femininity as equal to passivity, a view that seems prevalent in all the novels, and one that the women at the beginning of their narratives strive to uphold. The male characters are urged to be active and take control, even in situations where the female characters are controlling the events. Though negating this division by actively choosing their partners, they select a partner with the expectation that he will change their life. The masculinity they look for is active, assertive and able to carry the responsibility for his own actions. Through the shifting view on men and masculinity, the women's view of themselves changes from being needy and dependant, to believing that they have something to offer a potential partner. However, this does not mean that the novels offer versions of female masculinity or male femininity. It seems instead to be of the utmost importance that the characters divide between male and female conduct. Through their similar way of dealing with dream masculinity, they hint at a continuous view on male and female gender norms. However, the circumstances the characters want to escape from show a change in the formulation of literary masculinity. As the protagonist develops and gains experiences, her dream masculinity changes from being a saviour, whom she lives through, to becoming an equal partner with whom she can share her life. The novels thus seem to propose that masculinity is a complement to femininity rather than the answer to a better life.

The female creation of masculinity in the novels from this time period is thus not a direct critique of masculinity. On the contrary, even when the female characters at the end of the novels move on, they are not dissatisfied with the masculinities as such, but they have realised that this particular performance is not what will make them happy. Rim's initial thoughts on needing a man to be able to live *through* him is changed to her wanting to live for herself, but with a companion who needs her for what she is. As her relationship with Ziyad deteriorates, Rim reconsiders many of the characteristics she saw as necessary when first formulating her dream masculinity. Moreover, she begins to see her own role in making Ziyad the dream. While Rim is mourning her broken relationship, Nadya, her aunt, tries to explain to her what it is that has happened. During the discussion, Rim disagrees angrily, but at the end of the novel, it becomes evident that Nadya's analysis agrees with the events of the novel, and also with the other novels of this period.

> هي قصة الفتاة الشرقية التي لا تعرف شيئاً عن الدنيا فتنقاد لعاطفتها وتصب حياتها في وجود رجل! الفتاة التي تحب بكل قلبها وروحها وجسدها فتعيش حلماً لمدة وجيزة، وتستيقظ فجأة ليصدمها الواقع... الفتاة التي ترى حبيبها كما يصوّر لها الخيال وعندما يظهر الحبيب على حقيقته تسحقها المفاجأة.[72]

> It is the story of the Eastern girl who knows nothing of the world. She is steered by her feelings and pours her whole life into the existence of a man. The girl who loves with her whole heart, soul and body, she lives a dream for a short while, then suddenly wakes up to the shock of reality. The girl who sees her lover as her imagination presents him, and when he appears as his true self, the surprise crushes her.

The masculinity formation which, on one hand is seen as a dream masculinity, exemplifying how reality could be if real men were like the characters in the novels is, on the other hand, described as an illusion and not something that a woman can actually rely on. Through their characters, the female authors thus both experiment with positive and supportive masculinities and use the female characters to show that a woman's own development and strength is more important than finding a man.

2

Politically and Ideologically Influenced Masculinities

أليس الرجل الكامل الرجولة هو مَن يقف أمام التيار ولا يبالي؟ يفعل ما يمليه عليه ضميره ولا يبالي بالآخرينَ. يقول كلمة الحق ولا يهمّه رضي الناس أم غضبوا.[1]

Is not the man with a complete masculinity the one who faces the current without hesitation? He does what his consciousness tells him to do and does not care about others. He tells the truth and does not worry if people will be pleased or angry.

The novels discussed in detail in this chapter were all written during the late 1970s and early 1980s, the period named 'the Political Man' in the introduction. During this period, the politically engaged masculinity, or the revolutionary hero, became a feature in both men's and women's fiction in Syria.[2] When the political situation changed, the revolutionary hero consequently disappeared and in the novels of the 1990s the idealistic, ideologically influenced masculinity as a main theme is rare. The masculinities discussed in this chapter can thus be seen as an example of Syrian female authors' engagement, through their plots, with the social and political life in the country and region. As Iman al-Qadi notes, the novels of this period are influenced by the changing reality of Syrian society, with a larger number of women working outside their homes and thus mixing with colleagues, in addition to an increase in female students completing degrees at university level.[3] Due to an intensified interest in existentialist philosophy, socialist ideology and the development of independent new states, it is further a time in Arabic literature where it had become increasingly important to show an interest in political affairs.[4] The political and ideological masculinities created can therefore be read as reactions to the changing political landscape. Whereas the masculinities discussed invite the female characters to participate in the change, they also stand for promises of security and protection. In the previous chapter, new forms of masculinity construction were used as a way of showing how women's life could be different if the performance of masculinity changed. In this chapter the masculinity of the novels' young men can be read as being synonymous with the cause they are fighting for, and the female characters are seen to be infatuated both with the men and with the political ideas. As representatives for political trends, the novels' men are idealised and idolised by the women. The masculinities created can be said to craft a new ideology rather than simply new gender roles. The ideologically tainted masculinity of the main characters is contrasted with other types of masculinity in the fictional societies described, and although they are made out to be very different, they appear to rest on similar foundations. The political masculinity is hence more about how masculinity is performed than what it entails. The vantage point is that of the female protagonist who seeks the support and help of male characters in order to reach her goal. The connection between the male characters and social changes means that the male characters' traits stand for what is suggested to be a better society. The novels further demonstrate how, what is seen as outdated forms of masculinity, are contrasted with the new, transformative ways of performing masculinity and how, in this way, hegemonies change. In the introduction to their book on politically engaged literature in the Middle East, Friederike Pannewick and Georges Khalil write that "[l]iterature can be read as a transmitter of a certain political ideology but also as a kind of critique that primarily subverts established political and cultural orders'.[5] This also fits as a description of the literature women produce in this era, where they both formulate a political message connected to women and the nation, but by doing this on a personal level they subvert the prevalent orders of how things usually happen in their fictional societies, as well as the expected forms of fiction.

Although all the novels discussed in this chapter touch on political and ideological changes, they cover topics as different as the Lebanese civil war, Palestinian freedom fighters and the end of the French mandate in Syria. The political or ideological man takes a prominent role in all the novels. He is young and filled with ideas of change and justice, he is not put in opposition with the previous ideal father figure, but is seen as a modern, able and progressive version of the dream man. His primary concern is his country and his political cause. The characteristics exhibited by the political man are similar to those exhibited by the father figure previously discussed, and the actions expected from him by women (and other men) are similar, but the political man is portrayed in a context of political awareness. If the masculinities described in the first wave of novels could be seen as helping and supporting daughters and lovers, and functioning as role models in the novels, the political man talks of "woman's role' in the new society which his political ideas will build. The relationships described are no longer between a man and a woman but between two representatives of a better society where both will play their distinct roles. Like the dream masculinity or ideal father before him, the political man is the source of knowledge in the relationship. He is the one who introduces political and revolutionary ideas to the female characters and urges them to join the political movements, in some cases by taking up arms, in others by becoming nurses, teachers or messengers, occupations presented as more suitable for women in the novels.

The novels discussed in this chapter are *Kawābīs Bayrūt* (*Beirut Nightmares*, 1976) by Ghada al-Samman. This novel is divided into chapters of varying length where a reoccurring female 'I' often appears as the narrator; however, there are several chapters from other viewpoints introducing other characters trying to navigate life in the war-torn city, as well as inanimate objects such as shop mannequins, trying to deal with their new situation. The way of narration adds to the feelings of chaos that the plot describes. In *Bustān al-karaz* (*The Cherry Orchard*, 1977) by Qamar Kilānī, the scene is also Beirut and Lebanon but at the beginning of the civil war. The main character, Sūnyā, has begun to study at university and through her new friends she has become involved in a political group. She has never before thought about how society is organised or how wealth is distributed and the things she learns do not at all fit with the wealthy upbringing she has received. When the war begins, she decides to fight together with Sāmī, her boyfriend, and the person who has introduced her to political thoughts. Her brother also decides to take up arms, but on the opposite side to Sunya and with very different motives. Whereas both children take up arms to fight, their wealthy father decides to leave Lebanon with his mistress to escape the war. *al-Waṭan fī al-ʿaynayn* (*The Homeland in a Pair of Eyes*, 1979) by Ḥamīda Naʿnaʿ is concerned with Palestine and the resistance movement. The Syrian girl, Nadya, feels that she needs to do something with regards to the Palestinian cause, she cannot just sit and read about what happens there. She decides to join the resistance movement and, once she is accepted and has received her training, she starts to go on missions. When, for different reasons, the resistance movement decides that she no longer can serve them, she is cut off from the organisation. She marries and ends up in Paris where she tries to build a new life for herself, although her thoughts constantly return to her time with the resistance movement and she looks for a possible way back. *Man yajru' ʿalā al-shawq* (*Who Dares to Long*, 1989) by the same author is also set in Paris and the characters are a group of ex-freedom fighters and participants in various resistance movements. The main character in this novel is also called Nadya, although it is not the same character in the two books. This Nadya is disillusioned with the political leaders in all the Arab countries and the way they work against, not with, their people. To support her disillusionment, the novel moves between different characters and tells their separate stories before focus returns to Nadya who decides to move with 'Umar to fight against the occupation in a north African country. The final two novels to be discussed in this chapter are both set in Syria. *Dimashq yā basmat al-ḥuzn* (*Damascus, O Smile of Sadness,* 1980) by Ulfat al-Idlibī is set at the beginning of the twentieth century under the period leading to the end of French rule in Syria. The novel is presented as the diary of Ṣabriyya, the main female character, and tells of her life until she decides to commit suicide. Sabriyya has grown up with her three brothers in a traditional family. The youngest of the brothers, Sami, is interested in politics and social change and he and his friend, 'Ādil, inspire Sabriyya to educate herself in these matters too. Sami and 'Adil are against French rule and participate in the armed struggle against the French forces. Whereas Sami and 'Adil stand for a new and progressive ideas, Sabriyya's older brother, Raghib, insists that Sabriyya should lead a very traditional life. When both Sami and 'Adil die, Sabriyya is left without any support and it is as if she, too, has died. In the final novel, *al-Dawwāma* (*The Whirlwind*, 1983) by Qamar Kilani, Sāmiya is the main female character. She comes from an upper-class Damascene family but decides to marry Karīm, her tutor. Karim is an intellectual and politically involved. Samiya is influenced by his ideas at first and goes against her own family, but with time she feels that Karim can do very little for her personally and for the country as a whole. At the end of the novel, Karim expresses the same ideas of failure.

The Female Perspective

In the novels discussed in this chapter, the female characters are the main focalisors of the political and ideological masculinity described and it is through their reactions and feelings that the masculinities presented are evaluated and understood. However, that does not mean that the novels do not have other focalisors: in *The Cherry Orchard*, the narrative is split between several different friends, although it returns to Sunya and her view of Sami, while sections of *Beirut Nightmares* are from a different perspective than that of the first-person female narrator. The attitude with which the focalisation is done is very much coloured by the ideological or political viewpoint that is developed in the novel and that also has a bearing on the way the masculinities are presented. The focus in these novels, as with the previous novels, is still mainly the relationship between the main female character and one particular – political or ideological – masculinity. However, in these novels the structure has developed from mainly intimate conversations between two characters and internal monologues into one which allows more voices. This has led to the introduction and development of a larger number of secondary characters. However, despite the new plethora of voices, the main male characters, still the objects of focalisation in the novels are, for different reasons, killed or removed, which means that many of their actions only exist as memories or fantasies. Each of the main female characters uses what she thinks her ideal man would do in a specific situation to judge others' and, to some extent, her own behaviour. All the novels are set in a time of political unrest, where the female characters are working to change their respective societies. The man they describe is either the female's initiator into political thought or activism, or someone they meet through their political activities; they hence become their main contact with the cause for which they are fighting. The masculinity the male characters perform can therefore be read as a signifier for the political cause, not just as the individual traits of a single character. How the male characters perform their masculinity becomes symbolic of the political struggle and the female characters' wish for change. The novels further present a juxtaposition between the generation of fathers and other older men, who can be read to represent the former or failing governments and regimes, and the young men who represent the future. The masculinity performance the women meet in society, and see as real, is the one performed by their fathers, neighbours and relatives, whereas the political and ideological masculinities that form their hopes for the future are represented through young men of their own age. This connection between a man's performance of masculinity and a change of political and social life can be seen as a continuation from the previous chapter. However, whereas Rim and the other characters in Chapter 1 were concerned with their individual happiness, the characters in this chapter are concerned with social change. In *Who Dares to Long*, the main character, Nadya, makes a clear connection between her political ideas and the man Khālid when she describes him as the smell of the earth she loves, the awaiting revolution and the future filled with stars.[6] He is thus not just her dream man but an incarnation of a better future for the whole country.

Like the novels in the previous chapter, these narratives are set in societies that place the female characters' lives and happiness at the mercy of male relatives and relations. Especially, *Damascus, O Smile of Sadness* (henceforth *Damascus*) is a testimony to how a woman's life can turn into a catastrophe if a negative masculinity, as the main character Sabriyya sees it, becomes influential in it. The description of the political male characters in *Damascus* can be seen as instructive of how masculinity should be performed from a female point of view. The use of male characters as heroes and models for change allows the writer to approach areas that are otherwise off-limits for female characters at particular times. For example, in *Damascus,* set at the beginning of the twentieth century, it is impossible for Sabriyya to be allowed to join the fight or find the political material she reads. At the same time, the projection of change onto a male character is necessary as it enables the female characters to comment while they watch from afar. The male characters further become the personification of ideals and it is therefore symbolic that they die or disappear in the plot but remain alive in the minds of the female characters.

Like the ideal father before him, the political man is not seen as performing a common masculinity; on the contrary, he stands out, but in a positive way. He is the standard against whom other men are judged and whom the female characters support and long for. Nadya, in Hamida Na'na''s *The Homeland in a Pair of Eyes* (henceforth *Homeland*), is part of the militant Palestinian freedom movement where she meets Abū Mashhūr. He is strong, idealistic, helpful and honourable and, in her and others' eyes, the ideal man, who soon becomes Nadya's role model. When he later dies, and she is banned from fighting, she thinks that marrying and creating a new life for herself will make it easier for her to live on. But her husband, despite doing everything she asks for, cannot measure up to the ideal masculinity she expects and they divorce. Her next lover has also been a freedom fighter, but in Africa, and Nadya has read some of his work on revolutions. When it shows through their relationship that the man has changed, and he no longer believes in the armed struggle and the revolutionary ideas he previously fought for, Nadya leaves him. She is once again disappointed not to find the ideal masculinity exhibited by Abu Mashhur. If the dream masculinity discussed in Chapter 1 was placed within the family, the political man, though having relationships with women, seems to be so detached from the family setting that it is necessary for him to die before anything more serious than an engagement has happened. In *Damascus,* Sabriyya loses both her brother and her boyfriend, who were the novel's two ideal, political men, and she is left with the brothers that are described as performing variations of negative masculinity.

As dead, the men continue to influence the female characters and their masculinity is idolised even more. Having given their lives for their cause, they cannot be criticized. In *Beirut Nightmares* by Ghada al-Samman, it is not the revolutionary man who stands out as the ideal masculinity but the military which finally comes to rescue the main female character from the war-torn city. They, especially their commander, exhibit the same characteristics of idealism, bravery and determinedness as the previously discussed masculinities, this time literally saving the heroine from chaos and death. Even if the army is rarely described, all the political men sooner or later take up arms against their enemy, and their ability to handle firearms becomes another way to measure their masculinity.

Like the previous portrayal of dream masculinities, many of these novels do not really take what they see as poor examples of masculinity to task. But contrary to the earlier novels they are given more space during this period, and it is also clear how the main characters feel about them. In *Damascus*, Sabriyya gave her diary to her niece Salmā before committing suicide. For being a personal diary, it spends a significant amount of time on other family members, particularly those who are male. This has implications for these characters too, as, rather than developing into fully fledged characters, they remain stereotypes. The characteristics of the various male characters are repeated several times and it becomes obvious who is seen as bad or good within the novel. In case of doubt, either Sabriyya or her niece Salma, add comments, explaining the character or situation further. The characterisation comes mainly through Sabriyya's comments and plays a part in the ideological framework of the novel; the sharp division between 'good' and 'bad' supports the general idea of a new ideology that will change life for the better.

In the first wave of novels, the characterisation of the male characters was mainly through a direct description by the female characters with support from secondary characters. Their interest and appreciation made him stand out as different from others. Through direct characterisation, statements about individual characters, either by an external narrator or the characters themselves might seem reliable, this does not necessarily reflect more than one character's view. In this second wave, the characterisation is still direct but with the addition of more male characters for comparison. There is also more focus on indirect characterisation which focuses on actions, speech and style. Using these different types of characterisation, information about the characters, but also their internal relationships, disseminates. This type of characterisation is affected by both the fictional environment and the background information of the reader. With regard to masculinity and the novels analysed, characterisation, in its different forms, sheds light on what a certain environment and context see as expected characteristics in masculinity. The analysis of characterisation falls close to the content of the text and will be used as a basis for the discussion of types of masculinities and their hierarchical connections. Mieke Bal further points out the way characterisation can indicate ideological positions for characters and suggests a model of opposing characteristics as a way of analysing themes in the character composition in novels.[7] The reoccurring trend of opposing masculinity and femininity in the novels analysed, as seen in the previous chapter, shows for example how the characters express views on which characteristics are promoted, or demoted, in male characters.

Changing Hegemonies and New Men

The concept of hegemonic masculinity is never stable but constantly reworked, due to new influences and changing power dynamics. Sometimes these changes take place due to a number of disconnected events, whereas at other times changing the hegemony is seen as a project. In *Working Out Egypt*,[8] Wilson Chacko Jacob gives an example of the last type of change. He shows how a conscious, long-term reworking of what he calls 'Effendi Masculinity' leads to a new performance of masculinity within this particular stratum of society in Egypt. In his book he shows how this change was triggered by a discontent for the role of masculinity that Egyptian men felt the British colonisers had imposed on them, and how the change was fuelled by a sense of nationalism.[9] A similar scenario can be seen in the novels discussed in this chapter, where the younger generation of men reacts towards the older generation's way of performing masculinity. The Effendi Masculinity, as outlined by Jacob, is constantly contrasted with what 'it is not' and hence exemplified by its opposite. This internal dichotomy, the fluidity of the new masculinity and its fixation with what 'it is not' is also seen in *Damascus* where Sabriyya constantly compares what she sees as old masculinity, which is the 'real' masculinity she sees her relatives perform, and 'ideal' masculinity, which is what she believes her boyfriend would perform if he were still alive. In *The Cherry Orchard* by Qamar Kilani, it is the father who exhibits all the traits the main character Sūnyā and her new friends fight against. He is rich and does not seem to have made his money in an honest way, he has a mistress that he spends time with, and he is more worried about saving himself and his wealth than taking a political stand for the country. Sunya, who has never really thought about her father in this way before, comes to a harsh awakening through the political meetings she participates in at university. During the meetings she becomes attracted to Sami, who is the opposite of her father, and deeply engaged in political activism. Hamida Na'na's two novels, *Who Dares to Long* and *Homeland* similarly build on the dichotomy between the men who dare to take a stand, and later pay the price for their involvement in the fight for freedom, and those who do nothing. In *The Whirlwind*, Karim, who is the new political man, overshadows his father-in-law, who used to be a prominent fixture in Damascene society. At the latter's funeral, people refer to him as 'the father of Karim's wife', rather than his own achievements, showing how ideals have changed. Later in the novel, his daughter returns to her family values and seeks help from her father's friend, an army officer, because her husband has left her. In all the novels, taking action and standing up for one's beliefs are what is seen as accepted masculinity within the circles in which the main characters move.

The 'ideal' masculinities discussed in this chapter are all performed by participants in ideological groups of young men; the ideal masculinity is therefore as much a political stand as a comment on gender relationships. 'Adil, Sabriyya's love interest in *Damascus,* fights against the French colonising powers. His performance of masculinity is a stand against both the coloniser and the elder generation, whom he sees as silent supporters of the French. He, and consequently Sabriyya, wants to see a new performance of masculinity, one that acknowledges the role of women in society and rejects what are described as traditional and colonial values. This idea of masculinity as a political signifier is similar to the concept of the 'new man' used by Huda Elsadda and others in relation to Egyptian society and literature.[10] The concept refers to a well-read, nationalist man who sees social change as the only way forward for his country at the beginning of the twentieth century. This character from the beginning of the century is also common in Syrian literature. In her trilogy on Syria, Nadya Khust incorporates characters similar to the new man, as does Ghada al-Samman in her novel *al-Riwāya al-mustaḥīla* (*The Impossible Novel,* 1997) and he further appears in *Damascus.*

The idea of a politically influenced masculinity is, however, not limited to novels set at the beginning of the twentieth century. 'The intellectual', which is Samira Aghacy's name for the politically engaged masculinity, became a feature in both Arabic and Syrian literature towards the end of the 1960s.[11] He differs from the 'new man' by being engaged in contemporary politics, an active advocate for various ideologies and opposed to what he sees as old-fashioned governments. Through his political ideas and the radical, often militant, solutions he proposes, this character believes that he will change society for the better. This type of masculinity continues to be popular until the beginning of the 1980s, when the disillusioned hero suddenly takes over.

The politicised masculinity, though formulated by male and female writers alike, coincides with the period when Syrian female writers became more involved in politics in their literary texts.[12] Aghacy points out that the masculinity performance of 'the intellectual' includes virility and sexual ability[13] and hence does not differ greatly from the hegemonic norm. Many of the male characters she analyses are particularly active in their sexual relationships and she makes a connection between the potent man and an ability to save the virtuous motherland.[14] The male characters discussed in this chapter do not conform to this description; instead, they die or disappear before they can commence a sexual relationship with any of the female characters. Instead, the focus is on their ideological foundations and the struggle for a better society. Whereas virility, and the ability to father, appear in relation to other characters it never becomes an issue for the main male characters of the novels. This is particularly telling as women writers have dealt with these topics in other circumstances. It seems that in these novels, the masculinities are incarnations of a better society. The ideal men function as symbols for change, and are consequently removed from physical and bodily needs and actions, although they are able to confess love for their girlfriends.

In order not to confuse these concepts, and since the masculinities in the Syrian literature of the 1970s to the 1980s, are often fighting for political change, the concept of 'political man' is used in this chapter instead of 'new man' or 'intellectual'. This opens up the discussion to similar masculinity formations, published in the same era but with plots situated in different periods. In *Damascus*, the young men who are seen as performing the ideal masculinity are active members of the nationalist movement. The novel is set in the first half of the twentieth century, a time preceding Syria's independence in 1946. Qamar Kilani's *The Cherry Orchard* takes place in Lebanon at the beginning of the Lebanese civil war in the 1970s. Ḥamīda Naʿnaʿ's *The Homeland* does not give clear dates and disguises many place names, but it appears that the narrative moves between Europe, Syria, Lebanon and Palestine. Despite not giving dates, it seems to be describing events during the 1970s and is thus, like many other novels from the period, dealing with the reality in which it is created. *The Whirlwind* refers to 1948 and takes place during the Six-Day-War in 1967, an important factor in the plot since , as can be seen from the novel, the loss of this war is seen to have had a huge impact on Arab intellectuals.

Even though 'the political man' is used to dislocate the characters from a specific time, the discussion still draws on the concept of the 'new man'. The 'political man' in the novels above, like his brother 'the new man', calls for the education of women as a way of bettering the country. In the novels set at the beginning of the twentieth century, it is a question of basic education such as reading and writing whereas, later on, it is a question of political and military training. However, as Elsadda points out in her discussion of the 'new man', 'aspiring to a more egalitarian relationship with women does not, however, compromise male dominance and control',[15] something that is evident in all the novels discussed here. The female characters are invited and encouraged to take part in the men's world of knowledge and fighting, but by coming in as beginners and only being allowed to participate at the mercy of their male companions, they are never able to take control.

Male and Female Gender Roles

Despite new vocabulary and a new theoretical framework grounded in various ideologies, the internal dichotomy between male and female seems to be firmly in place within the characters' minds as described in all the novels. Aghacy even argues that the nationalistic discourses and the ideologically influenced characters distinguish, more firmly than previous literary trends, between what is considered male and what is considered female.[16] Signs of masculinity are still to be in control, to be protective and to take care of women, while at the same time criticising previous generations' ways of doing the same thing. The 'political man' is therefore a re-shaping of masculinity and internal power foundations rather than a reformulation of intra-gender relations. The political men in the novels use their relationships with women as a way of forming a new powerbase vis-à-vis the older generation, rather than changing the balance of power between the genders.

The fact that the expectations the female narrators place on their revolutionary men are very similar to what they, especially Sabriyya in *Damascus*, have grown up with and criticise as old fashioned, is a sign of the duality of hegemonic masculinity. There is a fixed idea of what masculinity is and all men, whether or not they agree, are judged against this; however, when times change and political ideas begin to influence society, the views on how to execute masculinity change. The ideal masculinity Sabriyya, Nadya, Sunya and the others dream of is a new manifestation of an old structure. The ideal masculinity they formulate is connected, through descriptions and discussions described in the novels, to their belief that they need a man to make them happy. Not just as a subject of love, but as someone fighting for their right to study, work and have an opinion. It is further a manifestation of how they want the whole society to change in order to become better for everyone: men and women.

The views of Sabriyya and the other characters on masculinity together form a hegemony that builds, first and foremost, on the differences between men and women. One of the arguments to urge men to fight is that only women sit at home – real men make a difference.[17] Secondly, men provide for those they are responsible for. Sabriyya's father makes sure there is food in the house even during the long times of bombardments and curfews.[18] Third, a real man has high moral standards and does what is deemed right for him, his country and family. Fourth, he protects those he is responsible for – both physically and mentally. Fulfilling these four expectations leads to power and respect. In all the novels, political activism functions as a fifth indicator for how characters should be judged.

The male characters are not only judged on the basis of performing elements included in the political or ideological masculinity, but also on *how* they perform them. The ideal masculinity the narrators formulate is hence drawn upon masculinity as the narrators see it performed in their encounters with different men in the novels. Similarly, Deniz Kandiyoti argues in a chapter on the paradoxical nature of masculinity in the Middle East, that being 'a new man' should be interpreted as a way for sons or young men to rebel against their fathers rather than as an actual male revolution for women's education.[19] The new man, as well as the revolutionary man, is preoccupied by freeing his country from external powers and defending what he sees as national values. External, political motives are incorporated into the concept of masculinity and used by the younger generation to gain power and position; this does not necessarily mean that the previous power structures between the genders have changed. In the novels it is clear that the ideal masculinity, as performed by the revolutionary men, is a new type of masculinity, but to some extent, these are only surface differences, the underlying structures are similar to those seen in the novels' portrayal of traditional or old masculinity. For example, in all the meetings between 'Adil and Sabriyya, he is the one who thinks, organises and understands. On more than one occasion, Sabriyya comments that she understands part of what she is given to read or writes about how happy she is when she thinks she has understood everything.[20] Her father, or her older brother Rāghib, would never have bothered to discuss anything with her or ask for her opinions, so the interest 'Adil and Sami pay her is certainly new. At the same time, she initially does not think of herself as an equal to them but as someone they educate – after a long holiday, when she has done her utmost to read and study, she hopes that she has come closer to their level.

سأصغي إلى حديث سامي وعادل وأتفهمه جيّداً. وسأشترك أنا أيضاً في الحديث. ألم أصبح قارئة جادة مثلهما تماماً؟[21]

> I will listen to Sami and 'Adil's discussion and understand it well. I too will participate in the discussion, have I not become a serious reader just like them?

This never happens because after the holiday Sabriyya is forced to wear a full veil and as a veiled woman she is not allowed to walk with men,[22] hence she is deprived of the chance to prove to Sami, 'Adil and to herself, how serious she is. Next time any discussions are mentioned in the diary, neither Sabriyya nor the boys are acting as if they were equals. To herself, Sabriyya admits that she is as good as the men, but when they meet, she awaits their invitation to participate. More importantly, she does not find it strange that she has to wait for an invitation; her subordination is still internalised by both her and the men. The equality she expects is by invitation only, as when her father invites her mother to talk to him after the children are in bed. The ideal masculinity she hopes for is therefore not so different from the real masculinity she wants to change.

The same pattern appears in both *The Homeland* and *The Cherry Orchard,* where the girls exercise and study in order to fit into their respective combat groups but are still, in particular Sunya, considered less-worthy members of their groups. Nadya, who at one point functions as the leader of a group hijacking airplanes in Europe, is quickly dispensed with when she disagrees with the leaders; the other members of the group are told that she has left to marry and have children. In *Who Dares to Long,* Nadya (the main female characters of Na'na''s novels are both called Nadya) is visiting her boyfriend 'Amr in his camp. When they are being attacked by the enemy, she gets dressed to go and check what has happened, but he immediately orders her to stay inside in case there are more attacks whereas he, as the man, will find out what is going on.[23] Earlier, when she has just arrived, Nadya is full of questions about the political and military situation in the country. However, that is not what 'Umar was looking forward to; he tells her that he was waiting for her to come to him as a woman, not as a bunch of questions.[24] Even within the struggle for the new society, there is a gender order that places males over females and presupposes that even women who participate or have participated in armed struggle should leave certain matters to the men. In *The Whirlwind*, Samiya receives a letter from Nājī, Karim's friend, with whom she has had a brief relationship. In the letter he describes himself as the thinker, Karim as the intellect and Samiya as the heart. He admits that all three are necessary, but it is obvious that the heart is the least valued of the three and the gender stereotypical division is clear.

The connection between performing male activities and power is evident in all the novels. As is the reference to armed struggle as something masculine. In *The Cherry Orchard*, Sunya is at first shocked when she sees this aspect of the fight and she wonders if weapons must be the sign of strength and masculinity and heroism.[25] Later in the novel, another character, Ilyās, expresses that it is the duty of all young men to learn how to use firearms and taking part in battles is seen as proving one's masculinity. In *Beirut Nightmares*, the connection between masculinity and weapons is also clear. In the final chapter, the only one labelled Dream instead of Nightmare, a grandmother is saying good night to her grandson. She sees his guitar and looks at him like a child, but she fails to see the gun he has hidden and the signs of masculinity in his eyes. The connection between the gun and masculinity as opposed to music and childishness is telling, since it defines both what masculinity contains and what it does not. In *Damascus*, it is also the shift between reading and discussing ideological change and taking up arms to fight for the ideas that change the perception of Sami and 'Adil from boys to men, even in the eyes of their opponents.

When 'Adil is back from fighting, he and Sabriyya take to meeting in an orchard close to Sabriyya's school. One week, Sabriyya does not turn up and 'Adil is very upset with her for not attending. When he hears that the reason for her absence is that her mother was ill and that Sabriyya needed to take care of her, he immediately advises her to do as much of the work at home as she can. He does not ask what her brothers are doing to support their mother, nor does he suggest getting help so that Sabriyya can concentrate on her studies. It seems that women's education and work are only important if there are no pressing needs, such as ill mothers or babies, to keep them at home. Sabriyya herself, who has previously complained about the unfairness of her doing all the housework while her brothers are sleeping or being out with friends, now agrees. It is her sense of duty towards her ill mother that later hinders her from eloping with 'Adil, a decision that effectively changes her future. The fact that she herself has played a part in her broken dreams is never analysed by Sabriyya, who lays the blame solely on her brother Raghib and his wish to see her unhappy. This is also a clue to her perception of gender. She, as a woman, has no agency to act and influence things, so the acting – and the responsibility – must be placed on her brother.

Ideological Masculinity – the Political Man

To give up everything to fight for 'the cause' is brought out as the core of masculinity in these novels, whether it is Syrian nationalism against the French or Arab nationalism against Israel. The male characters, as well as the female ones, take an active part in forming these values. In *The Whirlwind*, Karim describes himself to Samiya when they are at the beginning of their relationship by saying:

أنا يا سامية إنسان بسيط ومخلص. همي هذا الوطن المسحوق المكبل بالقيود.

> Samiya, I am a simple and devoted person. My only concern is this crushed and fettered homeland.[26]

However, rather than looking at the political man and his own interpretations of what he wants, the novels discussed in this chapter present women's views on these men and what they stand for. Samiya, for example, marries Karim not only because of his views on the homeland but also because she believes that he will be an injection of fresh blood into her cold family. In order to explain what is new and different, the female characters need a model for comparison and it is often the father or older brothers who play the role of symbols of the past. In *The Whirlwind*, Samiya's brothers do not want her to work and one of them, Fā'iz, would prefer for her to live with him, rather on her own, to protect her and the family from gossip. After Samiya has married Karim and begun to be more and more influenced by his ideas, many of which criticize the choices and lifestyle of her parents, her father first questions and argues with her, but then later turns quiet. Sami, the youngest of Sabriyya's brothers in *Damascus* and the one who represents ideological masculinity is put in contrast to the two other brothers and the father. Sabriyya cannot find fault with his behaviour therefore he becomes the ideal against whom she judges everyone else. He sees the value in education and he is interested in politics. He brings home books and articles to read and shares some of them with his sister. Even when his father and Raghib argue with him, he stays convinced of his principles and ideas. In the end, he decides that in order to not just talk, but actually work for a change, he needs to take part in the armed struggle, so he runs away from home to take up arms.

Sami's conviction influences Sabriyya's views on the future and on society. She welcomes the changes promised by the nationalists and sees how they will shape a new man and masculinity as opposed to what her father and two older brothers stand for. In *The Homeland*, Nadya sees her father and brothers as examples of old and dictatorial types of masculinity but, like Sabriyya, although she finds it difficult to cope with her brothers' wish to decide for her she, too, finds excuses for her father. And when she later needs help and support she turns to her father and mother and takes their advice on getting married as a way of solving her problems.

In *Damascus*, Sabriyya finds another ideal masculinity in addition to her brother Sami, namely Sami's friend ʿAdil, who later becomes her boyfriend. She sees them as very different from what she labels old masculinity and she is excited about their ideas and discussions. Both Sami and ʿAdil are among the nationalists and take part in the uprising and fighting against the French. In addition to the fight for a free Syria, their political ideas include things like education for women, the removal of class boundaries and a revival of the Syrian nation.[27] For example, Sami is adamant that his sister should be allowed to finish her schooling and not be married off to someone. When the mother keeps on saying that Sabriyya's only chance for a happy future is if a good man comes to ask for her hand, he tries to persuade her to change her mind.

أرجوكِ يا أمي أن تفهمي كلامي وتقتنعي به: إياكِ وإن تقبلي بزواج صبرية ولو جاءها ملك الزمان قبل أن تنال شهادتها.[28]

> Mother I beg you to understand and be convinced by what I say: Do not agree to marry off Sabriyya before she has her degree even if the king of all times would ask for her hand.

Furthermore, Sami and ʿAdil are against the veil, and believe that marriage should be a private matter for the individual, not something for their family to decide. Sami confides in his sister about his girlfriend and supports her love for his best friend ʿAdil. The father, in contrast, does not even acknowledge his love for their mother and the way the two of them look at marriage is as a business deal. The first mention of ʿAdil in Sabriyya's diary is when he and Sami follow Sabriyya to school. She walks between them, protected, not speaking in order not to disturb their conversation. ʿAdil is described as sometimes asking her to participate in the discussion despite the fact that she is both younger and a girl. All the ideas she hears make Sami and ʿAdil stand out as new and different in comparison to her father and her other brothers. Sabriyya spends time with her brother and boyfriend reading and discussing. She is filled with the new nationalist ideals they teach her and sees a great role for women as educators for future generations. Since mixing between genders is difficult in the fictional historical society, the summer vacation brings a halt to the daily conversations and the novel never presents deeper political or ideological debates between Sabriyya and the male characters. In novels that are set in a later period, for example *The Cherry Orchard*, *The Whirlwind* and Hamida Naʿnaʿ's two novels, the characters, male and female, spend a lot of time in ideological discussions, exploring different angles of a topic. The historical setting in *Damascus* might also be why Sabriyya has two ideal men, her brother who acts as a facilitator, and her boyfriend who is described as the performer of political masculinity and the one with whom she wants to build a future. In the other novels, the narrators have the freedom to study at university and come and go as they please. Since they are not confined to the house in the same way as Sabriyya, they have more opportunities to meet men performing different types of masculinities and do not need an ally at home to allow them to meet. This further accentuates the changing roles of the female characters who, with time and education, are portrayed as more able to form opinions on their own, although the structure of being informed and initiated to the topic by a man still remains.

The next time ʿAdil is mentioned in the novel, Sabriyya is older and he comes to give back some books to Sami. Sabriyya opens the door to him and they have a quick and secret conversation. ʿAdil recommends novels to Sabriyya and when she appears sad after having read a particular novel, he warns her about another one that might upset her, confessing that he himself cried when he read it.[29] Through this confession he is described by the text as both sensitive and at the same time protective of Sabriyya's feelings. It is interesting here to contrast Sabriyya's reaction to ʿAdil's tears with how she reacts to her brother Mahmud when he is crying. In this context, she sees the crying as a sign of sensitivity and a demonstration of how ʿAdil is connected to his feelings. In the case of Mahmud, Sabriyya pities him since he is unable even to see blood without crying.[30] The act of crying is hence closely connected to the circumstances. As a sign of fear and weakness, it is seen as a fault by Sabriyya, but as a sign of the new, more sensitive man, it is welcomed. Sabriyya looks for empathy in her new man, not the cowardice and hysteria she finds in her brother. Both Sami and ʿAdil are described as being fearless and firm towards those who oppose them. The empathy they feel is with the poor and weak, groups that will be redeemed and looked after as soon as the new nationalist government is in power. The new, sensitive man still looks after and protects but the objective is different. He protects out of care not out of obligation, which is how the father is described in the novel. Later on, when Sami is killed, 'Adil writes to Sabriyya, explaining how much he hates to see her sad and tells her that he will now step in to look after her.

> أشعر أنني مسؤول عنك أمام سامي، أتساءل كيف أستطيع أن أمسح الحزن عن عينيك وأعيد إليهما ألقهما الذكي؟[31]

> I feel responsible for you in front of Sami, I ask myself how I can wipe out the sadness in your eyes and bring back their clever sparkle?

In *The Homeland* and *The Cherry Orchard*, Nadya's and Sunya's political men are very similar to Sami and 'Adil in their interest in their different political causes, the way they have read and studied the topic and their decision to later take up arms. Nadya joins a radical group, which fights for the right to a Palestinian state and she uses Abu Mashhur, the most experienced fighter in the group, as her model. Like Sabriyya's model masculinities he stands for a new society where old injustices are going to be wiped out, he supports Nadya's fighting and practicing and discusses political and revolutionary texts with her. The same feeling of renewal that fills Sabriyya when listening to Sami and 'Adil fills Nadya when she thinks of Abu Mashhur. In *Who Dares to Long*, Nadya is also filled with a sense of hope when she thinks of Khalid and how they, together, will transform society into something better. The idea of being at the centre of an historical change appears in all the novels, even if *Who Dares to Long* and *The Whirlwind* focus on the characters' distress when this change does not happen.

In *The Cherry Orchard*, Sunya is also living through a transition. The novel is set at the beginning of the Lebanese civil war and Sunya has, thanks to her boyfriend, joined an armed left-wing, Palestinian group. Like Sabriyya and the two Nadyas, she is swept away by the idea of men and women working together for a better future. They all think of new gender roles where women are no longer just wives and mothers but companions and comrades participating in a joint life, not just as a part of a man's life. As discussed in the previous chapter, part of the changing masculinity is an allowance for women's advancement. The female characters see a need for the male role to change so that women can take up important roles in society.

In all the novels, the revolutionary men disappear after a while. Sami, Sabriyya's brother, dies during one of the French attacks and Sabriyya has no way of knowing how he would have behaved as a grown man. His 20-year-old idealist self becomes, for her, the real Sami. She thinks of him every time she feels unjustly treated. To support herself she thinks of what Sami would have done and how he would have helped her had he been alive. She turns her dead brother into an ideal masculinity through which she judges the rest of the world. When his former girlfriend suggests that Sami would not have mourned over her for more than a few days before he found a new girlfriend, had she died instead of him, Sabriyya is outraged.[32] In her world, ideal masculinity equates to high moral standards and fidelity and she is sure Sami would have behaved accordingly. She herself cannot imagine marrying someone else when 'Adil is murdered, and she assumes he would have felt the same. 'Adil, though surviving longer than Sami, is turned into another ideal masculinity for Sabriyya. She imagines their life together and how they would have lived happily in a small village. As with Sami, she plays out different scenarios in her diary about how her life would have been with 'Adil and how he would have reacted to different events in their life. Her fantasy of 'Adil is transformed, in her mind, to reality and she laments the future she believes that she is missing.

In *The Homeland,* Nadya and Abu Mashhur are separated having completed both training and a successful mission together. When they are reunited, they are only allowed a short time together before Abu Mashhur is reported missing after an attack in Israel. Nadya constantly thinks of him when she later marries, she wishes her husband were more like how she thinks Abu Mashhur would have been as a husband. Having only lived with Abu Mashhur in combat situations and training camps, she still sees him as the ideal man in any situation and he, or her own image of him, influences her life and decisions.

In *The Cherry Orchard,* Sunya is separated from her boyfriend Sami on their first mission; she does not find him until the end of the novel, but she soon loses him again. For most of the novel, Sami functions as the ideal revolutionary man for Sunya. She does not know what he is doing, but she assumes he is the perfect fighter and she judges herself and others on that basis. The female narrators create characters that cannot be negated, since they are either dead or not present, nor can they disappoint the narrators by behaving differently from what they expect. It is also significant that the men die and the women live, but in a world that does not change in the way they were hoping. Sunya finds that the group she has been fighting with begins to treat her as a servant, exactly what she was working to avoid. When she leaves them, she leaves for a world of chaos and different armed gangs, one of which later kills her. Both Nadyas, in *Who Dares to Long* and *The Homeland,* want to return to the fighting and do something for the cause, but they, too, are held back by the changing world. Sabriyya, on the other hand, becomes a voluntary prisoner, staying by her father's bedside to look after him without leaving the house.

Another example of the mix between new and old can be seen in Sabriyya's participation in a demonstration. As an advocate for a new society, 'Adil encourages Sabriyya to participate with the other girls.[33] Her father, when he later finds out about the demonstration, states that no daughter of his would demonstrate with boys.[34] His problem is not with the political ideas but with the fact that Sabriyya has been talking to, and walking with, men. Had he been present at the demonstration he would have been pleased. The girls do not take part as equals to the men, but as symbols to convince the French that the entire population is against them. The girls are driven around on a lorry while the men and boys act as their protectors, making sure that nothing happens to them and that no one can reach them: not the police, not the French and certainly not unknown men. Sabriyya, initially excited that she, as a woman, will be able do something for the revolution and not just wait around patiently, is pleased to see that the women are looked after. She wants to participate but she also wants the security of being protected. This wish echoes the ideas brought forward in the novels of the first era, where protection played an important role in the formulation of dream masculinity.

Sunya and Nadya, who unlike Sabriyya are used to mixing with men, also expect to be protected and looked after by their men. Sunya trusts Sami to look out for her and save her. When the roles are reversed and she saves him from the guarded wing of the hospital where he is kept, they are both uncomfortable and their relationship crumbles. Sunya starts to question her motives for participating in the fighting and, when Sami leaves on a mission without giving her any details, she decides to leave. No longer protected and looked after by Sami, she can just as well look after herself somewhere else. When Nadya in *The Homeland* has a breakdown after Abu Mashhur's disappearance, she is pleased to see her father and mother come to her side to look after her. Her parents, who were previously a hindrance, now provide welcome comfort and protection. When she begins to feel better, she agrees to accept her doctor's proposal and they get married. One of her reasons for accepting is that he makes her feel secure and looked after. Samiya, in *The Whirlwind*, who marries Karim because his behaviour is different from the customs and traditions she is used to, is still disappointed when he spends all his time working for the cause and she is left alone, without protection or the married life she wanted.

Nadya and Sunya express similar ideas. They want to be looked after and cared for in addition to being appreciated for what they do. They want a new society and, at the same time, they expect that parts of the previous hegemonic masculinity will stay in place so that they are looked after and feel secure. What

Sabriyya expects from 'Adil is essentially what she has grown up to expect from her father. She does, however, want the execution of these things to be different. She agrees to the what – what a man should do –but wants a change in the how – how a man should perform these things. She is also certain that a woman on her own has a very small chance of living a good life. In her world, the man stands for power and decision-making.

In *The Whirlwind*, Karim has left Samiya and she is not sure what to do. However, she remembers her father's old friend, an army officer who she is sure will help her. When she describes him, she says that he is strong and able, a true nationalist and he is, furthermore, performing perfect masculinity.[35] She has exchanged her previous ideal man and now relies on a friend of her father, who at the beginning of the novel stood for old-fashioned ideas that she opposed. When she meets the officer for the first time, he says that he had been expecting her to come to him. He then goes on to ask about Karim, a question which Samiya ignores and instead answers that what is important for her now is the people of her country who are suffering. The political man is portrayed to be unable to help and the state, personified through the masculine officer, is what can be relied on.

The Death of the Political Man

Other than being the personification of a new social order, whether political or ideological, there is one other point that most of the male characters discussed in this chapter share: an untimely death. This means that the ideal masculinity of the novels is never properly tested, the young men disappear or die before their masculinity can be accurately implemented. The worldview they propose remains a fantasy for the female characters and can be said to signify a utopian society. On one hand, this leads to a possibility for the characters to glorify them even more, since they can no longer do or say anything that will contradict the ideal picture painted of them. On the other hand, this leads to a crisis for the main female characters. When 'Adil is killed it is as if Sabriyya's dreams die too and she says:

مات عادل، وانتهى كل شيء![36]

'Adil died and everything ended!

She no longer goes out and refuses to take up her studies, even though her parents change their mind and allow her to go back to school. She stops following the developments on the political scene and no longer mixes with people. Without the support of a man like ʿAdil or Sami, she sees no possibilities for herself. Her previous ideas of women taking part in society are completely forgotten when she needs to support herself. Her earlier critique of her mother, who did not dare to leave the house without her father's permission,[37] could now be directed towards her own life. She does not allow herself to carry on with her life without the necessary (male) support.

No one of the characters has built her ideal masculinity on imagination alone. In Sabriyya's case she knows the way both Sami and ʿAdil looked at masculinity and masculine ideals when they were alive[38] and the same is true for Sunya and Nadya. What they do not know is how time and circumstances would have shaped the men had they lived to marry and complete their lives as fathers and husbands. Based on what they know, they imagine what the men would have done and said and they form a picture of ideal masculinity. The ideal masculinity of the revolutionary men is contrasted with other men's behaviour in the novels. In some cases, the narrators reflect on the differences while no comment is made in others.

In *Who Dares to Long*, Khalid turns his back on the revolutionary and idealistic ideas that attracted Nadya. When she finds out that he is no longer her revolutionary hero but trades weapons and sells the names of previous comrades to the enemy he becomes a dead man to her.[39] Rather than become more motivated to continue the fight herself, she loses direction when Khalid stops and she can no longer fight or help her comrades with other things.[40] As a final symbol, her friend ʿAsim, whom she describes as a real idealist, is killed and there are no revolutionary men left for her to use as inspiration until she later meets ʿUmar.

The revolutionary man is hence not a revolution, he is a new version of the masculinity previously performed. He is nonetheless important, because in these novels he is half-real and half imaginary. The absent boyfriend performs the ideal masculinity and becomes the measuring rod for everyone else who does not just quite measure up. The female narrators have created their own hegemonic masculinity which no one, probably not even the idolised absent boyfriends, can live up to. The fact that the boyfriends disappear and leave the female characters to continue the struggle, with varying results, is also significant. The hopes and changes they were eager to implement are still alive in the memories of their girlfriends, but the hegemonic masculinity, the real masculinity, which they worked to change, still prevails at the end of the novels.

In the narratives, the political man stands out as a fantasy. He states his goals, makes his plans and fights for them, but he is not around to see them materialise.

As a result, the political man becomes connected to a utopic version of reality that even the fiction cannot produce. However, he does inspire the female characters to, in a sense, take control over their own lives. In *Damascus,* Sabriyya uses her power to commit suicide. She defies the wish of her brothers to live a quiet life so as not to disturb them and instead punishes them by creating a scandal that exposes them as incapable of taking care of her. Through her death and her diary, she orchestrates her revenge. Nadya, in *The Homeland*, uses her power to enjoy sexual relationships. When she feels she is ready, she challenges the orders of the group leaders and goes back to the Arab world to take up the armed struggle. Sunya, in *The Cherry Orchard*, leaves the group she is fighting with when they begin to treat her as a servant and sets up her own life in the midst of war-torn Lebanon. However, although Sabriyya's suicide is indeed staged as a revenge and is very much her own choice, it is also a choice that means that she sees no other way forward for herself or possibly her country. In *The Cherry Orchard,* Sunya is killed by a sniper at the end of the novel and what are presented as corrupt values are then allowed to take over. Towards the end of the period, this theme is developed and the failed revolutionary hero becomes a topic, as can be seen in Qamar Kilani's *The Whirlwind.* In this novel, Karim becomes so absorbed by his political struggle that he neglects his wife Samiya. His commitment to the cause is contrasted with his lack of commitment towards her and is described as a fruitless attempt to reach impossible dreams rather than working and building a family. The novel spends several pages discussing the danger of dreams and how they can make a person hope and believe in things that are not true. In a study of male-authored Arab novels from 1985, Aḥmad Mashūl states that there is a crisis for the fictional, revolutionary hero.[41] He bases his argument on the changing political reality that it is no longer credible to believe that one politically committed person will be able to change the world. He then shows how the revolutionary heroes he examines all fail to live up to their own and others' expectations. This is clear in *The Whirlwind* where Karim, despite his involvement and connections, can do nothing to protect the country or his wife and, when Syria is attacked by Israel, the novel ends in chaos. The reception and characterisation of Karim in *The Whirlwind* compared to the view of the revolutionary men in the previous novels can further be seen as an example of the changing hegemonies. Whereas Sabriyya and Nadya were not pleased to be left alone, they accepted that their lovers were fully occupied with their political cause and patiently waited for them. In *The Whirlwind*, Samiya is, at the beginning, taken in by Karim's worldview and his ideas to the extent that she goes against her family and begins to fight against her class background. However, with time, it is clear that Karim's words are just that and there is no real change. Towards the end of the novel Karim describes the same feelings: he still sees that both his country and his wife need him, but rather than taking the active role he had at the beginning of the novel, he now decides to sit back and wait to be asked to help. The novel further portrays both Samiya and Karim as intellectual and learned characters, living in a different world from reality and not appreciating the real problems of the other characters. The failing revolutionary hero ignites the trend of the 1990s with troubled or aggressive masculinities where the function of the male characters in the female authors' narratives moves from potential partners in the struggle of changing society, during the period of the 'political man', towards being confused in their performance of masculinity and the adversaries of the female characters in the period of 'problematic masculinity'.

3

Changing Masculinity – a Transformation from Solution to Problem

بابا، هل أنتَ حيوان؟[1]

Dad, are you an animal?

Whereas the specific characteristics for an ideal masculinity are interpreted differently from novel to novel the greatest change over time lies in the female characters' perception of men and their performance of masculinity. The earlier novels generally assumed that the male characters should, and would, take on the role as provider and protector and guide the female characters in the right direction. However, the first two waves end in disillusionment. In the first wave, most of the male characters, although formulated as ideal, are discarded by the female characters by the end of the novels. In the second wave, the politically and ideologically coloured masculinities die or disappear as do many of the female characters. It seems that the two first attempts of creating and hoping for a change through a divergent and progressive masculinity are not entirely supported by the writers themselves and in the third wave, written at the end of the 1980s, the themes and styles of masculinity formation change. Novels written after the 1980s instead begin to assume that the female characters understand what is good for them. Although they are still described as being in the same position of dependency on male characters, they are given a more critical voice in the novels. The changing representation of masculinity in the fiction of Syrian female authors is closely connected to their views on their female characters and their ability, which reflects their relationships with male characters and their expectations of them. This period overlaps with what Faysal has called 'rebellious discourse' where she identifies various ways for the formulation of female characters that do not conform to the expected gendered behaviour.[2] Rather than using masculinity as a symbol for change and hope, these authors use masculinity to analyse and critique problems in society by, on the one hand, fore-fronting social problems such as poverty and class differences, while, on the other hand, questioning what the ideals of hegemonic masculinity really stand for. In addition to these two topics, where subordinated and complicit masculinities play a major role in the narratives, a third theme, that of oppressive and aggressive masculinities, appears in the fiction of the last two decades of the twentieth century.

Iman al-Qadi traces the changes that appear in the last wave of novels to the emergence of writers from other areas and classes than previously represented, with new agendas for their writing. This can be seen in the 1990s when a number of writers from the coastal area became prominent and woman writers with specific interests in certain groups in society began to publish their novels, a trend which has evolved during the twenty-first century. The new perspectives can further be traced in the female-authored novels both as a dichotomy between countryside and city and between conservative values and those with more open-minded views. The novelist Mayya al-Raḥbī sets her novel *Furāt* (*Euphrates*, 1998) in the poor areas of Damascus, Haifa' Biṭār situates some of her novels in Latakia with a mix of main characters ranging from doctors to prostitutes. Writers Anīsa 'Abbūd and Umayma al-Khush both explore the countryside and examine the relationships between the poor farmers and the wealthy landowners; many of the novels place their characters abroad for a period of the novel or as a background story.

Buthaina Shaaban further argues that, near the close of the twentieth century, the Arabic novel in general, and women's novels in particular, were entering a new stage in terms of both theme and technique.[3] This can be seen in the structure of the narrative. Whereas many of the previous novels had a restricted gallery of characters, often limited to a small circle of friends and family members, many novels, written after the 1980s, are opening up the narrative to a larger group of secondary characters. Sometimes these characters only have the function of adding opposing views on topics the main character is concerned with or they may represent different viewpoints in political debate. The last usage can be seen in Ghalia Qabbani's *A Woman's Morning* where the characters represent the political perspectives of different countries. Another aspect in women's novels of this period is the added interest in the male perspective, with male first-person narrators as the main characters for parts or sometimes the whole narrative. In her study on masculinity in the novels of the 1990s in Syria, Maysun al-Jurf concludes that the female writers' negative representation of masculinity in this period is connected to a changing worldview and what she calls traditional masculinity cannot adjust.[4] She argues that, regardless of the number of masculinities existing in a novel, there are only two types which female writers can create; either the monstrous man or the female alter ego, ie a male character written as a female character. She has a point: the number of disagreeable ways of performing masculinities has risen and the ideal masculinity, presented by, for example, Nadya Khūst, is different from previous generations of masculinities. Despite this, the multitude of masculinities and the fact that they are mostly presented as problematic must be seen as more complex than this division.

The uncertain, worried and unstable masculinity performed can be seen as the first signs of a changing representation of men in Syrian women's writing. From having generally been seen as the support and help for less capable characters, both male and female, the main male characters of the late twentieth century and the early twenty-first century are often portrayed as unable to handle the outer (and inner) pressure of performing the role of masculinity. A change that, in turn, leads to fictional masculinities who oscillate between weakness and inability or aggressiveness and a wish to dominate. On the one hand, this leads to a formulation of masculinity that has become more divergent and could destabilise previous hegemonies. On the other hand, it introduces the ability to critique the patriarchal system and point out ways in which it is misused and exploited by individuals or groups. The multitude of masculinities further offer an ambiguous understanding of masculinity and show the relational nature of how it is shaped, and received, by society. What is also of great interest is that the masculinities of the final wave, ending around year 2000, are not just problematic they are also problematised to a higher degree than before. The behaviour of the husband in *Imraʾa fī dāʾirat al-khawf* (*A Woman in a Circle of Fear)* by Ḍiyāʾ Qaṣabjī is discussed and partly normalised by a psychiatrist, while half of Anisa ʿAbbud's novel, *Wild Mint,* is devoted to the male main character ʿAlī's perspective on things, his dreams, memories and background. The male character in the most recent wave of novels has become human in the sense that he can be criticised and stereotyped as a despotic patriarch and shown with faults and problems, far from the ideal and idolised political man who preceded him. Another new addition to the description of the male characters and their masculinity in this time period is the focus on their sexual activity, or lack thereof. Whereas the first two periods described variations of love relations, the description of physical contact was limited to kisses between the characters. In this period, several novels focus on the sexual act and describe it in some detail. There are, furthermore, descriptions of male characters who carry out what would be labelled rape in a contemporary discourse and female characters who realise that they enjoy sexual encounters.

Idolised masculinities still appear, but often with an opposite masculinity, in order to make the point about what is right and wrong in historical events. In addition to this changing view of masculinity and to challenge patriarchal structures through the reformation of the father figure or a re-examination of traits previously seen as inherent to the performance of masculinity, women writers, toward the end of the century, also attempt what Hanadi al-Samman labels a reformulation of the understanding of the nation.[5] In this reformulation, the construction of masculinity has an important role, often as a carrier of a specific message where agreeable, strong and well-respected masculinities represent the good and the opposite is true for the enemy. Nadia Khust's novels *Shuhadāʾ wa ʿushshāq fī bilād al-shām* (*Martyrs and Lovers in the Levant*, 2000) and *Ḥubb fī bilād al-shām* (*Love in the Levant*, 1995) are examples of this use of masculinity and, as Zeinab Zaatari claims in relation to TV series, when used like this, the novels' constructions of masculinity are mainly tropes in a specific narrative, rather than fully fledged characters. Another example of this trend is Ulfat al-Idlibi's *Ḥikāyat Jaddī* (*My Grandfather's Tale*, 1990) which presents the story of an immigrant moving from the Caucasus to Syria generations before. Like in Khust's novels, the man is presented to perform a perfect masculinity as seen by the other characters when it comes to chivalry, generosity and strength and he becomes a symbol of both the ideal immigrant and the shared Islamic background between the countries. This trend of writing the history of previously ignored minorities is continued by, for example, Mārī Rashū and Hanrīyit ʿAbbūdī (Henriette ʿAbbudi). They also use a form of ideal or positive masculinity for their heroes, while their male enemies are portrayed as cowards with no respect for others. Hence the writers make use of an existing hegemonic masculinity, which is used to guide the reader as to which characters to like and which to dislike.

In this time period, which forms the third and largest wave, authors such as Nadya Khust, Mari Rashu, Haifāʾ Bīṭār, Malāḥa al-Khānī and Anīsa ʿAbbūd create male characters who perform masculinities perceived by the other characters as one, or a mixture of, the following: weak, oppressive, traditionalist (meant in a negative way), aggressive, feminised, misogynistic or idealistic. The themes featured in these novels are historical events, biographical tales, divorce and male/female relationships. The problematic masculinity can be performed by all men, the father figure, which previously has not been directly criticised, is now openly blamed for the misfortunes of his daughters and wives. In addition to the father, a gallery of unreliable lovers, incapable brothers and hypocritical husbands is created.

This chapter will look more closely at *Furāt* (*Euphrates*, 1998), by Maya al-Rahbi, which tells the story of Furat, from her childhood in a village near the Euphrates, to her life as a mother and grandmother in the capital. A young Furat marries a man she does not know and travels with him to Damascus, a city she has never visited. There she is forced to form a new life for herself under very squalid conditions. Through her hard work, wit and later the help of her children, she can enhance her situation. At the beginning of her story, Furat lives her life according to what she sees as the norms of society, even when that means that she has to accept being hit and humiliated by her husband. However, the more she sees of life the less she cares about these norms and, by the end of the story, she does what she thinks is best for herself and her children instead. In Haifa Bitar's novel *Qabw al-ʿabbāsīn* (*The Abbaseen Basement*, 1995) Khulūd's parents are divorced. Khulud blames her father, but rather than just blaming him for his actions, she directs her hatred towards all men and decides to take revenge by driving young men to suicide. She begins sexual relationships with them and then ends them abruptly, thus hurting the men as she believes that her aunt and mother have been hurt. In a second novel by the same writer, *Afrāḥ ṣaghīra afrāḥ akhīra* (*Small Joys, Final Joys*, 1998), Hiyām meets her husband, who remains nameless throughout the novel, while they study in Paris. When they move back to Syria, the relationship changes, mainly due to social pressure. Hiyam discovers that she is unable to conceive children, something that affects both her and her husband negatively. After years of marriage, they divorce and Hiyam moves to another city. Although she is determined to live the rest of her life on her own, she falls in love with one of her customers, Tawfīq. Tawfiq is already married, but Hiyam believes that he will leave his wife for her. However, when she later realises that he has children, she breaks up with him. In *A Woman's Morning* by Ghalia Qabbani, Nadā, a doctor working in Kuwait, witness the invasion of the country by Iraqi soldiers. The sudden switch between normality and all-out war puts several relationships under strain and the novel examines how various characters, many from other countries and only working in Kuwait, navigate the days following the invasion. Mari Rashu's novel *Harwala fawqa ṣaqī ʿ tūlīdū* (*Hurrying Over the Frost in Toledo*, 1993) tells the story of Hind who travels to America to marry her cousin Jād. She sees no future for herself in her home city and believes that life in America will be easier for her. However, Jad is not the type of husband she had hoped for nor is her new life what she had expected. Once she realises that Jad is not going to be of any help, Hind learns the language and finds herself a job; when things deteriorate further, she asks Jad for a divorce and moves out of the house, together with her daughter. In *al-Tawq*

(*Longing*, 1997) by Umayma al-Khush, Thurā has lost her job as a pharmacist because a child died due to the medicine she has administered. As the story unfolds, it becomes clear that Thura, her brother and previous boyfriend are all fighting for political freedom in different ways and have been targeted by the secret service. When they decide to take up the fight against the wealthy landowners in their home village, they meet with even more resistance. In the end, they win over the landowners, the farmers get the right to use the water freely, Thura's new boyfriend contrives a daring plan and scares off the secret service agent and it seems like the characters can return to a normal life once more.

The focalisation in the novels discussed in this chapter is less stable than in the previous two periods discussed. The number of characters in each novel are bigger and the focalisation does not necessarily stay with the main female character. This leads to a more dynamic view of the masculinities presented and has further implications for characterisation. For example, a character's actions might mean one thing, a secondary characters' judgement might mean something else while the main female character provides a third viewpoint.

The use of focalisation and characterisation in this way further puts the focus on society and the social norms in a way that has only been hinted at in the previous two waves. To read the novels written in this period, but placed in the 1950s or 1960s, and the way they portray the upbringing of children, the view of pre-marital relationships, or women's education is very interesting since they are often in stark contrast to the benevolent fathers and husbands of the novels written in the 1960s. To read the novels from the different periods together illustrates the idealness of the earlier masculinity formations but also shows how the choice of perspective changes them.

Changing views on the Father Figure

Authorisation can be a specific position or background that makes a certain man's masculinity performance valued and respected more than others. Authorisation consists of the factors that help a group of men keep power through asserting their close relations to hegemonic masculinity and can be explained as positive stereotyping. By being part of a specific group, or holding a certain position, a man is automatically assumed to behave in a certain, approved, way and can enjoy power accordingly. In the Syrian context, this could, for example, be religious men, or men from specific families who are respected on grounds disconnected from their behaviour. In a hierarchal society, age is also a factor of authorisation where the eldest son is singled out as being special. The men who benefit from authorisation have a certain leeway in their performance of masculinity; due to their already powerful position in society they can compensate for 'shortcomings' in their performance and still preserve their elevated position in relation to women and other men. This is often seen in the portrayal of the father figure who, until the 1980s, is usually excused when he acts in a way that are not seen as part of the female characters' expectations of masculinity. The explanations and excuses they offer are based on the authorisation the position of 'head of the family' gives the fathers. Brothers or husbands, who lack their father's authority, are not excused in the same way when performing similar actions. In her book *Fathers and Sons*, set in the Middle East, Dalya Cohen-Mor discusses the position of the father as a figure who has absolute power over all members of his household and describes how this, in turn, has a negative effect on other family members.[6] This can also be seen in *Damascus* by Ulfat al-Idlibi. During the memorial service that Sabriyya organises 40 days after her father's death, two women discuss whether Sabriyya is truly sad, or just relieved that her father has passed away. One says to the other:

مَهما يكونُ الأمرُ فالأبُ عزٌّ.[7]

Whatever the circumstances, the father is [a source of] power and dignity.

The other woman immediately agrees. The word *'izz* emphasises the importance of the father figure and the power of this position. The fact that the sentence is agreed as a general statement shows that it is not specific to Sabriyya's relationship with her father, even though it applies to her. In Haifa Bitar's novel *The Abbasseen Basement*, Khulud cannot forget the way her father has treated her mother, but she is repeatedly told by her aunt that since he is her father she must forget and forgive rather than create problems within the family.[8] For her mother, and this is also the opinion of her aunt, it is more important that the father returns to the family and they can live together again than to delve into the past.

In a Syrian setting Lisa Wedeen has shown how this understanding of the father as a source of absolute power is incorporated in the political discourse to gain acceptance and credibility.[9] To position oneself as the father of the nation carries with it obligations and also a promise that people can expect to be looked after but, more importantly, the role demands respect. As the utmost symbol of the patriarchal system, the father is a fundamental part of the power structures in Syrian society, as discussed by Kamal Abu Deeb in a study where he analyses the links between power, fatherhood and divinity.[10] He connects the elevated position of the father and how he is treated as a small God, and how that is then transferred to society through the political system. The connection between fatherhood and goodliness further means that it is difficult, or even impossible, to criticise the father and his actions, whether in the family or as symbolised through a state apparatus. Despite this, Hartmut Fähndrich argues that,[11] from the 1950s, a trend of descriptive novels with despotic father figures has emerged in the Arabic literary tradition, scrutinising both the personal relationships between children and fathers and those between the state and the citizens of a country. Fähndrich contends that the father figure is the best representation of power exerted by society upon the individual,[12] hence the commencing critique of this character is telling for the period. Looking at Syrian female-authored fiction, the start of this trend appears somewhat later, after the 1980s, and even then, not all novels chose this option. Novels such as *Euphrates* and *The Impossible Novel* keep the father figure as an ideal masculinity against which other men are measured. In *Euphrates*, the father is, however, described in contrast with others and his love for his daughter is compared to their strictness and hardness, making him stand out.[13] Despite these exceptions, it is illuminating to see the change in the position of the father figure over the time period studied. In the first wave, the focus is on an ideal father who advocates for the right to study and work, or at least does his best to give his daughter a good future. In the second wave, the father figure is still respected but becomes, to some extent, a symbol for old-fashioned ideas while the third wave sees the appearance of father figures who are despised and depicted as despotic brutes. In the patriarchal societies described in the novels from all three waves, contesting the role of the father implies contesting the social system and, furthermore, the hegemonic masculinity, which is exactly what the female writers attempt to do, but from different angles.

The fact that a position gained through authorisation can be lost is exemplified in *Khaṭawāt fī al-ḍabāb* (Steps in the Fog, 1984) by Malāḥa al-Khānī when Haytham, the main male character, decides to leave university and concentrate on his work. His mother disagrees with him and brings up the topic in front of the father. The father, who before his illness exercised absolute power in the home, now says that the choice is up to Haytham, who is surprised.

هل تعني أنك موافق؟
لم أقُل أنّي موافق أو غير موافق. هذا شأنك ومستقبلك...وفي مثل حالي ووضعي لا يسعني أن ألزمك بأمر تاباه. أقول لك من وجهتي فقط؟ فكّر مرتين أو ثلاث قبل أن ترفس الجامعة نهائياً.[14]

> Does this mean that you agree?
> I did not say that I agree or disagree: This is your matter and your future … In my situation and circumstances I cannot attempt to force you to do something you refuse. Shall I say my view? Think twice or three times before you give up university completely.

The father acknowledges that even though he still holds a privileged position in the home, his wife turns to him for important decisions and he has the final word in key matters, he has lost his powerbase. Unable to provide for his son and look after him, the father feels that he has neither the right nor the ability to interfere in his son's life. This needs to be contrasted with the beginning of the novel where the father is constantly telling Haytham what to do, when to be home and how to behave. Now, the roles are reversed and Haytham, who is suddenly the breadwinner of the family, is also the decision maker. To avoid a similar loss of power the father in *Damascus* does not rest until he has made sure that he has an income, so that he can still support the household despite being bedridden. Despite his physical state, he feels that he needs to fulfil his obligations towards his daughter and feels that he cannot allow his sons to take over the finances and consequently the right to make decisions on family matters. He knows that he cannot afford to lose any more of his power: having lost all other ways of gaining respect, being unable to provide for his household would be the final blow to both his masculinity and his power. The father in *Steps in the Fog* does not put forward any claims on power. Being a man and a father he benefits from the patriarchal dividend and is respected by his wife and son, but he can no longer force them to do what he wants. Haytham, who is described at the beginning of the novel as disagreeing strongly with his father, but still obeys him, is now seen to ask for his father's advice, but then acts upon his own ideas, for which he then gains respect. The performance of masculinity here becomes a conscious, or unconscious, agreement between the members of the family. The collective behaviour of and reactions from the mother, father and Haytham allow, or force him, depending on how the events are read, to perform a grown man's masculinity.

In all the novels discussed in this book, the father figure stands for a power which has an immediate effect on the female characters' lives, whether that is interpreted for good or bad. The link between the father's power and the daughter's life is examined further in Līndā ʿAbd al-Raḥman's *Tamthīlāt al-ab fī al-riwāya al-niswiyya al-ʿarabiyya al-muʿāṣira* (*The Portrayal of the Father in the Contemporary Arabic Female Authored Novel*). She shows how the fathers in the novels she has analysed influence their daughters' lives, not only as role models and caretakers but also through their decisions over their daughters' lives based on their own political and religious motives.[15] The choice of the father as a symbol for change and an advocate for new values in relation to their daughters is hence not a strange choice in the first wave of novels, nor is the choice to vilify him in a period when absolute control is no longer seen as an acceptable way forward.

As the master, the father deals with the members of his household as he sees fit. In *Damascus*, Sabriyya does not question his right to do this or the way in which he executes his orders. On the contrary, she seems content to be part of a family where a strong and decisive father looks after its members. When she comes home late after participating in a demonstration, she knows that she is in trouble, but she does not expect her father to hit her repeatedly. Nor that he, when her brother Raghib insinuates that she might no longer be a virgin having mixed with boys, should demand to have her virginity checked. Both these acts infuriate Sabriyya who sees herself as innocent. However, when she has calmed down, she reasons with herself and decides that her father is the victim of traditions and a 'wrong masculine ideal'.

> يخيّل إليّ أنّه الآن يتعذّب، يتمنّى أن يأخذني في حضنه، يمسح آلامه التي سبّبها لي، أنا أدرك تماماً كم يحبّني وكم أنا غالية عليه ولكنّه لن يستطيع أن يفعل ذلك لأنّه يجد فيه ضعفاً يمس رجولته. كلّ شيء عنده أهون من أن تمس هذه القديسة. أي مفهوم خاطئ للرجولة هذا![16]

> I imagine that he is tormented now, he wants to take me in his arms and wipe away the pain he caused me. I know very well how much he loves me and how dear I am to him, but he is not able to do it because he sees it as weakness that would undermine his masculinity. Everything is easier for him than for this sacred thing to be harmed. What a wrong concept of masculinity this is!

Despite her bruises, both physical and mental, she convinces herself that her father is not responsible but an external power forces him to prove his masculinity and she has to put up with this. She restores her internal picture of the father as a man who cannot do her harm and always wants the best for her but who is misguided. His behaviour is explained by a wish to appear strong in front of his sons and neighbours. In the later novels, similar behaviour can be seen in *The Girls of our Neighbourhood* by Malaha al-Khani, with the difference that the men's brutal behaviour is not forgiven. In *The Impossible Novel* by Ghada al-Samman, fathers who behave like Sabriyya's father and brother are described as backward and problematic. In *Euphrates*, Furat does not agree with the fact that 'Umar hits their daughter, however she tries to convince herself that, as her father, he has the right to bring her up as he sees fit and she should not intervene.[17] However, instead of continuing with this picture of him as a father who wants the best for their daughter and hence punishes her for mistakes, one day she has enough, threatens him with his own gun and forces him to stop being violent.

Khulud in *The Abbaseen Basement* states that she enjoys when she can do the opposite of what her father expects, or when she manages to disappoint him.[18] The interesting point here is not the actual relationship between Khulud and her father in the novel, but the fact that the characterisation of Khulud is done with empathy, whereas previous female characters did everything in their power to please their fathers. In the later novels, the critique of the father figure is even clearer, for example in Usayma Darwīsh's novel *Three of Love* where the father is described, many years after the daughter has left home, as a heavy cloud above her head. He ran his household through fear and none of his children and definitely not his wife dared to contradict his orders before Madā, the main character, finally ran off with her husband-to-be. In Haifa Bitar's *The Abbaseen Basement*, the relationship between the father and mother is described through the eyes of the daughter, Khulud, who sees what damage the father's behaviour does to her mother, especially when he marries another woman. She has no way of justifying what her father has done, as previous generations of female characters are seen to be doing; instead, she decides to take revenge on all men because of what her father has done to her mother.

Another theme connected to the role of the father in the novels from this era is his absence from the narrative as an active agent, but still affecting the narrative by being portrayed as a missing link for his children. Hence showing the importance of a strong father figure and what happens if that role is not fulfilled. In an article on fatherhood in Syrian TV series Rebecca Joubin analyses the trope of missing fathers and how that leads to the breakdown of families,[19] enhancing the importance of a strong and able father figure, for the family and the country. Similarly, the fatherless figures in the novels are described as lost. In *A Woman in a Circle of Fear,* Hasnā', the main female character, wonders if she unconsciously has replaced her dead father with her older husband. And then she goes on to describe how she felt when she lost her father.

وأصبحتُ كعصفورة صغيرة الجناحين...توقف طيرانها ريح عاتية هبت عليها قبل أن تتعلّم الطيران.

I became like a bird with small wings, stopped by the raging wind before she learnt how to fly.[20]

Similar feelings of loss and lack of guidance can be seen in the other novels where the father figure has disappeared. In *Wild Mint*, by Anisa ʿAbbud, the main male character ʿAlī realises that he has become different in the eyes of the other villagers from the day his father dies. He is now, as his mother says, without protection in the same way as she is without support, the utmost image of insecurity in a society built on male protection. The mother is not the only one who is aware of the changes that will affect the family due to the father's death. When ʿAli's schoolteacher hears that he is fatherless she begins to cry. The older children, on the other hand, take the chance to pick fights with him and refuse to play with him, knowing that he has no one to support him and defend him. At the same time, ʿAli does not so much miss his physical father as much as he misses the idea of having a father in order to fit in with society and obtain the benefits of having someone looking out for him. ʿAlyā, the female character of the same novel also loses her father at a young age. Whenever she sees a man who could possibly be her father, she runs towards him and asks him to take her with him. Her siblings, especially her older brother, punish her and tell her that a person can only have one father, thus emphasising that once the original source for protection is gone, it cannot be replaced. When ʿAlya grows up and faces difficulties, her first reaction is to wish that she had had a father to turn to for help and support, reiterating that she lacks a support system. The missing or dead fathers are mostly remembered in times of need; even Thura in *Longing*, who reminds her mother of her father's aggressive behaviour, expresses several times in the novel that had her father still been alive, other male relatives would not have behaved in the way they now do.

Empty Promises and the Problem of a Changing Masculinity

A reoccurring theme in the novels of this period is the young man who seems to be open-minded and searching for a wife who is an equal who, after marriage, turns into everything he has previously taken a stand against. Amjad in *The Impossible Novel* puts it like this:

أعترف: كل ما قلته لها قبل زواجنا عن التضامن مع المرأة وتحريرها كان دجلًا.[21]

> I confess: All that I said to her about solidarity with women and women's freedom before our marriage was trickery.

These double standards are interesting from two perspectives. Firstly, because the initial young men presented, and liked by the female characters, can be seen as an ideal or dream masculinity. As Amjad explains above, this often includes supporting equal opportunities for men and women and supporting the right for women to study and work. The changes that later appear include restrictions on working and studying, expectations on household work and family obligations, restrictions in cross-gender relationships and in mode of dress. In Haifa Bitar's novel *Small Joys – Final Joys*, Hiyam meets a fellow Syrian man in Paris while they are both completing their doctorates. Without telling their parents, they move in together and live for a year in what Hiyam calls 'a dream'.[22] Before they move in together, they discuss the roles of men and women. Hiyam asks her boyfriend if he is not an 'Eastern man' to which he replies by pointing at his head saying that honour and morals are in there, ie by using his intellect not his feelings. When Hiyam puts pressure on him and asks if he is not at all concerned about his future wife being a virgin, he replies that this is just silliness and that he is completely free from what he calls the complex of being the first man.[23] When they return to Syria, both of them feel trapped by society's view of relationships and how they immediately have to get married in order to be together. Many years later, when he wants to break up their marriage, Hiyam's husband says that he should never have married a loose woman like her who lived with him for a year without them being married.[24] His previous views have completely changed and he now defends, as he puts it, high morals. A similar change can be seen in the character Abdallah in *Three of Love – Forest of Sadness*, who is described as open-minded and very understanding when he is living in London but later, when the couple move to Saudi Arabia, he changes and suddenly wants his wife to become someone else, someone who does not study, talk to men and have opinions, but rather stays at home and looks after him and their children. Although not making it the centre of the story, *A Woman's Morning* also brings up the same theme. Nada's husband is excited to have a girlfriend who is clever, interested in politics and writes poetry; and he portrays himself as a modern man, something that changes completely as soon as they are married.[25] When he later is made the narrator of a chapter of his own, he expresses surprise that Nada wants him to return to his 'old self'.[26] However, it is not only male characters that are seen to support these views. In *The Abbaseen Basement*, Khulud is curious to know why her brother is allowed to live with a foreign girl. Her mother explains to her that it does not matter as long as he is abroad, but she makes clear that she would prefer for him to marry an honourable Syrian girl who only gives herself to one man and respects the family.

In Mari Rashu's *Hurrying over the Frost in Toledo* Hind has just lost her father and she now looks for someone to save her as she does not see that her mother or siblings are able to do this. Her aunt in America suggests that Hind should get married to her son Jad and Hind, who has heard about women's rights in America, agrees. Once she is married to her cousin, she realises that he has no intention of letting her live the life she dreamt of back home; instead he abuses her and prevents her from leaving the house. In *A Sun Behind the Fog* by Nawāl Taqī al-Dīn, the main male character does not go through a change in the same way as the characters described above, but he slowly withdraws from Nadia, leaving her to wonder why one day he wanted to marry her and the next he cannot find time to see her. In the end this, as she sees it, inexplicable behaviour drives her to a personal crisis and she leaves Damascus. The novel is told in the first person and it is Nadya who is telling the story to her friend Samar. The structure of the novel is similar to those of the first wave – there are very few characters and one male character's behaviour is the focus of the whole narrative. However, the man described here is deceitful and unreliable and seems to use his contact with Nadya only as a way of enhancing his own feelings of power. Another similarity between this and earlier novels, is the portrayal of a woman's dependence on a man to become happy: Hānī manages to break Nadya's heart twice, the second time reducing her to a state of constant crying.

The changes in the masculinities portrayed in the novels are sometimes only explained as the male's way of tricking a girl into marriage; other times it is clear how pressure from neighbours, family and society at large, influences the relationship after marriage. These changing masculinities can be read as a comment on the first wave of novels with dream masculinities, a masculinity that takes up little space in the later novels. In *Euphrates*, Furat is married off to a man she does not know; when he sees that she is scared on their wedding night he asks her if she has something to hide, something she does not want him to discover. Faced with this threat, Furat can do nothing but give herself to him and the narrator tells us:

استسلمت وغاب الحلم والفارس، وحل مكانهما الجسد اللزج يفوح برائحة العرق والشهوة.

> She gave in, the dream and the knight disappeared, and a sticky body, reeking of sweat and lust, took their place.[27]

The way 'Umar is characterised, both directly through his comments and actions, and indirectly through how Furat sees him, presents him from the start as a disagreeable character. The dream knight is a mixture of a childhood sweetheart and the fact that her mother has told her that Umar has everything one could wish for in a husband and to refuse him would be foolish. The wedding party and later, the wedding night, proves that personal dreams and social norms are different.

In the other novels, where the male and female characters form their own relationships, the initial version of masculinity that the female characters fall for supports women's equal opportunities at work and in education; they are happy for their girlfriends to choose their own clothes rather than the other way around and they do not interfere in the female characters personal relationships. As such, they appear as copies of the dream men seen earlier and the hopes and expectations of the female characters seem to be similar. But whereas none of the female characters from the first wave actually ended up marrying the performers of dream masculinity, the female characters in this third wave do. While the novels of the first wave presented new versions of masculinity while hinting at the fact that they might be an illusion, the novels of the third wave show that this is the case when the performer of perfect masculinity drastically changes, making the earlier versions of masculinity function only as a comparison for the reader to understand how bad the 'later' masculinity performance is. As such, the novels in this period present a darker picture where men seem to know what gender equality means, but actively choose to uphold the patriarchal power structures. It can further be read as a comment on the power of society, where the men are described as happy and content with the more relaxed, less-controlling performances of masculinity that are expected in the European countries they live in, but soon change away from that to fit in when they have moved home again. This is also seen in a comment from Bushrā, one of Hiyam's friends in *Small Joys–Final Joys*, who wishes that she was able to return to Paris since relationships with men were less complicated and strict there and she could easily have lived with a boyfriend,[28] without taking any notice of the social norms she now has to consider. This restrictive and punitive masculinity can also be seen in other men, such as fathers and uncles, who often represent obstacles in the lives of the female characters in this period.

In this third wave, the portrayal of society and the supporting characters is somewhat altered. In the first wave it was clear that the dream masculinity was not the same as the hegemonic masculinity in society – that is what made it a dream – but the focus of the plot was the acceptance of these characters and how they gained support from the female and other secondary characters. The masculinities that were seen as undesirable were not given space and time in the texts and were not seen to be supported. In the second wave, with the political and ideological masculinity, the need for comparisons and a stand against the past led to more details of the undesirable masculinities, but these did not usually find support from the main characters; when they did, it is shown through the narrative that their actions are still not justified.

In this third wave, the opposite can be found, the masculinities described above, though seen as problematic and sometimes impossible to live with from the female character's point of view, find support in other characters, both male and female. In *Euphrates*, the main female character's husband is controlling and violent, but although Furat feels ashamed that he is hitting her, she also understands from her family and her neighbours that it is the man's choice to deal with her as he sees fit. His violence, though not seen as something good, is not seen as something strange. On the contrary, when Furat finally has enough and threatens him with a gun, the neighbour she runs to is more upset that she, the wife, considered threatening her husband than the fact that the husband has almost killed her and her daughter. In Umayma al-Khush's novel, *Longing*, Thura asks her mother if she ever loved her husband, who was angry and ill-tempered. Rather than giving a straight answer, the mother accentuates how well liked and respected the father was amongst his neighbours and friends, and how this now, after his death, reflects on them as a family. She downplays the aggressive side of the character since society's respect is worth more to her than her own feelings. Through the discussion between mother and daughter a difference of opinion based on age can be detected. For the mother's generation, social norms are more important whereas Thura seems more concerned with if she loves her boyfriend. When she figures out that she does not, she breaks up with him even though she is told it might affect her reputation. In *The Abbaseen Basement*, the same generational difference can be seen when Khulud asks her aunt about her marriage which only lasted for a year. She knows that her aunt's husband was extremely harsh with her – he had very elaborate sexual desires that he wanted his young bride to agree too, something which both scared her aunt and made her ashamed. Despite this, her aunt refuses to agree that her husband was particularly abusive; instead, she says: 'I don't know, he was a man'.[29] By showing how the women downplay the conduct of their husbands and remain unwilling to vilify the brutality they have been shown, the writers highlight the role of society in accepting and rejecting forms of masculinity. A similar change in worldview can be seen in *Hurrying Over the Frost of Toledo,* where the main female character supports a patriarchal gender role, but condemns the way her husband uses his privilege to live a very different life from that he allows her, whilst at the same time abusing her if she complains. Her problem is with a specific performance of masculinity not with the general norm.

Another masculinity which appears in this wave and is seen as problematic is described as a 'weak' form of masculinity. In Diya Qasabji's novel, *A Woman in a Circle of Fear*, the main female character accepts her husband's threats and restrictions but when she finds out that his wish for a child makes him dress up as a baby and play in their home when she is not there, she cannot stand the fact that he gives into his weakness, as she sees it, and loses all her respect for him. In Abbud's *Wild Mint*, the main male character, 'Ali, sees his inability to perform the strong and assertive masculinity of his friends as the main reason for his problems with women and the other characters seem to agree. The difference between this way of performing masculinity and those that are more aggressive, is that both male and female characters agree that this masculinity is problematic. Hence, the collective view presented by these novels can be read as depicting fictional societies that accept and, to some extent support, abusive and dominant masculinity, but find masculinities that are unwilling to perform an assertive and aggressive masculinity weak and lacking.

Changing Realities for the Formulation of Masculinities

By looking at the whole period from 1959 to 2000, what stands out is that it is not so much the characteristics of masculinity or male behaviour as described in the novels that change, but rather the female characters' interpretation of the behaviour. Actions that could be seen as a form of protection in earlier novels, for example being escorted by a man when leaving the house, is described in later novels as a restriction on the female characters' freedom. Hence the understanding of a character's behaviour and motives change with the society in which it is created and the female characters of later periods are less forgiving in their attitudes. This also plays out in the novels; actions that were condoned by the female characters during the 1960s and 1970s are now seen as problematic. Even though she might be the most outspoken character of the ones analysed in this book, Khulud's statement in *The Abbaseen Basement* that:

إنّ الرجال قذرون، وعلى المرأة أن تنتقم منهم.

Men are dirty and woman must take revenge on them.[30]

exemplifies the shift in the view on masculinity from the supportive helper in the first generation to an obstacle in the most recent period. At the same time, as a cultural creation, the notion of what is understood to be masculine and feminine relates to the cultural environment and certain core traits re-appear during every period studied. They might, however, be re-invented and re-interpreted in correlation with social change; the focus adopted in the different novels veers between praise and blame. In a Syrian setting, there seems to be a consensus of what is seen as an accepted performance of masculinity. In her study of masculinity in the Syrian novel, Maysun al-Jurf has made a list including generosity, chivalry and strength.[31] In a study of Arabic masculinity, Ruth Roded traces masculinity back to pre-Islamic poetry and lists traits like virility, martial ability and dignity as vital parts of masculinity.[32] Similarly, in the novels she analyses, Samira Aghacy connects the pre-Islamic use of Fuḥūla, which she translates as potency, virility and fertility and a strong and sought-after masculinity.[33] In other studies, provision, protection and procreation are often listed as essential to masculinity.[34] Whereas the same words might be repeated as signifiers of masculinity, their meaning will differ from time to time and place to place. Hence, it is not the traits themselves that are interesting, but rather the struggle between the articulated expectations and individual male characters' way of meeting theses expectations depending on their position and background that can be seen as the development.

In *Damascus*, Sabriyya's relations with her brothers, Raghib and Mahmud, shows how similar actions are interpreted differently depending on who performs them. Through her eyes, they are examined both in relation to hegemonic masculinity and to her ideal masculinity. In her judgment of them, she returns to the same core traits that she found important in her father. However, she thinks Raghib overplays his masculinity while she does not find Mahmud masculine enough. In an article on masculinity in a feminist text, Helen Nabasuta Mugambi makes the point that all the male characters are crafted around the same traits, however their position in the fictional society depends on how the traits are utilised and seen by other characters.[35] This is similar to the way the male characters are treated in the novels discussed in this chapter and how their behaviour is seemingly accepted by society but is described as being unbearable for the female characters. The male characters further use the social norms and expectations and pretend to fulfil masculine ideals to access privileges that they then deny the female characters. This is comparable to what one of the respondents in Farah Ghannam's book on masculinity in Cairo says when she suggests that there are two types of men: 'a raagil (a man) and illi bye'mil raagil (one who pretends to be a man)'.[36] The first type performs normative masculinity with the purpose of looking after both himself and his family. The second type tries to obtain advantages by assuming the role of normative masculinity when it suits him, then avoiding it when it does not. He can, for example pick fights to show off his manliness, but run away in a real fight or have many relationships with women to boast about his virility, but is unable to marry and build a family. The reaction of the female respondents and the views of the fictional characters are similar, since they take into account the underlying motive for specific actions and seem to accept only what they believe are genuine actions.

This can be seen in *Euphrates* where Furat has grown up well aware of what is expected from men and women. Although she might not agree, she listens to her mother when she explains to her that she can no longer play with boys and that it is time for her to get married. At the beginning of her marriage, she also follows her husband's rules and definitions of male and female behaviour. This, however, changes when she later sees him as a failure and a drunkard and she loses her respect for him. From then on, his behaviour is no longer seen as acceptable by Furat and she does not believe that he performs masculinity according to the norms, even though other characters treat him as if he does, since he upholds appearances in front of them.

Returning to *Damascus,* the novel discussed in Chapter 2, the clash between expectations and execution of expected traits of masculinity is pointed out by Sabriyya when she tells her brothers off after her father's memorial service. She tells them that the one thing they have in common is that neither of them has ever cared for her. As their sister, she has demands on them and these have not been met by the aggressive Raghib or by the passive Mahmud. Both brothers benefit from the patriarchal dividend and are treated differently by her parents. However, they have positioned themselves on opposite sides of the hegemonic masculinity she sees her father perform. Neither of them has changed in a way she approves of; instead, what she looks for seems to be a progressive version of her father's masculinity. The traits that Sabriyya has assigned to her father's performance of masculinity hence become negative :assertiveness becomes aggressiveness and protection becomes hindrance, in addition to the opposition formed by the inability to perform masculinity completely. She is not happy with Mahmud, who does nothing, but nor is she happy with Raghib who overdoes his masculinity. As Helen Nabasuta Mugambi points out, this can be used to criticise masculinity from within.[37] It further emphasises that the female character's point of view plays an important role in how the performance of masculinity is interpreted.

The creation of rejected masculinities problematises the idea of hegemonic masculinity as a set of actions or traits. The characters, both male and female, are not just interested in actions but how and why these actions are performed. The rejected performances are either attempts to use the patriarchal dividend and the idea of hegemonic masculinity to gain an advantage, or a failure to adhere to the performance. In both cases, the norm of the fictional society decides if a man is successful. It is clear that even though the fictional society does not grant the female characters power to change, or punish, the men who perform masculinity at the expense of the female characters' well-being, their literary depiction functions as a way of exposing them.

4

Masculinity – a Demanding Role to Play

“معك قِرش بتِسْوَى قِرش”. ولكنّ نقوده تكاد تنفد. إنّه لا يساوي شيئاً في هذه المدينة المفترسة.[1]

“If you have a penny you are worth a penny.” But his money is about to run out. He is worth nothing in this ravenous city.

The changing representations of men and masculinity, as seen after the 1980s, further entail a discussion of the problems faced by the male characters due to models of masculinity they must position themselves against. The masculinities discussed in this chapter can be described as subordinate and marginalised masculinities who, rather than enjoying the benefits of the patriarchal dividend, are plagued by trying to meet the expectations placed upon them based on their sex. Instead of focusing on the aggressive and oppressive masculinities that are part of the era of Problematic Masculinities, the portrayals here function as a social critique by showing the impossible situation in which some of the characters live. Kifah Hanna means that for Ghada al-Samman, and the writers coming after her, the aim was to revive the Arabic novel as a key way to address the social and political issues raised by the regional crisis of the Arab world.[2] They used their novels as a way of both representing and changing social and political reality.[3] This can be linked to the usage of masculinity and male characters as examples of the affects social changes have on citizens in general through the exploration of gender roles. Except for Ghada al-Samman's novel *Beirūt 75* (*Beirut 75*) from 1975, this way of using masculinities is mainly found after the 1980s and towards the end of the 1990s.

The novels discussed in this chapter are *Beirūt 75* by Ghada al-Samman which tells the story of five people living in Beirut and their struggle to survive in the city. Faraḥ and Yāsmīna travel from Damascus to Beirut in search of their respective dreams. Farah wants to earn money and a position so that she can get married, while Yasmina is looking for a less restricted life. In the car to Beirut there are two other passengers, Abū Muṣṭafā, and Abū al- Mullā. The novels link the characters through the car ride and their struggle to find a place in society, but their individual stories in the novel are told independently from each other and they do not interact. In *Imraʾa fī dāʾirat al-khawf* (*Woman in a Circle of Fear*, 1985) by Ḍiyāʾ Qaṣabjī we follow the childless marriage of Hasnaʾ and Sami. Hasnaʾ is content with her marriage, despite the fact that Sami cannot have children, but one day she begins to notice that things have moved around in the house when she is not there. Sami refuses to believe her and tells her that she needs to see a psychiatrist. Hasnaʾ agrees and, through her conversations with the psychiatrist and her friends it emerges that she is not as happy within the marriage as she appears. The main male character in *A One-winged Eagle* by Haifa Bitar, is Karīm, a doctor by profession, who have difficulties to make ends meet. The novel follows Karim through his daily struggle with his patients, but most of all his money problems and the way he feels trapped by the system although he, as a doctor, should have a high status in society. The novel contrasts the pressure Karim puts on himself with the demands his sister places on men in general to provide for her. Henriette Abbudi's novel *The Naked Back* has a male main character, Adham, a Syrian judge, on holiday in Paris. In a bar one night he gets to know Aliksi, who invites him to his home the following day, but when Adham turns up at the address he has been given, a beautiful blonde woman opens the door. Adham recognises her from the previous evening and, when he realises that she has just broken up with Aliksi, he decides to move in. The woman, Klīr (Claire), is surprised but does not seem to mind, and Adham has soon taken Aliksi's place. The novel could be labelled a relationship novel and the focus is on Claire and Adham as they try to carve out their respective positions within the relationship. In addition to these novels, the chapter returns to some of the novels from the first and second wave to discuss changes in masculinity construction.

Cross Writing the Male Gaze

Whereas the pioneering female writers were seen as using a female gaze to filter their experiences and present them in novels, the writers in this period use male characters to a greater extent. In this chapter, several of the novels discussed make use of male focalisors, deciding what to look at and how to see it. In many cases the 'objects' they focalise are the hegemonic norms for masculinity in their respective society and the focalisation takes place from the premise that these norms create obstacles for the men. The use of male characters seems to allow the authors to step away from the view that they are only writing their own lived experiences, as well as providing the opportunity to discuss masculinity constructs from within. Through the internal monologues of the male characters, in addition to their own negotiations with ways of performing masculinity, the characters offer their views on women in a sort of double exposure, where Woman is seen through the eyes of Man, but a man created by a female writer. Through their use of male focalisors some of the novels also employ, or play with, the male gaze.

The concept of the Male Gaze has been influential in analyses of visual art and literature since Laura Mulvey's 1975 article on 'The Male Gaze'.[4] In her original article, Mulvey demonstrates how the camera, the main male actor and the audience together transform into 'the viewer' and that the main female character serves only as the object and a symbol of 'the other'. 'The Male Gaze' can therefore be seen as a reification of male dominance over females. In novels, Mulvey's outline can be applied to the narrative in a similar fashion, to observe the relationship between subject and object and how power positions and gender are presented. The fact that the novels analysed are written by women does not mean that they cannot be seen as examples of 'The Male Gaze'. The ability to produce a narrative that identifies with, and supports, the patriarchal order does not correspond with the writer's own biological sex. However, it does not necessarily mean that the narrative reinforces a patriarchal structure. On the contrary, it is possible to read the narratives as a critique of a gender system that can be interpreted as restrictive and demanding. At the same time, the narrators in the novels are described in a way that corresponds with what is often described as stereotypically male, possibly in an attempt to authenticate their masculinity. Adham in *The Naked Back* is depicted as being concerned with women's looks and bodies, in what is presented as a conventional male way. At the beginning of the novel, Adham is mesmerised by Claire's naked back to the extent that he spills the whisky he is drinking.[5] He cannot focus on anything else and his newfound friend, who tries to get his attention, has difficulty breaking the spell Adham is under. He is described as a stereotypical, heterosexual male, lost in front of female beauty. The following day when Adham visits his new friend's house and finds Claire there, he describes how he looks at her.

وأنا أفترسها بنظراتي، عاجزاً عن تنحيتها عنها ولو لثانية.[6]

I ravish her with my gaze, unable to remove it from her even for a second.

He sees her golden legs under her kimono and begins to imagine her body. The language he uses enhances the image of him as the predator, and Claire as the prey he is getting ready to devour. Later, after they have embarked on their relationship, he watches her showering, dressing and undressing, always with admiration for her tall, slim figure and always with desire. Several times, he says to her that since she is so pretty it is impossible to refuse her wishes,[7] and because of her beauty she will always get what she wants. For Adham, Claire symbolises visual and bodily pleasure, he shows no interest in her thoughts, work or hobbies. Even when it dawns on him that they have a 'bed relation', as he calls it, he does not try to change it by taking a bigger interest in Claire's life.[8] He does not ask her where she works and, until the end of the novel, he does not have her work telephone number. He meets her friends briefly in different settings, but he does not use these opportunities to get to know Claire better. The way his view of Claire is described, he seems only interested in owning her, showing her off and keeping her to himself, all of which is negated by his actual actions. The duality in his character appears through the incoherence between what he sees and what he does. Through the way his gaze is directed, he lives up to the external views expressed in the novel of a masculinity built on strength, virility and ability, but his actions, according to himself, do not measure up to the same level. Hence the male gaze is shown to be empty, whereas what actually happens, bears witness to his inability to take decisions and assert power in his relationship.

A similar use of the male gaze can be seen in *Beirut 75*, when Farah waits in the taxi in Damascus, dreaming of his future in Beirut. He thinks of all the women he is going to sleep with, and enjoys looking at his fellow passenger Yasmina's white legs and short skirt. The anticipation he feels at hearing the name 'Beirut' is described as being similar to sexual excitement.

يرتعش لاسم بيروت كما لو التصق به الاسم جسداً لامرأة عارية.

> He shivers at the name 'Beirut' as though the name was sticking to him as a body of a naked woman.[9]

The image presented is that of a heterosexual man. Farah's enthusiasm for the trip is contextualised by using the desire of a man for a woman's naked body in a way that makes it the normative behaviour and the sentence sets the tone for the hegemonic masculinity that the novel presents. However, towards the end of the novel, it becomes clear that this is nothing more than a fantasy and Farah's main image of Beirut has changed to that of a hospital for mental illness. In these two novels the male gaze can be seen as a trope to create a text with a double perspective through its narrative structure, since the actual plot negates the importance, and consequently the value, of the male gaze.

A different usage of the male gaze or focalisation can be seen in *A Woman's Morning* by Ghalia Qabbani. The relationship between Nada and Majdī is mainly described from Nada's perspective and it is clear that she feels trapped and unhappy in her marriage. She hears from colleagues that Majdi has other women, he drinks more and more, and she describes their intimate relationship as him raping her.[10] When a chapter is told from Majdi's perspective, his view of things strengthens his wife's description of him as a brute. He asserts that he will not let her get a divorce, that he would rather see her dead at the bottom of the sea than together with another man, and that he indeed uses force to get to her body to show her that it is his to do with as he wants.[11] Through Majdi's comments and interpretations of what has happened in the relationship, Nada's decision to divorce him seems understandable to the reader and her feelings for him are justified, although society seems to think that she should stay and look after her husband as a good wife would do. The male voice in this novel thus functions as an authentication of what the female character already knows.

In *The Impossible Novel* by Ghada al-Samman, the question of how society has an impact on performances of masculinity are highlighted through a confession by Amjad, the main male character, who insists that he has killed his wife. It soon emerges that his wife has died during childbirth, but that it was his insistence on having a son, despite her first difficult pregnancy, which forced her to have another child. In addition to confessing that he sacrificed his wife for a son, he admits to himself that, in order to marry her, he pretended to be a different man, whereas all the time he was hiding his 'true Eastern self, deep inside him'.[12] Although the novel is set only in Syria, Amjad uses geographical stereotypes to explain his own behaviour. He, like many in his generation, has studied in France and seems to advocate a different, as he sees it 'Westernised', model for gender relationships. Like Ahmad in *Love and Mud* by In'am al-Musalima, discussed in Chapter 1, he confesses his previous mistakes and vows to become a different man. He then goes on to live a life in the service of his daughter to ensure that she is brought up with the same rights and opportunities as her male cousins. This use of the male voice in a confession breaks the mode of accusation that a female account of the same events would have rendered whilst, at the same time, it draws attention to the agency of the individual man to break the structures he disagrees with.[13] This way of writing, showing the male characters' awareness of the female perspective, can be interpreted both as a result of the female appropriation of the male voice and as showing the intricate and informative relationship between feminism and masculinity that Simon Gikandi pinpoints as one of the reasons for looking at female-authored masculinities.[14] The use of male characters, as discussed by Showalter, has, at times, also given women writers the chance to expand the possible settings for their fictional characters at a time and place when women, for example, did not travel or work.[15] Through their fictional male characters, they create a chance for themselves to explore arenas of life not open to them or to female characters. The first-person male narrator in the novels bring out controversies in their fictional societies through their internal monologues. The use of male narrators by the female authors further shows what Eve Sedgwick Kosofsky claims, namely that as women they are 'producer[s] of masculinities and performer[s] of them'.[16] Through their narrators, the female authors create an arena where they can link social problems and masculinity. They produce masculinities for different purposes and in the characters' monologues they tease out what they see as society's demands and how they relate to them, whether they negate them, or struggle with them, demonstrating that masculinity is a constant performance.

The female authors' creation of male characters can be read as comments on masculinity and how society's expectations influence individual behaviour. The characters, even though they act and speak differently, express their inner desires, in alignment with society's expectations, through their views on the world. This opposition within the characters illustrates various layers of masculinity formation and, at the same time, it breaks the illusion of a hegemonic, formative masculinity of the hero type. The dynamics of gender seen in the novels further problematise and make visible the position of men who are removed from power and authority. Women writers' grappling with this issue through their male characters demonstrate an act of cross writing, as Berthold Schoene-Harwood has labelled the action of women writing with male narrators and men writing with female narrators.[17] Cross writing, as both Diana Wallace and Sara Pearson have pointed out, often causes critical comments on female-authored texts, since the male characters are found not to be masculine enough.[18] Criticism of this type is interesting – not because it is necessarily true – but because it demonstrates how not even fictional characters can escape the expectations of normative masculine behaviour. The characters are lifted from their context and treated as living persons in the time and age of the critic and are subsequently judged using very different criteria from those they find in their own fictional societies. If the external criticism is left aside and the characters are analysed within their fictional society and through their thoughts and feelings, the result might, however, be different.

The use of main male characters in the novels further allows for men's views on men, by which the female authors can further distance themselves from the narrative. The main male characters are shown to formulate their identities, and masculinities, in cooperation with other male characters and not as individual projects of the author. In *The Naked Back*, this type of male interference can be seen through the insertion into the narrative of 'Azmī, the brother of Adham's colleague who has lived in Paris for some time. When Adham first tells him that he is going to stay in Paris to be with a woman he has met, Azmi approves of the idea. He thinks that a short relationship with a French woman will do Adham good. His reaction condones the practice that masculinity embodies sexual ability, which in his mind is the obvious attraction in a relationship with a French woman. A relationship in France will prove Adham's virility without carrying with it any complications for his further life at home. Azmi appears impressed with Adham and the fact that he has found a French girlfriend. However, when Adham insists that he is serious about Claire, and that he wants to change his life and marry her, Azmi becomes worried. In his world, it is one thing to have a casual relationship with a woman, but something very different to be married to her. This is especially true for Adham, since a longer period in France means that he will become dependent on Claire, not the opposite, which is what Azmi expects in a relationship between a man and a woman.

To put a stop to the relationship, Azmi begins to bring up characteristics of their shared views on masculinity that he believes that Adham is now ignoring. He starts with the financial aspect and says that he cannot sustain Adham economically for a long period, and then he asks whether he really wants to be dependent on a woman after that? Adham's wish to be in charge financially is a tradition he and Azmi share. To be dependent on someone else, especially a woman, is, in Azmi's eyes, emasculating. He then goes on to ask about Adham's loss of autonomy, how he can allow a woman to decide his life, what he does, where he goes and what he should do. He implies that the opposite is the norm that Adham should strive to adhere to. He then brings up the responsibilities Adham has to his friends and family, the fact that he has a life and a reputation at home that he cannot abandon in favour of a relationship with a foreign woman. His arguments are similar to the opinions Adham himself holds about masculinity and femininity, revealed by his expectations about Claire and his own behaviour.

According to the fictional societies, masculinity performance entails being the stable provider, in charge of decisions and with carefully thought-through reasons for his choices. To leave everything behind with no consideration for others, because of feelings or lust, is not what Azmi thinks of as a good performance of masculinity. Adham acknowledges that everything Azmi is saying is correct and that he is not performing what would be seen as acceptable masculinity in their shared culture. He means that he is no longer the man he used to be. He is sure that he does not want to change back – at least not as long as he is under Claire's spell.

In his encounters with Azmi, Adham takes an active stand against the masculinity he used to perform in favour of the way he now conducts himself. He is aware that it is not the traditional way of performing masculinity, but as long as it allow him to stay with Claire he is happy to perform this version. By this behaviour, he contradicts his own openly declared views on masculinity and femininity. It is as if Azmi, as a remote friend, has been assigned the role of opponent and it is easier for Adham to justify his behaviour in the face of Azmi's opinions than it is to convince himself of what he is doing. When Adham finally decides to go home, having realised that Claire is no longer interested in him, Azmi is relieved. In his eyes, by going home and standing up for himself instead of staying and hoping that Claire will come back to him, Adham has retrieved some of the masculinity he has lost during the relationship. A fling to prove one's sexuality is acceptable, but to give up oneself for a woman does not fit with the masculinity Azmi adheres to.

In *The Naked Back*, Adham refers to the freedom he now has to reinterpret his masculinity because he is not at home. This idea also features in some of the other novels discussed previously, showing that the social norms and expectations are described as burdens for the main characters too, even though they gain power from adhering to them. However, some ideas on what masculinity entails seem to be universal, at least in *The Naked Back*. Another man who watches Adham's transformation in his relationship with Claire is the elderly neighbour Jūstān. He tells Adham that his only way of winning Claire is to behave like a man.[19] Through this advice, he shows that he does not think that Adham is performing masculinity correctly. Like Azmi, and Adham himself in his internal monologues, he believes that masculinity entails being strong and assertive, something which Adham definitely is not. Justan is described as having had a great marriage and is still so in love with his (now deceased) wife that he plays her favourite melody on the piano every night, paying no attention to the neighbours' complaints. Nevertheless, he still does not understand that Adham is willing to change in the way he has done to live with Claire.

Adham is aware of the other male characters' views of him and his performance of masculinity; despite this he does what he thinks Claire will like. He is only concerned when he feels that she is not impressed with his way of performing masculinity and when she makes fun of him. When they go to parties, he believes the other people think of him as a fool, but he consoles himself with the fact that he is the one who will bring Claire home at the end of the night. He can live with what he feels are their condescending looks because he will prove them wrong by winning her.

On the other hand, Karim, in *A One-winged Eagle,* is constantly worried about what society and his neighbours and colleagues think of him. He does not, like Adham, have a girlfriend that he can show off to prove himself and therefore finds himself at the mercy of others' opinions. His desire to fit the traditional male role is what forces him to go against his own principles to earn some extra money. The two characters are both aware of the external pressure, but they deal with it differently. For Karim, it is important to obtain a general acceptance so that he can begin to live the life he thinks he deserves with a wife and family. Karim also has less leeway to form his masculinity performance since he lives in Syria and he describes the looks of pity he thinks he is getting from his neighbours and people in the street as a lack of trust in his ability. For Adham the situation is different, he has chosen to stay in France because of Claire, and he can afford, as a foreigner, to disregard others' opinions, even if he agrees with them.

Subordinate Masculinity

Because of the internal relationsships between masculinities, Connell divides masculinity into three groups: dominant, complicit and subordinate.[20] The subordinate masculinity includes groups of men who are not able to fulfil hegemonic masculinity and therefore experience loss of power and respect in their relationships with other men. Performing hegemonic masculinity has, in many cases, meant 'ways of gaining and keeping respect and power' for male characters. The previous chapters have demonstrated that both male and female characters make use of social expectations and traditions in their interactions with each other and in their formation of gender.

The groups that differ from the hegemonic norm and which are therefore excluded from the patriarchal structures or circles of legitimacy, are called 'subordinated masculinities' by Connell. Subordinate masculinity, together with femininity, functions as the binary opposition to the currently acceptable hegemonic masculinity. Connell mentions homosexual men as an example of subordinated masculinities in a Western/European setting in the 1990s. In an analysis of the Tunisian film, *Man of Ashes,* where Robert Lang and Maher Ben

Moussa discuss the main homosexual character and the way society stifles his life, the characterisation of homosexual men as subordinate is shown to be true also in a Middle Eastern setting. As a homosexual man, the main character in *Men of Ashes* is subordinated and he has limited possibilities of forming a position for himself in a society which values the performance of masculinity. Lang and Ben Moussa make the point that he has no chance of saying: 'get stuffed. I'll do what I'd like'.[21] He is bound to live his life according to the norms set out in the society of which he is part. The same can be seen in *Beirut 75*. The manager, Nishān, prefers men to women,[22] but when dining out he makes sure that he has young girls with him to give the impression of being heterosexual so that he does not lose his powerful position. On the one hand, Nishan can be seen as caught by society's rules and norms, which deny him the possibility of living life the way he wants. On the other hand, he himself supports the fictional society's normative ideas of a masculine and powerful man as someone with several girlfriends and an aura of (heterosexual) virility. This opposition of what can be seen as private and public discourse is, however, not very different from how many of the other men handle the expectations of hegemonic masculinity in the novels discussed in this book.

Nishan does not perform a weak masculinity in the novel, on the contrary, when he forces himself on Farah, Farah is the one who loses what is described as his masculinity, starts dressing like a woman and becomes confused about his identity. Nishan, only allows for those dependent on him to know about his preference, so he already has an advantage in the relationship. In his detailed analysis of homosexuality in Arabic literature, Joseph Massad discusses this dichotomy. In one way, desiring men is, as Nishan puts it, a truer desire than the one for women. Since men are strong and powerful, it is more rational to be in love with them than with weak women who can make no difference to one's life. A similar discourse appears in European male homosexual circles during the twentieth century as discussed by Arne Nilsson. He asserts that men who were described as 'real men' and dressed and behaved as heterosexual men in addition to being the active, penetrating partner in a homosexual relationship were seen as masculine. The partner who was penetrated was instead emasculated, especially where the man in question chose to wear different clothes or behaved in a way that differed from the hegemonic, male norm.[23] The men were not judged on the basis of their partners' biological sex but on what they did with, or to, their partners.[24] The same value system echoes in the events of the novel, which show that being penetrated, like Farah, is emasculating whereas performing the action, as Nishan, is seen as a sign of being powerful. Nishan's behaviour can, moreover, be read in the light of Michael Kimmel's statement that '[a]t the same time as gender shapes sexuality, sexuality confirms gender'.[25] As with many levels of masculinity the characters are judged on their actions, what they actually do, not their biological sex, asserting that the performance of masculinity is action centred.

In the same way as hegemonic masculinity changes with time, the reasons for deeming a masculinity subordinate also alternates. Thus, what can be understood as grounds for subordination in one place and culture might not be interpreted in the same way in another place or time. Massad shows, for example, how the view on male homosexuality has changed from being normal to abnormal in the Arab world.[26] Whereas men's sexual interest in boys was, at one time, seen as a sign of virility, in the twenty-first century it is interpreted as an illness. Subordination can also come from other factors, such as being unable to perform certain parts of what is considered hegemonic masculinity. Marcia Inhorn gives examples, in her studies from Palestine and Lebanon, of how the inability to have children severely changes a man's perception of his own masculinity, as well as others' views about him.[27]

Connell sees dominant, complicit and subordinate masculinity as internal to the gender order.[28] Since gender relations are always contestable and formed in cooperation with others, she adds two more concepts: marginalisation and authorisation. Whereas the three initial categories are more or less connected to actions performed, the latter two are outer frameworks that are difficult or impossible to change for the individual man. In the same way as authorisation asserts power, as discussed in relation to the father figure in the previous chapter, marginalisation comprises the factors that prevent a certain group from gaining power. Again in an American setting, Connell quotes race as one such factor and says:

> [t]hus, in the United States, particular black athletes may be exemplars for hegemonic masculinity. But the fame and wealth of individual stars has no trickle-down effect; it does not yield social authority to black men generally.[29]

Individuals from the marginalised group might be successful, but their individual success does not mean that all men from this group are accepted. In a hierarchical society, occupying a low-status job might be one factor that keeps a man marginalised or having a low-ranking position in the family (as the youngest son for example). Political ideas and activities can be other factors. By not being seen as equal participants by the majority group of men that make up society, the marginalised men do not enjoy the same privileges and are, as a group, looked down upon without any further investigation into what the individuals from the group actually do. Marginalisation hence works as negative stereotyping. It keeps certain groups of men subordinated in relation to the hegemonic masculinity in that society, but it does not mean that individual men of this group cannot perform hegemonic masculinity.[30]

A novel that uses marginalisation as a way of commenting on reality is *A One-winged Eagle* through its main male character Karim. Karim is aware of the expectations placed on the performance of successful masculinity, but he is hindered by poverty to meet the expectations of a commercialised society, and he confesses to performing actions he is not convinced about in order to maintain the respect he has. He is further described as being aware that because of the marginalising forces in his life, his actions are not valued in the same way as if other characters with more authoritative positions had performed them. Although being a doctor and, as such, enjoying a higher status in society, his struggle to perform masculinity and his marginalisation are telling of how masculinity, contrary to being seen as a source of power, can be turned into the opposite if one is hindered in different ways from performing the expected role. The masculinity created in the novel seems to function as a way of showing the cumbersome and difficult way of performing masculinity. The novels discussed this far do not deal with the patriarchal dividend and the privileges of masculinity. Their sole focus is how the benefits of masculinity are instead out of reach for the characters due to marginalisation. As such, the novels' formation of masculinity is not as a role model or new examples of hegemony but a critique of the hegemonic masculinity present in the fictional societies.

Performing a different type of masculinity than what is expected by the hegemonic norm can lead to a celebrated, 'new' masculinity, as shown in Chapters 1 and 2. Alternatively, it leads to a subordinate position vis-à-vis other male characters and a lack of respect from female characters. The constantly changing and collaborative nature of masculinity formation leads to 'man' becoming:

> [a] kind of artefact, and as such always runs the risk of being found wanting. [. . .] The result of the enterprise [to perform masculinity] is so uncertain that it has to be stressed if it is successful. In other words: In order to praise a man it is sufficient to say: He is a man![31]

The problem facing the characters discussed in this chapter is precisely this, the fear of being found wanting which, in turn, powers their pursuit of 'being a man'. Through this quest, the novels reveal versions of masculinity and how these are received. They further demonstrate how the importance of being 'a man' and of performing an accepted form of masculinity drives the characters to actions that seem contrary to their nature as depicted by the novels.

Hegemonic Masculinity as an Impossible Ideal

In the discussion of hegemonic masculinity in the introduction, subordinate masculinity is defined as the opposition of hegemonic masculinity, which is true in the respect of power, influence and position. It is, however, not true with regard to ideals. Subordinate masculinity either strives towards the performance of hegemonic masculinity, but is unable to succeed, or overacts to assert his own position without any foundation for his actions. In the same way as acting according to hegemonic masculinity gives power and respect, the inability to do so means a loss of power for the characters, and they are only able to perform a subordinate masculinity which contains very little power in relation to other men. It also means a constant struggle to keep up appearances and assert the small amount of power one has. Rather than being empowering, the performance of masculinity becomes suffocating for those who cannot live up to it and several of the characters in the period of Problematic Masculinity have been broken down by the expectations placed on them.

In their article 'Manhood in Crisis', Amirhussein Vafa and Rosli Talif argue that what causes the crisis in masculinity formation is the discrepancy between the lived reality and the inherited language of masculinity.[32] The masculine discourse depicts a masculinity that no longer exists or is impossible to perform in a modern society but remains as an ideal to strive towards. The same problem faces the male characters in *Beirut 75*, as they live a reality that makes it difficult for them to meet the expectations placed on them. When they try, they create chaos for themselves and others. 'Ali in *Wild Mint* not only feels the pressure from his family, but also from neighbours and friends. He believes that they all look on him as a failure and the higher he feels the demands rise, the more incapable of meeting them he feels. Sami in *Woman in a Circle of Fear* compensates for his inability to have children by being strict and demanding with his wife, showing her and society that he is a man through his words. Karim in *A One-winged Eagle* silently accepts the support of his mother but cannot bring himself to talk to her about his situation as that would be to admit his failure. Michael Kimmel suggests that this fear of failing is the problem that should be at the centre of masculinity studies.[33] According to him, the worry of not being seen as a real man is more important than the constant concentration on the power that hegemonic masculinity brings with it, when one discusses the formulation of masculinity. However, as seen in the novels discussed in this chapter, the two are intertwined. The fear of not being seen as a man is driven by a loss of power. Simultaneously, power is seen as a receipt of masculinity. It is the fear of not being 'man enough' that is the driving force for the characters, and which urges them to take certain actions, not always in alignment with what their believes and morals tell them. Samira Aghacy makes a similar claim in her book on masculine identity, arguing that masculinity becomes a masquerade where the construction of masculinity disrupts the self-autonomy of individual men and creates a sense of inadequacy and failure to measure up to the ideals.[34] Rather than attempting to recreate the hegemonic masculinity or perform a variant version, these characters carry on in their attempts to live up to the norm.

The internal duality – fluidity and fixation – embodied in the concept is what makes hegemonic masculinity useful in the discussion of male characters. In relation to the novels, common reference points that function as the basis for further discussions represent this fixation. Without a consensus on what masculinity was/is in a novel or a society, the research on changing, failing, dislocated and ambiguous masculinities would not be possible.[35] On the other hand, to look rigidly for pre-supposed patterns or to interpret hegemonic masculinity as a specific type of character, overlooks both the multiple ways masculinity can be performed and the power dynamics between characters. The fluidity hence appears in the development of individual characters' views on, and performance of, masculinity as well as in different characters' understanding of masculinity. The two contrary parts of hegemonic masculinity can be summarised by Pierre Bourdieu's argument in *The Male Dominance,* where he means that the privileges men have can quickly be transformed into a burden when virility must be proven, honour defended and dependents provided for.[36] He goes on to say that the added burden lies in the fact that these actions can only be valued by others. The 'success' of a certain performance of masculinity is therefore always relative to the reaction of the surrounding society.[37] The characters are constantly in need of approval from others to be assured that their performance of masculinity is accepted; when this approval is not given, they work even harder to perfect their image. At the same time, it is important to remember that, as Lynne Segal argues, even though masculinity is a form of unstable identity it is an identity that is powerful.[38] The combination of powerfulness, instability and a wish to live up to a certain form of masculinity can lead to a desire to overcompensate for what one sees as lacking in one's character. As miriam cooke shows in a discussion on masculinity in Naguib Mahfouz's fiction, this inability to meet approval often leads to the characters seeking another way of asserting their position through violence or in relationships with women.[39] In *Beirut 75*, this overcompensation to cover up an inability to perform the hegemonic masculinity is especially clear in the short episodes on Yasmina's brother who pretends to uphold the values of honour by killing his sister. His reaction does not so much reinstate his honour as it reinforces his performance of subordinate masculinity.

In *A One-winged Eagle*, Karim tries to prove to his sister that he is able to provide for her. When she comes to visit, he goes to the market and spends almost all his money on an expensive fish. Since he has used all his money on the fish, he cannot afford to pay for her present, a book, so he makes an agreement with the shop owner to pay for it in instalments. However, the sister's visit is delayed. Karim cannot afford to buy another fish, or other food for that matter, so he tries to preserve the fish in the freezer, smelling it every day to make sure it is good. Despite his efforts, the fish goes bad and after the first bite his sister declares that they will all get sick if they eat more. On top of having used all his money to please his siter and make her feel welcome, Karim must now bear the shame of his fish being thrown out and not being able to offer anything else to his visiting sister. Although Karim's situation is different from that of Yasmina's brother, he too attempts to act and spend money, in a way he cannot, in order to appear in a certain way that agrees with the hegemonic norm of society. However, as with Yasmina's brother, he does not gain anything but shame for his trial and his attempt cements his position as performing a subordinate masculinity.

In a chapter called 'Oedipus Deposed', Samira Aghacy analyses examples of what she calls fragile and vulnerable masculinity.[40] Her examples are explicitly written after, and about, the Lebanese civil war. Despite this, many of her arguments are valid in the discussion of the unstable masculinities discussed in the novels in this chapter. They illustrate that whereas certain historical or political events might bring about change or instability, gender roles are under constant reformulation. Under particularly straining circumstances as, for example, poverty in the novels discussed, and war in Aghacy's examples, the will or need to reformulate is intensified. It might further be that these circumstances force reformulations that are not condoned by the characters but become accepted because no other solutions are available.

The subordinate masculinities created in the novels are formulated in contrast to a hegemonic norm. Although all characters agree to the norm and do their best to adhere to it, the novels do not suggest that the hegemonic norm is correct. On the contrary, the hegemonic norm, though celebrated on the level of the individual characters, is presented as flawed, inhumane and corrupt through the overall narrative. The subordinated masculinities appear helpless and pitiful and through their entanglement with questions of class and work-migration the male characters further seem to function as a comment on society through their struggles with masculinity. The accepted truth in these novels is that the circumstances you exist within will form you and there is very little room for the individual character to display agency. In *Steps in the Fog*, Haytham's friends tell him:

أصبحتَ صاحبَ مسؤوليةٍ...ستخلقُ الواقعةُ منكَ رجلاً[41]

You have now got responsibilities . . . the event will create a man out of you.

Through this opinion, they stress that whether Haytham is ready or not he will have to become a man. Similarly, the other male characters in the different novels discussed do what they can to make the best of the situations they are placed in, whilst measuring themselves against a hegemonic norm of masculinity. Although the different levels of society depicted in the novels differ in their understanding of masculinity, they are aware of what is seen as the stronger hegemony. Therefore, rather than separating the characters, this chapter presents an internal hegemony that applies to the novel as a unit and fictional society. This approach highlights the relationships between the characters and how their views on their own and others' masculinity, materialise through the narrative. This further means that class differences and education, for example, become factors in the formulation of masculinity. The way money and position can be used to ease a man's performance of masculinity will be discussed, as well as the problems lack of money causes in the struggle to fulfil certain expectations. The analysis shows that the expectations on men re-occur over the class boundaries, as does the governing effect these expectations have on the lives of the male characters. In *Wild Mint*, 'Ali is, for example, extremely jealous of the young man Sami who is 'Alya's student. Sami is from a rich family and can therefore afford to have a car and to treat 'Alya to things 'Ali can only dream of. His connections with important people in society also make it easy for him to find a job and form a position for himself. His money will thus simplify his performance of masculinity in comparison with 'Ali who is poor and has no connections and who worries that he will lose 'Alya's interest because of this.

Varying Social Backgrounds

The class background of the characters plays a pivotal role in their ability to perform masculinity and their capacity to adapt to different social situations. As described by Connell, hegemonic masculinity cannot exist without the support of cultural and institutional power and it forms a sort of symbiotic support system between military, business and governmental practices, which founds and upholds the factors of authorisation and marginalisation.[42] With regard to Syria in general, Sally Gallagher has shown in her book *Making Do in Damascus* that the construction of gender in Syria is largely entangled in social structure, traditional culture and political economy.[43] Preventing certain groups of men to enter into business in a society where the successful performance of masculinity is connected to financial prosperity effectively stops them from performing hegemonic masculinity. Similarly, cultural institutions can promote specific cultural expressions at the expense of others and thus contribute to the creation of the solidification of hegemonies.

In this regard, many female-authored novels are examples of solidifying cultural hegemonies through their focus on the middle, or upper class, city man until the 1990s, when other types of men began to appear in their fiction. Nevertheless, the factors that are counted as authorisation and marginalisation are not static. When societies change and, for example, a different religious group assume power, what has been a marginalising factor might suddenly become the key to authorisation. What the novels of the 1990s plainly show is that the hegemonic norm is far from inclusive and when migration between the city and countryside increases, the clashes between variations of masculinities are intensified.

In *Damascus* by Ulfat al-Idlibi, discussed in Chapter 2, the male characters were homogeneous in the respect that they came from the same neighbourhood and had the same religious believes. Except for the age difference, they met similar problems and had similar advantages in comparison with other men. Their choice of either subverting or supporting the hegemonic masculinity as it appeared in the novel was connected to political beliefs and the performance of masculinity became a part of preserving or rejecting the political system as much as a performance of gender construction. In the novels discussed in this chapter, there are shifting ideas and ideals about gender roles between different generations within the families and between the male and female characters. Nevertheless, there are certain structures included in the development from boyhood to manhood. In *Live and Die Like a Man*, Ghannam uses the term 'Masculine Trajectories' to refer to the process of becoming a man.[44] In this process, she includes structures such as class and gender relationships, while emphasising that the masculine trajectories are different from a life cycle and intend to capture the shifting norms that inform the making of men.[45] Masculine trajectories further illustrate how class interacts with the expectations placed on masculinity. Men, and women, from the upper classes have more leeway in their performance of gender roles and a possibility to deviate to a certain extent from what is expected, without being seen by their peer group as losing in power or position. This leeway, however, never sanctions a major change of gendered behaviour, as the characters discussed in this chapter demonstrate. In *A One-winged Eagle*, the husband of Karim's sister is very wealthy and, although he does not divert from the hegemonic role of masculinity, his money protects him from blame when he does not interact and pay his respects to his wife's family to the extent one would have hoped. Before the wedding it is also clear that Salma, who appears to have had strict ideas on how her husband should be and think when she was younger, now accepts anything as long as her husband is rich.

In *Beirut 75*, the characters are from varying backgrounds and have very different possibilities of affecting their lives, which needs to be taken into account while discussing their approaches to masculinity. Though spanning a large group of characters from several levels of society, the hegemonic masculinity, which governs the fictional Beirut, seems very similar; what differs is the various characters' ability to adhere to it. This creates separate hegemonies on different levels of society. Abu Mustafa's fellow fishermen see him, for example, as performing masculinity according to the expectations and they respect him; at the same time, he is seen, and sees himself, as subordinate to Abu Nimr, the manager of the fishermen. Abu Nimr and his son Nimr are both very well off and they can use their money to coerce others into treating them in a way they want to be treated, whereas for most of the characters discussed here poverty is the main problem. The inability to provide for oneself and one's family becomes connected to how the characters look upon themselves and how others look at them. In this case, masculinity and the performance of gender roles are closely associated with the character's social position, which, in turn, hinders or enables him. Victor Seidler touches on this point when he discusses how, in some working-class cultures, the only tool the father can utilise to show love is by providing for his family members. Since caring words, touches and kindness are seen as signs of femininity, they are not possible options for the father, who is left with a material way of giving love. If he loses his job, it not only puts a financial strain on the family but the father's only way of showing love and care has been taken away from him.[46] In *Beirut 75*, it is Abu al-Mulla who is especially plagued by poverty. Not only can he not provide for his children, he has also had to send three of his young daughters to work as maids to support themselves. In the novel, his thoughts are constantly with his daughters. He thinks about how he can secure enough money to bring them back home again and to prove to them how he loves them and looks out for them. He sees his inability to provide for them both as a failure to perform masculinity and as a lost chance to show affection. Poverty has made it impossible for him to meet the expectations of hegemonic masculinity and he therefore sees his own performance as wanting, a problem that the characters who are better off never face. They are always able to use their money to at least create the façade of successful masculinity.

By locating the characters within a particular social stratum, the authors put the focus on social inequalities and financial problems and the created masculinity becomes a tool for social critique. As such, the male characters' actions are seen as the result of external pressure rather than their own free will. As noted in Chapter 2, the female authors utilise male characters, who are meant to hold strong positions in society, to further illustrate social inequalities and social burdens.

Virility as a Burden of Masculinity

In *Woman in a Circle of Fear* Hasna' is constantly asked when she will have children This question is repeated in *Small Joys* discussed in the previous chapter and in almost all the novels where a couple are newly married. In societies where children are a sign of virility and fathering a part of masculinity, marriage becomes a vital step to perform masculinity completely. Lang and Ben Moussa describe marriage and fatherhood as a man's graduation into real manhood,[47] and a father holds a specific position within the gender hierarchy as discussed previously. Regardless of how well a man fulfils other aspects of hegemonic masculinity in the Arab patriarchal society described by Lang and Ben Moussa, which is similar to that of the novels, an unmarried man is seen as having failed.

After marriage, childlessness can be a reason for subordination, as Marcia Inhorn has demonstrated in studies on Palestinian and Lebanese men. Even though she has shown that a majority of the men interviewed choose to look at their inability to father as an illness that can be cured, most of them acknowledge that this view has not yet spread to the rest of society.[48] Despite agreeing that it is a medical problem, deviating from the expected norm of fatherhood makes the men spend huge amounts of money on treatment or agree to take a second or third wife, against their own will, with the hope that the childlessness is the first wife's fault. The external expectations and the feeling of weakness of not being able to perform the role in a complete way governs their lives. The two poorest men in *Beirut 75* use this same notion to prove themselves as men. Each of them has ten or more children as a way of exhibiting their masculinity through virility. What is empowering for one man, to fulfil the expectations of masculinity, becomes a hinderance for another who is unable to do so.

In her discussion on masculinity in fiction, Samira Aghacy likewise brings up how the virile male body is the exemplary expression of masculinity.[49] In a section of her book she elaborates on how sexual ability is linked to a sense of power.[50] This is further elaborated in Evelyn Accad's analyses of sex as a symbol for war in Middle Eastern literature.[51] She argues that, consciously or unconsciously, a sexual discourse assuming man as the attacker and woman as the attacked is applied in the war literature. In *Beirut 75*, this type of discourse is used by Farah at the beginning of the novel. He sees the trip to Beirut as his chance to become the man of his dreams. He already holds himself as a potential performer of hegemonic masculinity, but he needs the right arena to be able to complete the role to perfection. He therefore looks forward to life in the new city, which he will overpower through his masculine force.

كلّهن وكلّهم يحلم ببيروت. لست وحدي، ولكنّي وحدي ذاهبٌ لإقتحامها.

> They all, men and women, dream of Beirut. I am not alone, but I alone am going to invade her.[52]

When the name Beirut is called out at the taxi station, he feels as if the man is presenting a dancer at the cabaret.[53] His initial presentation lays bare parts of the hegemonic masculinity of the novel, that of the virile, heterosexual man who proves himself through sexual acts. He is the active partner invading the woman, or in this case, the city. Farah's dream of the future is of himself as the performer of hegemonic masculinity, someone able to enjoy the privileges this role carries with it. By the end of the novel, when he has been treated for mental illness, Farah reminisces about his arrival to Beirut when he was still strong and able, and when he could have any women he wanted.

أه يوم جئتُ إلى بيروت كانت قامتي أطول من الليل [...] وكلّ نساء بيروت لن تكفيني.

> Oh the day I came to Beirut I was taller than the night is long [. . .] and all the women of Beirut were not going to be enough for me.[54]

His view of his previous self as 'a man' is closely connected to that of a womaniser and someone able to perform sexually. He is not the only fictional character that is described to expresses this view. In *Wild Mint*, the main character 'Ali's grandfather quietly accepts that he is not the father of his wife's children. Because of the view in his village that a man who is unable to procreate is not a man, it becomes more important for him to pretend that he is able to have children than to accuse his wife of adultery, especially since no one in the village knows. By accusing his wife of adultery, he would create a double scandal by admitting both that he cannot have children and that he cannot control his wife. In this way, he further cements the gender stereotypes by lying and pretending so as not lose his status.

Moving back to *Beirut 75*, the dreams of performing masculinity are not only expectations Farah has of himself. He expects this behaviour of men he thinks of as important. When he sees articles about his future manager Nishan, he is especially careful to look at the half-naked women dancing around him on the pictures as a verification of his manliness and success.[55] That the women are only signifiers of active heterosexuality and used as markers of a successful masculinity underlines the deception that hegemonic masculinity is made out to be in the novel. As the effective manager he is, Nishan knows his society and its expectations. When he later decides to make Farah into 'the singer of masculinity',[56] he works hard to make sure that this is the image Farah also lives up to.

The ability to perform sexually as a way of asserting one's masculinity is likewise seen in Abu Mustafa's behaviour in the same novel. He already has a number of children, eleven to be exact, and he still sees producing more offspring as a way of proving his masculinity. Every time he fails at work and is unable to bring home money to provide for his family, he has sex with his wife to prove to himself, and possibly her as well, that he is at least able to be a man in this respect. Similarly, Aghacy shows in her discussion of what she calls 'the politics of masculinity', that sexual activity can be used as a way of compensating for a lack of masculine behaviour in other domains.[57] Abu Mustafa's son is, however, not so impressed by his father as he is appalled at the result of the sexual activity.

كلما عجز والدي عن الصيد وعاد مدحوراً من البحر يذهب لصيد العصفور الذهبي في حدائق أمّي. والنتيجة فم جديد يجب إطعامه وجسد طفل جديد يرتمي في غرفتنا الضيقة.

> Every time my dad failed with the fishing and returned home defeated by the sea he went to hunt the golden bird in my mother's gardens instead. The result is another mouth to feed and another child's body to be thrown into our small room.[58]

The sexual ability is interpreted by the characters as such an important part of performing masculinity that Abu Mustafa can use it to compensate for his inability to perform other parts of the expectations placed on masculinity and

Nishan can build his public image on his ability to seduce women. This hegemony is further supported by Yasmina, who, on several occasions, thinks about the pleasure she gets from the male body. When her boyfriend Nimr decides to leave her, she is more upset about losing the bodily contact than his financial support or the emotional connection they have. For her it seems obvious that the performance of masculinity entails being able to sexually please a woman.

As demonstrated in the above discussion, the idea that virility is part of hegemonic masculinity reoccurs in several novels. In *Beirut 75,* it rests at the core of the performance of masculinity; however, as shown by the example from *One Night,* when Rasha decides to be unfaithful to Salim, an inability to live up to the hegemonic norm can also lead to a loss of power in a relationship. Returning to *Beirut 75,* Farah is unable to have sex with one of his girlfriends and, due to the huge expectations placed on his masculinity, the loss of respect is huge.[59] To gain respect from the masculinity that has become his trademark, he also needs to live up to expectations. Nevertheless, even for ordinary men, the expectations placed on them must be realised. The image created for Farah, which he himself cannot live up to, actively functions to idolise super-virility. It further strengthens the existing hegemony of heterosexual virile men as the norm. The importance of the hegemonic norm is exemplified in an argument between the parents in Bitar's novel *The Abbaseen Basement*. They throw insults at each other regularly, but when the mother one day accuses the father of being impotent, he strikes her, which has never happened before. He can accept other insults but not comments on his sexual ability.[60] Masculinity, virility and respect are closely connected when it comes to the characters' self-image and their views of others.

Since virility is seen as such an important part of masculinity, it becomes a hindrance not to be allowed to have sexual relations. Mustafa's frustration with his parent's sexual life can be read as a sign of his own inability to have a sexual relationship himself. He cannot get married due to the poverty the family is suffering from, and his own position as the oldest son, the one supposed to shoulder responsibility for his sisters and brothers, keeps him from forming a life for himself.[61] The poverty he experiences hinders him from fulfilling his own desires, and stops him from doing what, in the eyes of society, will make him a complete man: to marry and father children. In *Damascus* by al-Idlibi it is the younger brother, Mahmud, who is put under the pressure of showing masculinity through virility, having been married for a long time before finally having a daughter. The time waiting for his wife to become pregnant is filled with comments and suggestions, from relatives in general and his mother, in particular, about taking a second wife or different remedies in order to be able to have children. The assumption is that a couple without children is not normal. For Mahmud, who is looked down upon by his siblings for not performing a hegemonic masculinity, it is a huge victory when he finally has a daughter and is able to show that he can produce a child. Having a daughter is, however, not perfect in the eyes of society, but as the mother says: 'the one who has a daughter can also produce a son'.[62] This statement illustrates just how deeply rooted the expectations of having children, and explicitly male children, are. In *The Whirlwind,* one of the male characters recalls how he was tortured and states that, during the torture, he 'lost his manliness, or his ability to have children'.[63] In his view, a man must be able to have children to perform complete masculinity.

In *Woman in a Circle of Fear,* Sami, Hasna's husband is incapable of having children. Before they get married, Sami tells her that he thinks she will be a wonderful mother to his children. When Hasna′ finds out, she is prepared to stay with him and live without children, though admitting to herself that, had the roles been reversed, she would not have blamed him for leaving her. However, Sami seems to forget that he is the one who is unable to have children and when he is upset, he tells Hasna' that other women are so much better than her, just because they are mothers. Despite his pretence that it is Hasna's fault, Sami's need for a child becomes so strong that he develops psychological problems and secretly pretends that he is a baby himself. He does not tell Hasna' nor he does suggest that they adopt a child; instead, he books her appointments with a psychiatrist and tries to make her believe that she is mentally ill. When Hasna' finally finds out that Sami is pretending to be a baby, he decides to divorce her. While he still could pretend that the childlessness was her fault, and treat her as being mentally ill, he had no problem in staying married, but as soon as he appears weak, he states that he cannot bear the shame and leaves her.

On the other hand, in *Beirut 75*, Nimr, Yasmina's boyfriend, is aware that for his future wife and her family it will not be seen as a sign of virility that he has had a long relationship with Yasmina. He therefore does what he can, including bribing her brother, to cover up his relationship with her. His father does the same with his mistresses and states that he prefers foreign girls as they are less clingy, and do not place demands on him or threaten to inform his wife or friends about their relationship.[64] Nimr and his father both use their sexual relationships to show off for a select group of friends or co-workers, but their awareness of the social restrictions make them careful not to be open with their lovers. The hegemonic masculinity they know states that virility is part of masculinity, but at the same time the society they live in does not support sexual relationships outside of wedlock.

As with other parts of masculinity, virility is judged both on its own and in relation to surrounding circumstances. Inability to live up to the expectations can harm one's reputation as in the case of Farah and, to some extent, Mahmud. In this case, subordinated masculinity becomes the opposite of hegemonic masculinity and the characters suffer from a loss of respect and power in their interactions with other characters. Even though virility and the ability to have children form an important part of masculinity as demonstrated above, Yasmina is one of few characters in the novels examined that openly declares her satisfaction with the sexual act. Another character is Khulud in *The Abbaseen Basement* by Haifa Bitar, who has sex in order to take revenge on her father and then realises that she enjoys what she is doing. Furat in *Euphrates* enjoys her first sexual encounter with ʿĪd, a boy from her village, but is described as dislike the sexual acts of her husband. In the other novels, the focus is instead on the performance of the male, or fatherhood, the result of the sexual act.

The Ability to Provide as a Burden of Masculinity

In the formulation of masculinity thus far, the notion of providing is seen as an important aspect for all the female characters. In later novels, these expectations are looked at from a male character's point of view. In *Beirut 75*, Farah, for example, is travelling to Beirut in search of a job to earn money. In the fictional society described in the novel he first needs to be able to provide for himself and others before he can marry and perform what the novel presents as hegemonic masculinity. The idea of a financially independent man, who can look after his wife and children, is an aspect of hegemonic masculinity and forms part of the burden for some of the characters in the novel while it works as a sign of ability for others. In the same way as Nimr uses his virility to prove his masculinity in front of his friends, he also uses his ability to pay as a way of boosting his image. With his father's money, he can appear as the perfect provider and he takes pride in showing Yasmina off in expensive clothes in front of his friends, as if the dresses and furs she wears can vouch for his masculinity.

يحلو له أن يكسوني بالثياب الثمينة. أن يخرج معي إلى المطاعم الفخمة كي يرانا أصدقاؤه.
[...] ويحب اذلالي أمامهم تدليلا على سحره الرجولي.

> He likes to dress me in expensive clothes, to go out with me to superb restaurants for his friends to see us. [. . .] and he likes humiliating me in front of them as a sign of his masculine magic.[65]

When he later wants to end his relationship with her, he stops giving her gifts and money and tells her he will no longer pay her rent.[66] By refusing to provide for her, he shows that he no longer considers himself responsible for her and that their relationship is over. He feels no need to prove himself to her, he will soon marry and, through marriage, assert his masculinity and abilities in front of his friends.

In *Beirut 75,* Yasmina offers a female view on the matter of provision and she accepts that Nimr should be responsible for her financially. The fact that she has to support her brother financially means she looks down on him. As her brother, he should look after her, not the other way round, hence she, too, supports the novel's hegemony. In the other novels discussed, Yasmina's understanding of the different financial roles of males and females seems to be the prevailing view, which exaggerates the expectations on masculinity. This can be seen in *A One-winged Eagle* where Karim is seen to be struggling with his role. His mother understands his problems and tries to help him by offering the little money she has and does not ask him for anything more than what he manages to make available. She seems to realise the pressure he is under and does not want to make his problems bigger by demanding more than he can give. Other female characters, like his sister, are not so understanding. When Karim cannot give her what she wants, she is disappointed and shows no consideration for his circumstances. When he finds himself in a particularly stressful situation where he needs money to be able to pay the rent for his clinic, he musters up the courage to ask his sister, now very well off through her marriage, for money. She writes back telling him that his salary should be enough for him, especially since he is living in the family home, half of which should have been her inheritance. She then continues to say that if he is in desperate need, he should write again, and then she will send him 500 dollars.[67] Karim reads her answer as an insult, but he also thinks that it should be the other way around, her asking him for money, so he never asks her again. As in *Beirut 75,* this novel describes the female characters as active agents in the shaping of masculinity and part of Karim's frustration stems from the obligations he knows that he has towards his mother and sister. That his mother does not actively remind him only makes him feel worse, since he does not want her to pity him. Nor does he want to feel that he has failed her so much that she cannot ask him for what she needs. As seen by Karim, this female evaluation is thus another burden for him to carry.

In *Beirut 75,* the quest for money is plaguing Abu al-Mulla and Abu Mustafa who are both responsible for their families. The need for money is also what kills each of them in the end. Abu Mustafa, whose health is getting worse and who knows that soon he will no longer be able to go out fishing, decides to try one last time to find the magic lamp he has spent his whole life looking for. The lamp, with its magic spirit, will secure the economy of the family even if he cannot fish anymore. To get hold of the lamp he decides to fish with dynamite, something that he himself has forbidden others to do previously and, in the explosion, he is killed.[68] The fact that Abu Mustafa, who is described as very rational and down to earth, believes that a magic lamp is going to save him and his family from poverty suggests the impossibility of the situation. Nothing he does can change his life and he has to resort to magic to find a solution to his problems.

Abu al-Mulla, in the same novel, is similarly forced to change his habits in order to achieve his goals. He, who has been honest his whole life and guarded the archaeological site he works on dutifully, finally decides to steal a statue and sell it to earn money so that he can bring his girls back home from service again.[69] He steals the statue, but shame overpowers him and he dies from a heart attack. Reading these two fates only as the result of poverty, even though that is a major part of the problem, leaves out the social expectations that are placing extra strains on the men. Neither of them, as described in the novel, has asked his wife to take on work. Instead, they shoulder the whole financial burden themselves. Both of them have a number of children, even small children, though they are described as being old and having grown-up sons and daughters and neither of them is considering asking for help. Both men seem to think that provision is the man's duty. Furthermore, Abu Mustafa is introducing his son to the trade in order for him to take over the boat when he gets old enough and thus have an income to support a family.

Karim, in *A One-winged Eagle*, is described as having a similar mindset. Towards the end of the novel, when he is described as completely destitute, he decides to do something that he has previously refused to do, but which he describes as very common; namely to claim that a patient is more seriously ill than he is in order to charge more. The next patient that comes to his clinic is a small boy and he tells the father that the boy needs an operation, although this is not true. He charges the father for the operation, but he agrees to take only half the original price, since that is all the man has, and takes the child to the hospital. Before Karim has even started the operation the boy dies because of the anaesthetic administered to him. Karim, who knows that the operation was completely unnecessary, sees himself as having killed the child; however, he still uses the money he gained to buy food.[70]

Abu Mustafa, Abu al-Mulla and Karim all prefer to take risks and do things they are not at ease with to make things better for their families instead of asking for help. For them, as for the rest of the characters in the novels, it is more important to maintain the appearance of a strong and able family father.

In *A One-winged Eagle*, Karim is troubled by his poverty, not so much because it puts restraints on what he can buy for himself but because he cannot support his mother. Furthermore, Karim's sister takes for granted that she is to be looked after, first by her brother and then by her husband. She abandons her university sweetheart to marry a rich man, something she explains to Karim as being every girl's dream, a statement that makes his despair over his own poverty even greater. Karim tries to reason with her and says that love and understanding is more important than a big house or enormous amounts of money. He continues to say that a bigger house will come with time and together a man and woman can build a future. His sister does not listen and in the end, Karim screams at her to stop.[71] He is not upset on behalf of his sister's previous boyfriend, but rather at the fact that he himself has nothing to offer a woman other than a a room and the hopes of a better future. If his sister is right, then no woman will accept him. The burden of provision hence determines his future as well as his present life. When he witnesses a scene in a café where a man tips a shoe polisher with the equivalent of Karim's daily income, he solidifies his view that had he only been rich he would have been a perfect man, but social circumstances make it difficult to perform what is expected of him.

Karim's understanding of masculinity as being honourable, truthful, generous and helpful is supported by the novel's characters. It is also the role he wants to have at home. As a student, he can live up to the demands placed on him, but as a practitioner with his own clinic the demands rise, but not his ability to meet them. Karim feels the injustice in his sister living a good life due to her rich husband. Rather than analysing these gendered expectations, *A One-winged Eagle* critiques the social and governmental system which, in Karim's mind, means that one must either be connected to influential people or accept and administer bribes to achieve an acceptable position in society. A man like himself, with no powerful connections and no wish to use bribes has no chance of advancing. Hence, society reduces and marginalises men into performing subordinate masculinity, while those who are able to bend the rules can buy a position in society. Instead of changing the expectations on men and women, a social change that enables them to perform their roles successfully must be set in motion.

Whereas the masculinity construction is formed in correspondence with the hegemonic masculinity of the fictional societies, the inability to provide is described from the viewpoint of the characters themselves. The subordination the characters suffer from is thus presented as unjust and it often leads to the use of violence, as will be discussed in the following section.

Violence as a Burden of Masculinity

As seen in the chapter on political masculinity, the ability to use violence and defend oneself and one's country has been described as a vital part of masculinity. Zeina Zaatari further brings up violence as a key concept of masculinity in the Syrian Drama Series *Bāb al-Ḥāra* (*The Neighbourhood Gate*).[72] The connection between firearms and masculinity was discussed in Chapter 3 and in *Beirut 75*, the same idea of protecting oneself, and in this case one's honour rather than one's country, appears, for example in the section about Ṭa'ān. However, as with the provision discussed before, it is rather seen as a burden and a problem than something that leads to glory and the descriptions of violence can be understood as a critique rather than an addition to the hegemonic ideal. Ta'an's relatives have killed a man from a neighbouring clan and, since the murdered man had a degree, the other clan decided that they would kill the first man who obtained a degree from Ta'an's family, who happened to be Ta'an. He is therefore living under constant threat and suspects everyone he sees on the streets of being his potential killer. One day, a tourist taps him on the shoulder to ask for directions and Ta'an turns around and shoots him, believing that it is the hitman from the other clan who has found him. At the police station, he realises that even though the other clan has not managed to kill him physically, they have destroyed him mentally by scaring him and turning him into the killer of an innocent man.

> لقد نجحوا في النتيجة في قتله. بطريقة ما. أرادوا قتله لأجل رجلٍ لم يرَ وجهه قط. ودفعوه ليقتل بنفسه رجلاً لم يرَ وجهه قط. ثم ها هم يشدّونه إلى المشنقة ليقتله رجلٌ لن يرى وجهه قط.

> They had succeeded in killing him in the end. In a way. They had wanted to kill him because of a man whose face he had not seen. And they pushed him to kill a man whose face he had not seen. Then, here they were, dragging him to the gallows to be killed by a man whose face he would never see.[73]

Ta'an and his family are described as having no choice but to accept the vendetta they find themselves in. There seems to be no way of solving the problem other than by Ta'an's death which, although not killing him in the course of the novel, still ruins his life. Despite being worried, Ta'an knows that the result of him backing out of the challenge is to be considered a coward, which is worse than death, both for himself and his entire family. Whereas Ta'an sees the hegemonic norm as a justification for using violence to protect oneself and others, the narrative illustrates the meaninglessness of his actions. By not actually killing the men who are after him or meeting them in a proper fight, Ta'an has lost his chance of proving his masculinity. Instead, his fear has i led him to use violence in a way that leads to ridicule rather than respect.

In a short study of violence in female-authored Arab fiction, Angela Abdel-Malek suggests that violence has become an internal part in the depiction of masculinity by women writers.[74] She means that in the binary opposition created by female writers, physical violence becomes a signifier for male behaviour. In the novels discussed in this book, this might be true for the ideological men who use violence to save their countries or support their political ideas. It is also one aspect of the novels produced in the period called 'problematic masculinity' where violence becomes a male strategy used to control women. However, as shown in the above example, Ta'an is forced to use violence in a way he does not welcome. As with other traits, it seems that the act of violence does not signify masculinity as much as the reason why it is performed. This is particularly telling in the case of Yasmina's nameless brother who uses the pretext of honour to rationalise the murder of his sister.

When Yasmina no longer brings home money for him to spend on himself and his friends, he suddenly realises that he has nothing. He has no job, no family and no girlfriend. The only reason his friends have spent time with him is because of the money his sister has given him. Without this money, he has no chance of forming a position for himself. He accuses Yasmina of trying to build a new life for herself where she will keep all her earnings from him. In a rage he starts hitting her, screaming that she must give him the money she has hidden. When he cannot find any money, he kills his sister. He kills her, not because she has a boyfriend, but because she is unable to give him money. Nevertheless, when he goes to the police station, he says he is there to reclaim his honour.

لقد قتلتُ أختي دفاعاً عن شرفي، وأريدُ أن أدلي باعترافات كاملة!

> I have killed my sister to protect my honour and I want to present a complete confession.[75]

To confess that he has killed his sister for not providing for him would make him both a murderer and tell of his lack of ability to provide. Killing her to protect his honour makes him grow in the eyes of the police officer, who is described as being impressed.[76] In the same way, Ta'an's supposed killing of his perpetrator would have been seen as sanctioned violence and would have earned him respect. In *Beirut 75*, cleansing one's honour through violence is seen as normative behaviour, supported by the police. Yasmina's brother uses the expectations placed on hegemonic masculinity to cover for his true motives for killing his sister. Rather than being crippled by the expectations on masculinity, he uses them for his own purposes. By killing his sister, he has also ended the expectation that he, as her brother, will take care of her.

The next step for Yasmina's brother would be to attack Nimr, and he makes threats at the police station. Nimr can, however, when accused of having had a relationship with Yasmina, afford to pay off her brother. He also manages to persuade him to say that his sister was a prostitute, despite the fact that he knows that her only relationship was with Nimr. Position and money play a role in creating leeway for oneself concerning what are regarded as strict codes of honour and moral rights. This sudden switch in Yasmina's nameless brother's behaviour emphasises that, for him, the talk about masculinity and demanding his rights is more a show for society than based on his own convictions. For money, he accepts to work under the man who used his sister, the man he should really kill.

أنا زلمتك، يا بيك. اخترتُ. اخترتُ. نسيتُ اسمك. وينهار شقيق ياسمينة باكياً.

> I am your man, sir. I have chosen. I have chosen. I have forgotten your name. Yāsmīna's brother collapses crying.[77]

At the same time, the fact that he collapses indicates that he knows that he has lost. He can no longer claim to be the righteous man he was when he walked into the police station. He is now weak and at the mercy of Nimr and his men. The exact image that he tried to avoid when coming to the police station, that of a jobless, moneyless man with no control over his sister is now registered in the police protocol for everyone to read. Through money and contacts, Nimr was able to save himself and destroy the image Yasmina's brother had created. The situation at the police station further shows how the novel depicts hegemonic masculinity as a deception that one can buy for money or paint with words.

Another example where the characters are seen to use violence as a sanctioned way of performing masculinity can be seen in *Damascus* when the Raghib, the oldest brother, has his sister's boyfriend killed to stop her from eloping with him. The brother is not described as considering other options, such as agreeing to the marriage or discussing the relationship. His only thought is to get rid of him to put an end to the relationship. He does not boast about the murder, but neither does he exhibit any signs of regret, despite seeing how upset his sister is at the news. He sees the murder as his duty as the oldest brother to protect the family name.

In these cases, despite the fact that Nimr got away with his actions, the expectation that the men protect their rights and the family's reputation become, on the one hand, actions to be proud of (as seen by the policeman's reaction) but, on the other hand, they are cumbersome burdens that have to be taken care of so as not to lose face. The male characters are aware of the expectations and how to bend the rules, as shown by Nimr, but they all submit to them, even if it means killing or causing harm to others. The harm to their own pride is more difficult to bear. In the eyes of the characters, their use of justified violence enhances their masculinity and proves that they are able to protect themselves and those who depend on them.

Physical violence is an example of how actions seen as embodiments of masculinity move from being righteous to blameworthy actions. Bo Nilsson's definition of masculinity as 'a collection of changing conceptions, practices and positions, forming the foundation of male identities',[78] can be seen in the fact that the same actions are displayed by all characters but used and interpreted differently. When the father in *Snow Under the Sun* hits a man, it is seen as brave and the right thing to do to save his and his daughter's honour. When the freedom fighters use violence, it is seen as a sign of their bravery and ability to defend themselves and their country. However, when violence appears in the later novels it is seen as a sign of brutality and demonstrates an inability to control oneself.[79] The conception of what is acceptable behaviour in society has changed and with it, some of the notions of masculinity. 'Correctly performed' masculinity is still the key to power and influence over women and other men, but the framework has changed with time and place.

While the hegemonic masculinity characters in *Beirut 75* adhere to seems to sanction the violence used, the narrative exposes the murders committed by Yasmina's brother and by Taʿan as unnecessary acts of brutality. Taʿan's victim is an nameless tourist, while he himself is driven to murder by the fear of being killed. Yasmina's brother also remains nameless throughout the novel. This could be explained as them not being very important to the plot, however, there are other characters, with significantly lesser roles, who are named. The fact that the characters are nameless can instead be seen as a representation of a violent system, where both perpetrators and victims are not so much individuals as parts of a structure. The critique is hence of the system, which is allowed to continue with more and more people caught up in the consequences of these actions.

In relation to providing, virility and violence, the male characters are struggling with an external pressure over which they have no control. At the same time, the characters seem to be aware that the expectations are empty and flawed. Farah can be made into a singer of masculinity, his whole appearance and fame is produced by him and his manager. Nimr can use his position to cover up his actions and pretend to be the perfect husband-to-be while, at the same time, living another secret life. Ta'an tried to create a different life for himself through study, but is still caught up in the old traditional ways of proving oneself as a man and protecting the family honour, something which, in the end, ruins his life.

While being aware that the expectations are flawed, the characters actively use them to form positions for themselves in relation to others. The emptiness does not stop them from reaping the benefits of power connected to living according to the rules. Farah enjoys living the life of a rock star that he dreamt of during his childhood. He likes the women and the fame and the power, but when the demands become bigger than he can handle he goes mad. For Nimr and his father, their money is what saves them, but they, too, buy into the expectations and produce images of themselves as providers and protectors as well as virile men. For Abu Mustafa and Abu al-Mulla, the fact that they can sire many children demonstrates their ability as men, even though one or two children instead of 11 or 12 would have solved the problem of provision. The simultaneous acceptance of and struggle with the expectations make the hegemony, as presented in the novel, both extremely strong and extremely vulnerable. It will last as long as everyone accepts it, as all the characters do. However, since they all more or less deviate from it in their personal life, the possibility of the hegemony changing is ever present.

As the quote from Bourdieu at the beginning of this chapter stated, the privileges have, for most of the men turned into burdens and because of their dependence on others' approval they have very little agency in changing their position unless the norms change. As pointed out by Ben Moussa and Lang, the room for movement by the characters is very limited and they have no way to reject the social norms that govern them. On the contrary, they work to reinforce them – Abu Mustafa even organises for his son to take over the family fishing trade so that he, too, can one day provide for a family and live a similar life to his father. The discrepancy between the reality they live in and the norms they are striving for, as demonstrated by Vafa and Talif as the main cause for a subordinated masculinity, is not acknowledged by the characters, even though the narrative makes it clear that they cannot achieve the goals they have set for themselves.

5

Female Masculinity and Male Femininity – the Exploration of Gender Formulation

فضحكتُ من نفسي، من سلوكٍ جعلني أتصرّف وكأني أنا المرأة وهي الرجل.[1]

I laughed at myself, at the manners that made me behave as if I was the woman and she was the man.

In addition to an exploration of the burdens of masculinity another trend that appears in the novels towards the end of the twentieth century is to investigate the meaning of masculinity and femininity. In the works of some authors this is examined through an insecurity in the gendered behaviour of a character and in others it is explored by making characters consciously perform actions traditionally assigned to the opposite sex and the use of other characters to discuss this. Yet other authors deal with gendered behaviour through the upbringing of children and as such explore both how gender is communally formulated and what is seen as masculine and feminine in the fictional worlds of the novels. All the novels discussed in this chapter place their characters in relationships where their behaviour is affected and judged by others, but also has the (dangerous) potential of causing change. Whereas the novels of the pioneers and their ideal and political masculinities can be read as attempts to influence society, these novels instead acknowledge the role of social bonds and the power of society and weave these factors into the plot. As such, instead of formulating role models and good examples, their questionable and deviant masculinities form a critique against society and the ways they perceive gender roles as both something children are fostered into and something that grown-ups are forced to maintain.

The novels further highlight the role of women in gender formation and, contrary to the image that women in general are victims of the patriarchal structures, they exemplify how grandmothers, mothers, aunts and neighbours are crucial in upholding the power structures surrounding the gender roles. By showing the importance of a correct performance of masculinity for the reputation and survival of the immediate family, they emphasise how masculinity becomes an essential project for mothers and sisters, who have the educational responsibility. The female perspective is thus, more than just a woman's view. It is the counterpart against which masculinity is created. If it is unclear then masculinity is unclear, if its supportive masculinity becomes strong if it is too demanding, masculinity is unable to cope. The writers have created masculinities that are not solely influenced by homo-social settings. On the contrary, the masculinities presented are calculated around female reactions to their way of behaving. The male–female interaction and power play in the novels support Connell's claim that masculinities do not first exist and then encounter femininities,[2] but rather they are developed together.

In this chapter the following novels will be discussed. *The Impossible Novel* by Ghada al-Samman revolves around Zayn and how her father decides to bring her up as a boy. The novel is built around al-Samman's own childhood and is the first part of her semi-fictional biography. In the novel, Zayn gripples with what it means to be a girl and tries to make sense of the rules her aunt, grandmother and cousins impose on her in relation to the freedom she is granted by her father. The chapter further deals with *Steps in the Fog* by Malāḥa al-Khānī. The main character in this novel is Haytham, a spoiled young man whose only concern is that he is not allowed enough freedom by his parents. He is fighting with his friends to be seen as masculine enough and he works to uphold a manly façade in front of his girlfriend. When his father falls ill, Haytham is expected to take up his position as the provider of the family and his role changes completely. Through the changing expectations on Haytham, the novel shows how the fictional society shapes masculinity. In *Wild Mint* by Anisa 'Abbud the novel is divided into sections where 'Ali and 'Alya alternate the narration. 'Ali is a poet and has moved to the city to find work, 'Alya is a university professor and they meet through friends. Through their relationship and their struggles with life between the city and the countryside, the idea of what it means to be a man and a woman is explored. The novel makes use of myth and traditional tales and, towards the end of the novel, the two characters appears as two faces of the same creation. *Cyclones in the Levant* by Nadia Khust starts with a preface where the writer explains that the novel builds on memories, reports and historical documentation and the plot is indeed full of references to important historical figures, years and places. The main character Qays was born in Palestine but has lived large parts of his life abroad as a refugee. At the start of the novel, he decides to move back to his homeland. However, the move back stirs up memories and through flashbacks of varying length Qays' childhood and youth are described in detail. The chapter also discusses sections of *The Naked Back* by Henriette ʿAbbudi, partly covered by the previous chapter. The last novel to be discussed is, *Yawmiyyāt muṭalliqa*[3] (*Diaries of a Divorcing Woman*, 1994) by Haifa Bitar. The novel is told from the first-person perspective of an unnamed woman who, at the beginning of the novel, is back at her parents' house because she and her husband have separated. Since they are Christian, she is not divorced but is waiting for a final decision. During this period of waiting, she goes through old memories, trying to figure out where her marriage went wrong. She further discusses, in her diary and with her mother, how society looks on a divorced woman, and her family, as a failure. Towards the end of the novel, she has found a job and is attempting to live life as a single mother even though that puts both financial and social strain on her life.

The focalisation in these novels is similar to the discussion in the previous chapter. There is a mixture of male and female focalisors, and the perspective is shared between several characters. Like in many of the novels of the third wave, gender relationships are created and described via a web of characters which makes allowances for the different views that are normative in different societies, whether that is the opposition between the city and the country or between Syria and other countries.

Creating Gendered Bodies

Connell states that gender performance is connected to the biological sex of the person.[4] This is similar to Candace West and Dan Zimmerman who propose that '[g]ender activities emerge from and bolster claims to membership in a sex category'.[5] In the matrix of everyday relationships, certain expectations are put on bodies due to their biological sex; these expectations then influence that individual's behaviour. In this understanding, gender appears as a reaction to outer stimuli in the form of a social context's expectations on the individual. These are often founded on an assumed knowledge of the individual's biological sex. The conscious, or unconscious, agreement upon these expectations means that members of society will try to change themselves accordingly to be part of a homogeneous society. This is particularly important in the upbringing of children and is seen through actions and reactions to an individual's behaviour. The transition from childhood to the world of grown-ups includes learning a new coding system for how to behave. Not conforming to these expectations can, in some cases, as for Zayn in *The Impossible Novel*, lead to opportunities she would not have had, if she had followed the expected behaviour of girls. However, Zayn meets with opposition to her behaviour from her close family and society.

As discussed in Chapter 3, some of the novels from this period make use of a male narrator or main character as the focaliser. *Wild Mint* by Anisa ʿAbbud sets the scene for her exploration of gendered behaviour by starting the novel with an ungendered 'I' which makes the text ambiguous. The ambiguity continues until the first descriptive words appear in the text and through their grammatical form show her gender. As noted by Candace West and Don Zimmerman, not knowing for certain the biological sex of another person creates anxiety. In order to avoid this anxiety, gendered behaviour becomes the code used to both send out our own signals and read those of others.[6] Through these signals, one's own gender is established, and it is clear how others should be dealt with according to the gendered norms of society. Henriette ʿAbbudi does the same thing in *The Naked Back* and, by not immediately positioning the 'I' of the novel in one of the binary gendered positions, the actions performed by the character are the only possible keys offered by the text. Once the text has revealed that the 'I' is a man, the actions he performs are no longer evaluated based on being feminine or masculine; instead they are compared to an imaginary ideal of masculinity. In *Wild Mint* the "I" turns out to be female something we do not discover until the second chapter. In the rest of the novel, the narrative perspective moves between different characters, but it becomes clearer to the reader to whom the voice belongs. These narrative choices show how even the reader searches for the gender of a character in order to know how to evaluate him or her; paired with the novels' content which discusses similar questions, the authors clearly show the relationship between expectations of a specific behaviour and gender.

Even if the masculinities in the novels appear similar, the setting shows a development in the relationships between men and women. In *Cyclones in the Levant* and *The Impossible Novel,* education is not for everyone, especially not for girls. In *The Impossible Novel,* this is seen from a girl's perspective and with jealousy. Though supported by her father, all the things Zayn achieves, such as climbing trees, swimming, going out, publishing poetry and studying are things she has to fight for, whereas they are seen as natural for her male cousins. In *Steps in the Fog,* the interaction between girls and boys mainly takes place at university where they participate as equals. In the rural society described in *Cyclones in the Levant,* the distribution of labour is based on gender and, from an early age, boys and girls are quickly divided into two separate spheres. Whereas it is evident from the novels that the opportunities for girls have changed with time, the expectations on masculinity are very similar.

The mother in *Steps in the Fog* describes the father as 'the oak of the house'.[7] To her, he is the one who is strong enough to carry all the burdens, despite the fact that she too works outside the house and shares the obligations of the family. When he becomes bedridden, it is as if her whole world has fallen apart, not only because her husband is ill, but also because, without him, she believes that she is unable to continue her life as she used to. Her solution to the problem is to turn to her oldest son and instigate him in the role as head of the family. In *The Impossible Novel,* Zayn's aunt laments the fact that her husband is dead, again not so much because of her love for him, but for her loss of support and position. Her son is still young, but she does what she can to introduce him to the role of family head. In *Cyclones in the Levant,* the mother tries every possible way to keep her husband, including magic. Even though she is hurt by his affairs and the fact that he stays away for long periods, she still prefers to be married and have a husband than to lose her male support. When the husband is not around, she turns to her young son for support instead.

Despite the difference in time setting, the elder female characters, though described as very capable, turn to their young sons to take on the responsibility their fathers previously had. In this fashion, they reinforce the expectations that males, even at a young age, should be able to shoulder responsibility and family burdens. In addition to the demands they place on the boys, they also treat them with new respect and make sure they feel the privilege of performing masculinity. As a result, the boys are moulded into what the mothers' hope will be copies of their fathers and masculinity, as performed by the fathers, is reproduced. However, it is not always the case that these ideals will be the same everywhere. In *The Naked Back*, Adham tries to apply the gendered behaviour he learnt as a child and young man but these are not accepted by his French girlfriend Claire. He has ideas about who should perform the household chores and, as with his ideas on cooking and cleaning, he has divided the world into outer and inner space. Marriage would be a way for Claire to leave the outer world of work and instead be cared for by him. However, Claire does not agree, which she makes obvious to him. Every time he tries to apply any type of pressure on her, she tells him that she will not live in a prison and that if he wants to have a relationship with her, he has to make himself agreeable.[8] For Adham, who seems to see women as belonging to men, this is difficult to grasp even after being with Claire for several weeks. When she makes up an excuse not to go to a dinner, he tells her that she should have simply said that the man she loves forbade her to go. He thinks it is a perfectly reasonable thing to say, whereas Claire's reaction is literally to kick him out of bed.

Female Masculinity and Male Femininity

Even though there is a connection between the biological sex of a person and the gendered expectations placed on him/her as a set of actions, masculinity is not necessarily performed only by biological males. In her book, *Female Masculinity* Judith Halberstam argues that, throughout history, women have been involved in formulating, but also performing, versions of masculinity.[9] Through the discussions, court protocols and accounts she produces, it becomes clear that reactions to women's female masculinity have not always been welcoming. The gap between the expected and actual female behaviour of the woman has been too wide for the societies studied to accept. As a result, it can be said that the making of gender roles is not only the individual person's actions, but also others' reactions to them. Marie Nordberg has instead coined the concept 'masculine femininity', where she looks at how men exhibit traits usually coded as feminine.[10] The two concepts by Halberstam and Nordberg capture the difference between biological sex and gender by referring to a biologically sexed male performing actions conventionally coded as feminine and vice-versa. The two concepts highlight the expectations put on a body and the individual's struggle to live up to these expectations, whether as a male or a female. In the novels discussed, male and female characters perform perceived masculinity and femininity with varying degrees of success. Their level of success is not connected to their own perception but to others' reactions to their behaviour. In a different study, Nordberg argues that the discussion of female masculinity and male femininity is no longer useful in a modern debate, since it conserves gender stereotypes rather than breaks them.[11] She states that in order to talk about male femininity, a set of traits considered feminine has to be agreed upon and then looked for as alien in a man's behaviour so that he can be seen as performing male femininity.[12] She proposes a different approach, which would be to free characteristics from their connection to a specific gender and then only talk of different humans. This would further remove the pre-defined value attached to male and female actions respectively.

Whereas Nordberg's later study is an addition to the work on gender equality, the concepts of male femininity and female masculinity lend themselves as suitable tools for the analysis in this chapter. The characters in all the novels discussed are concerned with the performance of gender. The main male character in *The Naked Back*, Adham, is engaged in what he understands as the relationship between biological sex and gender roles. The emphasis put on various actions, because they are not normally expected from a man or a woman, serves to highlight the gender norm in the novel. Whilst stressing the expected norm, the novel does not safeguard the gender roles as much as it displays how the rules are socially constructed and hence can be broken. In the novel this is shown by what the characters themselves see as a reversal of gender roles. Adham describes himself as the obedient housewife and depicts Claire as the husband. As shown by the initial quote from the novel, Adham finds the position he is in funny and awkward, but despite this, he goes on behaving 'as if he was the woman'. This dichotomy, described and lived by Adham, offers clues to what the characters see as hegemonic masculinity. Through an examination of Adham it appears how masculinity is shaped in relation to the idea of ideal masculinity as it clashes with the everyday events in the characters' lives. Adham's inability to perform hegemonic masculinity and the affect this has on his life exemplifies the hierarchical levels of masculinity performance. Claire, in *The Naked Back*, is not aware of performing female masculinity, but in the clash between her values and behaviour and Adham's expectations on what a woman should do, her idea of everyday life is masculinised. For him, working in advertising, travelling, eating out, taking decisions and being the main earner are all things men, but not women, do. Whereas Halberstam's aim with *Female Masculinity* was partly to seek an end to gender binarism and replace it with more flexible forms for gender preference,[13] the female masculinity (and male femininity) that appear in the novels are anchored in the binarism Halberstam wants to distort, as seen above. However, the variations within the two accepted gender categories still deconstruct some of the biological and cultural expectations the characters are working in and around.

The discrepancy between reality and expectations of the roles of men and women can further be seen in *Steps in the Fog*. In the beginning of the novel, Haytham's inability to take decisions is pointed out by his girlfriend, Muna, who wants him to invite her home. Haytham replies that it is impossible because of his parents and their views and restrictions. Muna, whose mother sees Haytham as a harmless experience for her daughter, laughs at him and says that it seems she is the male between the two of them.

> انقلبت الآية إذا، تبادلنا الجنس، صرْتُ أنا الشاب وتحولتَ أنتَ إلى فتاة. لا أعرف أن شخصيتك مهلهلة إلى هذه الدرجة.[14]
>
> So, the verse is turned upside down. We have changed gender, I have become the boy and you have turned into a girl. I did not know that your character was weak to this extent.

Muna's comment illustrates the expected rules for males and females in their society, where the males traditionally have the freedom Haytham lacks, or is too afraid to exercise. It shows that this 'weakness' is not seen as an asset – she expects someone who is assertive and powerful and stands up for what he wants. Soon after this discussion, Haytham feels that he needs to find a way to meet privately if he is not to lose his girlfriend.

Since Judith Butler's seminal work *Gender Trouble*,[15] the concept of individuals doing gender rather than performing predetermined acts based on biology has become the domineering view in gender research. Connell adopts this view when she writes that '[g]ender is social practice that constantly refers to bodies and what bodies do, it is not social practice reduced to the body'.[16] The body, the biological sex, places certain expectations on an individual. In the novels discussed, this becomes flagrant when, in one scene in *The Impossible Novel*, it is impossible for a group of boys to tell if a new child they meet is a boy or a girl. They then decide it is a boy who can safely be included in their group. When they later find out the biological sex of the child, a girl, whom they were about to make their leader, they are utterly appalled. Their confusion illustrates their distinct preconception, based only on sex, of what girls and boys can do. When they face a girl who can run, swim and jump as skilfully as they can, they do not know how to handle the situation. Zayn's grandmother feels that this confusion could destabilise the relationship between the children and therefore decides to pierce her ears. By this clear marker of which sex Zayn belongs to, she has strengthened the binary gender structure and placed a visible reminder for the girl herself, and others, that she is doing something wrong if she performs actions that are gendered male. Connell says that: 'gender relations, the relations among peoples and groups organised through the reproductive arena, form one of the major structures of all documented societies'.[17] By her use of earrings, the grandmother reinforces the structures of her immediate society and makes sure that the division between the genders stays intact.

Gender can thus be said to be both context bound and performed in a symbiotic fashion with the surrounding society or, as Oystein Gullvåg Holter puts it, 'a social psychological link between the individual and the collective'.[18] At a specific moment, an individual action can be interpreted as either masculine or feminine, but the general division rests on social structures. These are something one has to learn and later adapt to. In *Cyclones in the Levant*, this is pointed out by Qays when he sees a little girl playing. Though still a small girl, her game concentrates on finding a husband and having children, a game he himself was never encouraged to play. To perform the expected masculinity (or femininity), is a process that starts at a young age and goes on for the rest of one's life. In their article 'Boys and Men in Families', Michelle Adams and Scott Coltrane maintain that the patterns of play in separate groups of girls and boys lay the foundation for later adult behaviour. They further quote examples of how boys and girls choose gender-separated playgroups, even when they are not prompted to do so by caretakers.[19] The fictional scenario involving Qays and his reflection on games demonstrates the texts' awareness of children's ability to create gendered worlds. In *Live and Die Like a Man,* an anthropological study from Egypt, Farah Ghannam shows how this process involves all members of the Egyptian families she has interviewed, rather than just the children.[20] She asserts how enactments of masculinity are observed, critiqued and evaluated by other members of society, including women.[21] This communal construction of masculinity guides children from an early age into what is seen as correct masculine and feminine behaviour. In *Cyclones in the Levant,* Qays would prefer to be with his mother and listen to the stories she and her friends tell. Rather than inviting her son to join, the mother tells him that he is big enough to go and sit with his father and the men in the other room. He is no longer allowed to take part in the women's conversation and she thus signals both to him and to her female friends that he has become a man. His own desire to stay is not important and the mother tells him that, as a man, he will find more interesting things to listen to in his father's company.

All the novels discussed in this chapter show this intertwined relationship between the genders and how the female relatives often stipulate the masculinity the boys are taught to perform. The gender dichotomy that appears in the novels cannot be said, therefore, to be a male creation but is rather formed in collaboration. The female characters are in charge of the day-to-day education and upbringing of the children and the expectations that make up gender roles are formulated and learnt at a young age. Another example of this is *The Girls of Our Neighbourhood* by Malaha al-Khani where the boys and girls are separated from an early age and treated differently within the household. Whereas it is seen as natural that the boys leave the house and study, the female protagonist must fight for a chance to educate herself. The awareness of gender differences from a young age is demonstrated in, among other places, a study on adolescent boys in rural Egypt by Nadia Zibani and Martha Braidy. The study shows that schoolboys have a clear view of what they think masculinity entails. They divide the roles of masculinity into conduct, responsibility and privilege. The boys are further aware that there are certain obligations that must be met in order to perform successful masculinity, ie, they mention earning and spending money.[22] The concept of being the breadwinner of the family is also discussed in Aghacy's *Masculine Identity in the Fiction of the Middle East* where she argues that a young boy's ability to bring home money gains his parents' respect and admiration.[23] This can be seen in *Steps in the Fog*, where Haytham changes his position within the family by becoming the main provider. In these cases, it is hence not to be born a man that leads to a respected position but the actions one performs. Moreover, it is others' approval of the actions that actually counts and leads to a change from childhood to manhood in Haytham's case. In *The Girls of Our Neighbourhood*, mentioned above, Sami, one of the main character's brothers is seen as good-for-nothing. When he runs away to join the army the father is enraged at how the boy can throw away his life in this way, but the action still shows agency and bravery, which later serves the boy well in his transition from boyhood to manhood.

Another example of how boys are eased into future performances of masculinity is given by Deniz Kandiyoti. She shows how young boys are jokingly treated as the head of the household when other men are absent.[24] This game primes the boys from a young age towards a certain behaviour, including a feeling of power when sisters and mothers obey their orders. As noted by Adams and Coltrane, the family circle is often the first place where boys understand that they are different from girls and begin to exercise their power.[25] It is, however, not only a fun game; young boys without older male support are expected to take up the responsibilities preserved for the male of the household from an early age. In *Steps in the Fog*, Haytham is not placed as the head of the household as a joke. It is, on the contrary, a demand from his mother when his father falls ill. In *The Impossible Novel*, Zayn notices how her male cousins are tasked with looking after her, even though they are the same age. Her aunt also treats her son, Zayn's cousin, whose father has died a few years earlier, as the head of her family unit. In this case, the aunt is priming her son to take on the responsibility he will later shoulder on his own. She further creates a position for herself by using her son, whom she can control, as the head of the family rather than turning to her brothers. In a conflict, however, her son is subordinated to his uncles due to the age difference, even though he has power over his immediate relatives.

Consequently, children's upbringing can give an insight into the dominant views on gender relations in a society and the roles prescribed for each gender. At the same time, the transition from boyhood into manhood and the performance of masculinity is not always easy, despite the early preparations that mothers and family members make for their sons. While mapping out the field of masculinity studies Stefan Horlacher notes that '[m]asculinity, as a notion, [...], is not a simple fact but has to be acquired through struggles, painful initiations, rites of passage, or long and often humiliating apprenticeships'.[26] Through various tests, the young boy proves that he is able to perform masculinity and learns the values of his society. As part of a specific group or society, adhering to the social rules or breaking them becomes, not a personal choice, but a decision which determines your position vis-à-vis others. Whereas, as stated above, the family setting is often the first place where a boy realises that he is different, it is outside the everyday life of the domestic setting that a boy, later a man, has to prove his masculinity.[27] This can, for example, be done in school, at work or in other social circumstances.

Bo Nilsson examines the same notion in his study of boy scouts and their rules and regulations. He too argues that boys can obtain masculinity by winning competitions and handling challenges.[28] Even though masculinity is always performative, the transition period between boyhood and manhood seems particularly focused on being able to prove oneself worthy of being a man. This is reflected in all the novels, where the boys constantly wait for others' approval to be accepted. Moreover, they participate in actions with the sole purpose of appearing better than other young men and boys, in order to improve the image of themselves in front of the others. In *Cyclones in the Levant*, Qays' father is a womaniser, something which plagues his mother but gives him status. During his son's upbringing, he explains to him several times the right of a man to have girlfriends in addition to a wife. When he sees that his son seems to be as interested in women as he is, he feels proud. Qays himself soon realises that having girlfriends is a way for him to appear manly and grown up in front of his friends, something that als features in *Steps in the Fog*. At the beginning of the novel, Haytham's mother is strictly against her son having relationships with girls. When Muna calls the house, she says that Haytham is not at home and, in front of Haytham, she pretends that the caller had dialled the wrong number.[29] When she later sees Haytham as a man, it becomes part of his performance of masculinity to have girlfriends and she jokes with him about the girls calling and discusses relationships with him.[30] While she now supports her son's right to see girls, she feels sorry for Muna, whom she assumes has to lie a lot to her parents in order to see Haytham. Like most of the other characters in the novel, she believes that girls and boys should not meet before they are married and she knows that society, as a whole, does not support this type of behaviour. At the same time, she likes Muna and does not try to stop her from visiting. What she does not know is that Muna's mother does not mind her daughter visiting her boyfriend and sees it as a way for her to try out her femininity. The social norms are cancelled out by class, but only within Muna's immediate family, not society as a whole. In all the novels examined, heterosexuality is seen as normative and young boys are described as being intrigued by sexual relationships with girls, something that is described as giving them status and a sense of pride even when their sexual appetites and actions are different. In *Steps in the Fog*, Saʿīd who is described as coming from a poor rural area, is seen as unable to handle his attraction for women. He is depicted as standing in front of a clothes shop, stunned by the plastic female mannequins and their flimsy clothes. He then goes home and, on the stairway, meets his young female neighbour. He feels that her lips are talking to him and silently drags her towards him and kisses her passionately, unable to resist the temptation. This action is neither condoned nor condemned by the all-knowing narrator, just presented in a matter-of-fact kind of way. Interestingly, these sudden pangs of attraction never affect Said at university. He, like the other students, has adapted to the mixed university environment and how to behave in it, but outside it, he lives by his old rules. The other male characters in the novel, all city boys, are never troubled by this raw desire for women and are happy to kiss their girlfriends or hold their hands, but do not feel the need to attack their female neighbours to get kisses. Said's action is, at the same time, a sign of heterosexual desire and a signifier that he is not a sophisticated city dweller who is used to the presence of women.

In her anthropological work on Damascene women's lives, Sally Gallagher has exemplified precisely that the particular gender expectations on men and women are the same over class boundaries, but that the enactment of them might vary.[31] This is verified by Dalya Abudi who, in a discussion on the Arab family as a miniature of Arab society, pinpoints education and wealth as two key factors for change. She particularly connects these two factors and more liberal views on marriage and gender roles in the Arab world, in comparison with the dominant views in society.[32] In *The Impossible Novel*, Zayn's mother comes from an upper-class family from the coastal region and she marries a man from an old Damascene family with a moderate income and position. Whereas the way things are done vary between the two families, the general demands on the role of a man and woman are very similar. The expected masculinity includes being the decision taker and money maker of the family. When Zayn's mother buys a flat with her own money, the father refuses to move there since he does not want people to think that he is dependent on his wife.

This division between provider and provided for, which hinders Zayn's father from accepting his wife's offer, is further enforced by the law which forces Zayn's grandfather to make his nephew, rather than his daughters, the beneficiary of his inheritance. As the male of the family, his nephew is supposed to look after the females, and he therefore has a right to the family money and land. The gender regime discussed in the introduction is not just based on culture and tradition but enforced legally. Whereas the Syrian constitution stresses the equality of its citizens regardless of biological sex, the personal laws regulating, for example, marriage, inheritance, travelling and childcare are gender specific and vary between the religious groups.[33] These laws, which are reinforced by the state, support a division of gender towards which the citizens must position themselves. This creates a hetero-normative society where distinctive gender roles are important; women have to be women so that men can be men.[34] Any violation of the hegemonic behaviour thus becomes not only an individual expression of lifestyle, but also a threat to and a questioning of the social, law enforced, order.[35] In a study on feminism in Syria, Mayya al-Rahbi has touched upon the effect these laws have on womens' views of themselves and their possibilities of shaping their lives.[36] She argues that the laws can be seen as discriminating against both men and women; women since they are not seen as equal to men and men since they have the burden of providing for and protecting their female relatives.[37] Rahaf Aldoughli argues that the new Syrian constitution of 1973 and the following personal laws not only force women into a subordinate position but also changes the state into a masculinist project. This book does not examine the different Syrian personal laws, however, since the writers engage with society, its laws and the social and legal frameworks within which the writers produce their fiction is known to both themselves and their readership. Different approaches in engaging with this reality can thus be read as ways of supporting or denouncing existing social structures both on a personal level, and, building on Aldoughli's argument of the state as a symbol of masculinity, on a state level. In *The Impossible Novel,* this division is, for example, critiqued through Zayn's confusion about what she interprets as inequality, whereas the grown-up characters do not think it odd that the male relative inherits all the money. Similarly, Haifa' Bitar discusses the influence the specific divorce laws for Christians have on the main character's life and how they delay her being able to free herself from her loveless marriage in *Diaries of a Divorcing Woman*. In *Sidewalks of Tedium,* discussed in Chapter 1, Maria takes a possible future court ruling over the custody of her son into account when she considers if she should ask for a divorce. Hence, even where the characters themselves want to free themselves from the gendered behaviour others expect from them, they are regulated by laws that are based on their biological sex.

Country-explicit laws hence inform the performance of masculinity, but specific locations can also impose their own rules. Particular places, such as military and educational institutions, can also, to a certain extent, negate the importance of class and other markers. In *Steps in the Fog*, the university stands out as a world of its own. It is an area closed to outsiders, such as parents, and the young men and women live the mixed social life they are not able to have outside the university gates. This suggests that gendered behaviour is somewhat situational. Class and regional differences are not forgotten, but they are not as prominent as in life outside the gates. Despite this, the structures of the relationships between male and female students are built on the same foundation as in their lives outside the gates. However, the expectations on the male character to be active, assertive and protective still linger in discussions and actions, in addition to the heteronormative distinction between those who have a girlfriend and those who do not. What is considered normal, even expected, within the university gates might not be seen in the same way outside. Having a girlfriend is one of these things. Whereas it stems from the same idea of male virility as part of masculinity, the way to display it in society is through marriage whereas, inside the gates, it is sanctioned behaviour to have a girlfriend.

In *Cyclones in the Levant,* the fields at the outskirts of the village form this place of freedom for the children and offer the possibility to meet and play without the grown-ups constantly watching. This is an area where the normal gender rules do not apply as strictly as in the rest of society. It is, however, clear through the interaction between the children, and the elaborate games played by the boys to show off their courage and strength, that the general norms are not forgotten. Girls are allowed to participate to a certain extent, but the main purpose of the games is for the boys to find a place in the hierarchal order. This determines their position in the group and the amount of respect they are shown.

Male and Female Influences on Masculinity Formulation

In *Steps in the Fog*, the Haytham's mother plays a major role in his life. She is the caretaker and, simultaneously, the executioner of the father's ideas. However, she is able to intervene with the father on behalf of her son. In Ghannam's interviews, she proves that women, contrary to what many previous studies have suggested, have a fundamental role in the formation of masculinity. As mothers, sisters and other close relatives, the behaviour of the family's men reflects on their status and position, so it is of utmost importance that the male performs masculinity as expected.[38] Through advice, help and their own conduct they influence their male relatives' behaviour.

The male–female relationship places a further burden on the women, since their behaviour affects the male characters' perception of themselves. In *Diaries of a Divorcing Woman* the main female protagonist knows that, by asking for a divorce, she will not only break her father's heart but his view of himself. Even though she is the one who has been unable to complete her marriage, he, as the one who brought her up, is held responsible by society. Although he does not oppose her decision, she feels that he has changed his habits and ways of dealing with people since he no longer sees himself as respectable. She is unable to continue her marriage, but she does everything else that she can to reinstate her father's feeling of self-worth.

Returning to *Steps in the Fog*, it is not just Hytham's mother who has influence over his behaviour. Muna and the girls at university exert power over him and the other boys and indicate what is accepted and expected behaviour from them. In one part of the novel Haytham and a friend discuss girls and the friend says that anyone can get a girlfriend these days since girls only want to get married. Haytham disagrees and points to the many demands modern girls have on their future spouses, demands he feels he must live up too.[39] Whereas his friend seems to think that *being* a man is enough to find a wife, Haytham instead advocates that *acting* like a man is what counts. He adds that modern girls have specific ideas about what this means, which cannot be overlooked, something that previously might have been possible. The boys' discussion can be read as a sign of a changing society, where girls have won more power over their life choices, which affects their men's performance of masculinity.

That the female characters decide what is considered acceptable might be interpreted as an overly direct way of changing society. In a study of ideal masculinity in English novels from the eighteenth century, Shawn Lisa Maurer finds the masculinities created by the female authors in her study unrealistic in their over-positive form.[40] She asserts that the fictional masculinities are too far from reality to be credible even as fantasies, which make them a humoristic, rather than a serious, contribution to the discussion of gender roles. Simultaneously, humour can place the spotlight on particular types of behaviour. In *The Naked Back*, many of the conversations between Claire and Adham are humoristic and play on the general notions and stereotypes of male and female behaviour, in addition to the opposition between local and foreign. The reversed stereotypes are, however, never stretched to the extent that the novel loses credibility and the characters transformed into mock characters in the way Maurer indicates; instead, they lead to questions on what 'male' and 'female' really mean for the characters involved.

The boys in Zibani's and Braidy's study go on to discuss masculinity and conduct, which is connected both to their own behaviour and their ability to control the conduct of female relatives.[41] The third component, privilege, was seen as integral to being born male and includes the right to be looked after by female members of the family. Whereas the researchers suggest that the same ideas the boys put forward are internalised by society as a whole, they mean that the time of adolescence is a period when these notions are intensified and the young boys feel a need to prove their masculinity and thus strictly adhere to what they see as the hegemonic norm.[42] In *The Impossible Novel,* the behaviour of Zayn, a female character, enrages her male cousins because they feel that what she does implies that they cannot control her which, in turn, leads to a loss of masculinity. In the matrix of gender relations, they are depending on her gendered behaviour to prove their own success. When she does not adhere either to their wishes or to society's norms, they try to scare her into behaving in a way that they see as being correct. Whereas the boys' sisters take pride in the male wish to protect the family's honour, and thus play the expected female role in the gender game, Zayn refuses. Her refusal to conform illustrates how gender roles are formulated by mutual agreement. When one party no longer performs the expected actions, the other party loses his (or her) ability to perform the opposite and a form of gender confusion appears. One way of avoiding this confusion is by enforcing gender using role models. The aunt in *The Impossible Novel* is therefore worried that her fatherless son will become less manly than his friends. Despite herself being influential in the children's upbringing, and very authoritative on what is masculine and feminine, she fears that her son is less equipped than other children to perform gender correctly. She is therefore careful to make use of her brothers in the children's upbringing. One example is when the aunt tells off the girls, and then asks her brother to tell off the boys, adding that they will listen to him because he is a man. Like this, the boys are told off twice, indirectly through hearing the aunt tell their uncle and directly by the uncle. They are also given the information that the aunt, though commanding her brother, does not give herself authority over them. In *Steps in the Fog,* the father is used as a final judge or authority more than as a role model for his children. When Haytham's mother sees that he will not listen to her, she seeks support from the father, not as an equal parent but as the head of the household, someone who has more power than both of them. The mother in *The Girls of Our Neighbourhood,* who is described as knowing everyone's secrets and being the one who keeps the family together, refers certain matters to her husband if she thinks that they need extra weight. In all three cases, the women are verbal about what they want and what they think is correct behaviour, but they refer the actual action to a man.

A role model does not necessarily have to be the biological father. In *Steps in the Fog,* Haytham's manager, a wealthy estate agent, tries to act as a father figure for his young employee. The father–son relationship invoked by the manager is used as a way of socialising boys into men. Since he holds a higher position in the hierarchal system of masculinity performance, he can support Haytham in his struggle with masculinity. He can help the younger man with money, work, and even marriage. By using his position to help Haytham reach all the material aspects of masculinity performance, the manager strengthens his own position by creating a network of young men who are dependent on him. Qays, in *Cyclones in the Levant,* is put in the same situation when he moves in with an elder man in the city who takes it upon himself to educate Qays and show him how a man behaves. Through his contacts and financial position, he can influence the young man and affect his life choices. The influence of older men does not necessarily need to be described as an active act. In *Diaries of a Divorcing Woman,* the main character looks back at her marriage and remembers that her husband always wanted to be in control, to the extent that she believes he wanted to destroy her just to prove that he was the man and she the woman. However, she does not blame him for this behaviour; instead, she believes that her husband had seen and inherited this behaviour from his father and grandfather. This points to the role of social factors in the shaping of masculinities.[43] Hence pointing at the social factors in the shaping of masculinities.

Thus far, the role of society, individual characters and external circumstances have been discussed as instrumental in the formation of masculinity. The transition from boyhood to manhood is usually described as more complicated than just a long adaptation process aided by society. David D Gilmore points out that: '[t]his current notion that manhood is problematic, a critical threshold that boys must pass through testing, is found at all levels of sociocultural development regardless of what other alternative roles are recognised'.[44] The change from child to man, from dependent to provider, builds on a set of tests showing that one is worthy of the new position. This can to some extent explain Haytham's hesitation. He knows that there is a possibility he will fail and he further knows that there is no going back once he is accepted as a man.

In *Imagined Masculinities: Male Identity and Culture in the Modern Middle East,*[45] the first section addresses institutional and social practices that function as tests for manhood. These can be religious rituals that one has to go through, or stages in social life such as obligatory military service, which is seen as a way of initiating a boy into manhood. These rituals or practices are important not only for the boy himself but also for the whole family. In the novels discussed, this is seen to a varying degree through games and religious and official ceremonies. In *Steps in the Fog*, Haytham is not put through any type of official testing, but there are still two trials that shape and distinguish him as a man. Firstly, when his father falls ill and he is forced to step in and take responsibility for the family, a role he does not really want. The second time is at his work. Having performed simple tasks for a while, he is asked to accompany the owner on a late evening tour. He is, however, told that it is his own choice and that he can leave if he wants to. Haytham chooses to go through with the tour. When he has accomplished what is asked of him, Haytham has passed the test, and his manager tells him that they are now equals. The trials function as symbols of the transition from one world to another, manifested in both Haytham's own behaviour and how others treat him. However, as Connell emphasises, masculinity is not something one earns by one specific act, but it is rather a constant struggle, something that Haytham also learns in the novel. Having been told he is a man and an equal to the manager, an angry outburst at a colleague reduces him to a child again in the eyes of his superiors.

In his study on boy scouts, Nilsson elaborates on the way infantile behaviour is used as an accusation of femininity in stereotypical accounts and can be equated to castration.[46] He concentrates on its usage in stories with the purpose of teaching moral values to young boys. In the transmission period between boyhood and manhood, while working actively to be seen as a man, to be judged as childish or even infantile results in a great loss of self-confidence and masculine identity. In Haytham's case, this is evident in his arguments with his parents before his father's accident where he feels reduced to a child. He is torn between his life as a boy and the possibility of being a man. He is attracted by the privileges he sees in manhood, but at the same time he is not willing to take on the responsibility associated with it.

However, whereas a man's position within the hierarchal structure of masculinities can be affected by his behaviour, there are certain rituals, which initially allow him to enter manhood: as shown in *Imagined Masculinities*,[47] one such rite is circumcision. To be able to endure the circumcision without crying or screaming means that the boy will turn into a strong man – the opposite shames the boy and the family for the rest of their lives.[48] Abdelwahab Bouhdiba and Abdu Khal describe how a mother, though worried about her son, is still filled with pride when he asks the circumciser to cut off a bit more, showing that he can handle the pain inflicted on him. Her feelings of pride acknowledge that her own position is affected by her son's behaviour. In *The Impossible Novel*, Zayn witnesses the preparation for, and later the festivities after, her cousin's circumcision. Though too small to understand properly what happens, she realises that her cousin has, through a ritual she herself is excluded from, suddenly obtained a much more important role in the household and among the children. Though technically still a boy, he is now half included in the category of men and, as a result, his power increases, something he makes sure the younger children, particularly the girls, are aware of.

Bringing Up Boys and Girls

The way the different novels treat children's upbringing and gender formation suggests an acceptance of male privileges as the norm. With the exception of Zayn in *The Impossible Novel,* the female characters are content to support this performance. Even Zayn does not demand a change in masculine behaviour, merely the right to behave like her male cousins. With respect to both male and female characters, the masculinity formation in these novels can hence be seen to uphold, rather than problematise, the patriarchal gender regime. As caretakers and relatives, the female characters are given the possibility to form a masculinity they support and wish to see in their fictional societies. The masculinity created and promoted is one that is caring, supportive and strong and a sustenance for the female characters. When *Steps in the Fog* begins, Haytham is spending the evening with some of his friends. It is getting late, and he decides to go home. His friends mock him and ask whether it is free will or fear which motivates him to leave.[49] Haytham's reaction and his thoughts on the way home confirm that he does not find their comments funny, on the contrary, he sees them as a sign of his own lack of power and self-command. What his friends are implying is that he has no ability to assert his free will but is under the power of his parents and, as such, he is still a child. Masculinity, as seen by Haytham and his friends, includes being responsible for oneself without having to answer back to anyone. The following morning, Haytham's father tells him off for having arrived home late the previous evening.

> عليك بفهم الأمور: طالما أنت في هذا البيت يجب أن تخضع لقوانينه. تصرّفْ كرجل، كفاك هزلاً.[50]
>
> You have to understand: As long as you are in this house, you have to follow its laws. Behave like a man, stop fooling around.

The subsequent conversation between father and son is illuminating in two ways. The father demands that his son follows the rules and stops fooling around.

He then demands that he behave like a man. Haytham's reaction to this is to point out the contradiction in his father's words.[51] How can he be treated as a child, ie without any respect or responsibilities, and then be asked to act like a man? The conversation shows firstly how both the father and the son have an idea of what it means to be a man and to perform masculinity and, secondly, that it is something desirable, something to aim for. It is also a state, which gives privileges denied those not included. Still considered a boy, Haytham must follow the rules laid out, accept the pocket money he is given and deal with his friends' mockery. The juxtaposition of father and son clarifies the hierarchal positions between boyhood and manhood. It is further used to show Haytham's initial reluctance and disgust at his father's power, a feeling that turns into desire for the same position during the course of the narrative. The father–son relationship, though not elaborated on in detail in the novel, can thus be taken to exemplify how Haytham gradually builds up his performance of masculinity.

In *Steps in the Fog*, the family consists of two sons and does not allow for comparisons between the upbringing of sisters and brothers in the same family. However, the parents' expectations of their sons, as well as what they do not expect, give an idea of gender-specific behaviour. After the mother falls ill and is bedridden for two weeks, she gets out of bed to find the house in need of cleaning. Neither her sons nor her husband have done any cooking and cleaning while she has been in bed. She does not complain about this or find it strange. Her only concern is whether Haytham has eaten properly and been able to change his clothes while she has been ill.[52] In her division of gendered behaviour, it would have been stranger if any of the male members of the family had taken care of the household while she was ill. When she does ask her sons to help her with household tasks, it is always actions located outside the house, such as buying bread or collecting things.[53]

It is not just Haytham's family who sees the division of labour like this. Said, who has his own small room, lives in a mess of dirty clothes, plates, cigarette butts and left-over food. Haytham reflects on his friend's untidiness and though he would his freedom, he prefers his clean and tidy family home, kept in perfect condition by his mother. The idea that he could live alone, and clean and tidy by himself, does not cross his mind. When Muna visits Said, she cannot stop herself from immediately beginning to clean up. This could be explained as being part of her character, but the all-knowing narrator explains the cleaning with the fact that her femininity pushed her to start tidying up.[54] Cleanliness is thus connected to femininity in the novel's presentation of gendered behaviour. Said, as a man, can only be pitied that he has no woman to help him look after the house, not really blamed for his inability to organise his life. In *The Naked Back*, similar views on cleanliness are held by Adham. Adham's first impression of Claire is that of a desirable woman. When he gets to know her further, he realises that she does not fit what he assumes to be the female gender role. He is shocked when she, on their first night together, shows him the guest room. The room is full of boxes, clothes and books and Claire simply points at the bed without apologising for the mess; something he is sure a woman from his country would have done.[55] When he is later left to roam the house on his own, he is again appalled that, as a woman, Claire does not tidy her house. He compares this new situation and what he is used to at home.

فقد اعتدت على الترتيب في بيت أمّي، ووجود امرأة في الدار هو، بالنسبة إليّ، رديف نظافة وبريق ولمعان.[56]

> I was used to the order in my mother's home, and the presence of a woman in the house is, for me, synonymous with cleanliness, lustre and brightness.

He does not generalise about French people as being untidy; he criticises Claire. Nor does he take into account that her husband, Aliksi, had lived in the house until the previous day, and thus could have participated in the cleaning and tidying. His association between gender and activities illustrates that in his world it is not part of a man's job to clean and tidy. Consequently, it is not an action that can be seen as part of performing masculinity. When he later asks Claire about the untidiness, she does not seem to care. He sees the lack in Claire's behaviour but cannot, at this stage, see that he could perform a woman's chores. As the narrative continues and he begins to change, he cleans and tidies to the extent that Claire can no longer find her things. In addition to cleaning, a woman, in Adham's mind, is meant to be interested in cooking,[57] something that Claire could not be less concerned about; she prefers to eat out. Adham's logic behind the idea of cooking follows that of cleaning. As a woman, and in charge of the house, cooking food should be a natural part of a woman's life. However, whereas Adham does not take care of the cleaning, he does prepare dinner for Claire, but only because she has been working and is tired. The fact that Adham does not work adds to the confusion he expresses about the different activities he does. He codes cooking as a female activity, and then still performs it, only to meet with Claire's disapproval since he did not take her out to a restaurant. By acting against his own coding of actions, he subverts the gender roles he has set up for himself, something that is not condoned, either by himself or Claire. It is as if the circumstances force him to do things he feels uncomfortable with, but that he cannot resist in his quest to impress Claire. His appropriation of what he sees as feminine behaviour can be read as the external influences on gendered behaviour, which the individual cannot withstand. Since Claire, as the female voice in the novel, disapproves of the behaviour, the novel lends itself to be read as a critique of male femininity.

In *The Longing,* Thura falls for Ghaith, an artist who introduces her to the importance of artistic expression. When she comes over to visit him, he opens the door in an apron and soon leaves her with his brother to finish the cooking. Thura expresses great surprise at this, she is used to her brother who does not enter the kitchen. As an answer she is given a lecture on how much fun cooking is and hence it should not be just for women. As in the *The Naked Back,* the traditional gender roles are clear, but Ghaith's reply flips the roles by describing cooking as desirable.

The opportunities that Haytham, as a boy, takes for granted are similar to what boys in *The Impossible Novel* can assume. The deceased mother in the novel wanted the best future possible for her daughter and the father decides to give her the freedom he would have given a son. This conscious choice highlights the differences in girls' and boys' childhoods and hints that the femininity which pushed Muna to start cleaning Said's room, might be taught rather than essential to her being. The problem that Zayn faces is that other characters, such as Zayn's grandmother and aunt find it difficult to know how to react to her behaviour. They do what they can to rectify what they see as the father's careless upbringing – Zayn is forcefully included in the household chores and is prevented from playing with the boys. For most of the other characters in the novel, it is inconceivable to bend the gender rules in the way Zayn's father does with his daughter. They, especially the grandmother, are worried about what will happen when Zayn grows up and has to function in a wider social reality than their home, and between her closest relatives. The novel leaves Zayn before this happens and the text never gives an answer. What is clear, however, is that for a girl to adopt what are seen as masculine traits alienates her, to a certain degree, from her society. The same can be seen for Haytham; when he is indecisive and, as his friends see it, too obedient to his parents, he is teased for not being manly and accused of being a girl. To distinguish what is accepted and expected behaviour for each gender enables the characters to live in relative harmony. For Haytham, both his close family and society as a whole prime him towards a specific behaviour. Similarly, Qays in *Cyclones in the Levant,* acknowledges that he needs both his mother and father, but accepts society's division and realises that in order to form a place for himself he needs to follow the example of his father and older brother and become a man.

The overall view presented by *Steps in the Fog*, through events and conversations, is that of a normative heterosexual society where there is a clear division in gendered behaviour. It is a society where male characters are more likely to be in charge, especially if they conform to what is socially expected of them. The mother in *Steps in the Fog* refers to the father as the foundation of the house and she does not know what she would do if he were to die.[58] The same type of society crystallises in *The Impossible Novel* and in *Cyclones in the Levant*, especially since Khust's articulated goal with many of her novels is to remind her readers of the golden days that have passed. Qays becomes an historical character from a time when masculinity and femininity were still easy to understand and the roles were clear-cut, not complicated and difficult to formulate. The novel seems to suggest an understanding of life that was simpler than present-day society with its many obligations. At the same time, a return to the time of Qays' childhood includes a loss of the equality that Zayn fights for and which Muna takes for granted.

Breaking the Strict Gender Boundaries

The concepts of male femininity and female masculinity build on the breach of conventionally expected gendered behaviour. This section will discuss how the characters make use of these expectations in their dealings with each other. Some critics have pointed to the fact that the theory of hegemonic masculinity builds on a heteronormative concept of male/female dichotomy and does not clearly account for differences within the gender categories.[59] This is interesting, since this was one of Connell's critiques of the sex role theory and one of the reasons why she constructed the theory of hegemonic masculinity in the first place.[60] In the novels analysed in this chapter, many of the narratives present a blurred version of the male/female dichotomy. In words and thoughts, most of the characters describe the difference between male and female gender roles as very important. However, in their reported actions, they repeatedly transgress the gender roles.

The exploration of gender formulation through the upbringing of children has fore-fronted the role of the close family but also society as a whole in the construction and upholding of gendered identities. The characters who aim to transgress these boundaries, whether male or female, often face difficulties. Whereas Amjad, Zayn's father, fits the description of ideal father from the 1950s and 1960s, his choices and behaviour are not welcome in the fictional society of the novel, on the contrary they are seen to create problems. He, especially in comparison with his brother, is seen by the other characters to be too lenient and soft. Rather than portray Amjad as performing an accepted and successful masculinity, the novel, to some extent, problematises the choice of being different and doing masculinity in one's own way.

A deviation of masculinity performance, or rather a merge between femininity and masculinity, is further seen in *Wild Mint* where 'Alia states that she is:

أنا الأم والأخت والزوجة والقديسة والعاهرة، والرجل مني وأنا منه.[61]

> I am the mother, the sister, the wife, the saint, and the whore and man comes from me and I from him.

Through this statement 'Alya not only pinpoints the traditional female stereotypes but also the close relation between man and woman and their shared origin. In the context of the novel this becomes even clearer since the two main characters, 'Ali and 'Alya, not only share a name, but they also have a similar background, upbringing and experience of life. They come from the small villages outside Ludosia and moved to the city to find work. They are torn between the traditional village life and the demands of the city. During the novel, their intermingling voices, dreams and worries make them appear as two faces of the same character. Or rather, 'Alya appears as the missing part that 'Ali needs in order to become complete. As such, they represent aspects of the same character and 'Alya's words echo through the text: 'Man is from me and I am from him'. At the same time, the characters of the fictional society presented are extremely preoccupied with what it means to be a man and woman respectively.

However, the configurations of practices, performed knowingly or unknowingly, which make the surrounding society see and accept the character as a man or a woman vary between time and place in the novel. Hence, the understanding of masculinity in the village is very different from the demands placed on 'Ali once he moves to the city. By being different and not able to follow the rules laid out, 'Ali is, to some extent, marginalised both in the city and in the village. When Ali's voice takes over the narration, the reader follows how he judges his own behaviour in relation to what he thinks is accepted masculinity. He measures the outcome of his actions and others' impressions of him. Through the variation between male and female voices in the text, the view on how masculinity should be performed is highlighted from several angles and is then distilled into an idea of ideal masculinity, which 'Ali is far from able to perform.

Village life, as described in the novel, is designed around each character knowing his or her role in the hierarchal community. In this environment, the correct gendered behaviour is key in order to be accepted. The gendered conduct is often presented in a binary opposition between two poles, articulated through the worry of assimilation between male and female, winner and loser, grown up and child, and fear and bravery. The two poles are most openly described by 'Ali's grandfather's advice on how to be a man, namely by simply 'not being a woman'. The same expectations appear in the male–female relations described where man stands for stability and reasoning and woman the opposite.

'Alya, repeatedly returns to the fact that she needs a man to talk to, turn to for help or just rest her head against when she is in difficulties. It is obvious from her and her friends' comments that they feel that they need male support to function fully in society. Some of the women even mean that this is the man's sole role and refuse 'Alya's ideas of romantic love and partnership. Their interest is instead only in how well the man fulfils the outer, visible aspects of the expected masculinity. This ideal can also be invoked as a way of pledging with a man to do something. Salwa, 'Ali's colleague, uses it with 'Ali to pressure him to do what she wants. When he seems uninterested in providing her with what she is after, she asks him to show his manliness by looking after her and giving her what she requests. Although not convinced that he should give her what she wants, 'Ali is still affected by her talk and realises that his choice is to be deemed unmanly or fulfil her request. He complies with the specifications included in the role of being masculine in order to be accepted and benefit from being seen as 'a man'. Since 'Ali is not convinced that what he does is the right way of behaving, he does not perform the actions convincingly and thus does not persuade either Salwa or himself that he performs masculinity successfully. He is not able to be the protector and provider she is looking for and, as a result, he is no longer interesting for her. The treatment of gender relations in novels is connected to the fact that the writer has an opportunity to create not only a character, but also the surrounding society's reactions to this version of masculinity and, more importantly, the character's own reflections on the demands and expectations put on him. The hegemonic masculinity governing society at the time and place of publication can therefore be subverted or, if similar, reacted to differently.

In *The Naked Back*, Adham believes a man should be strong; however, this is in contradiction to his own abilities; while trying to carry his suitcase up the stairs he exhausts himself in front of Claire.[62] He is troubled both by his own weakness and by the fact that Claire so openly disapproves. They both expect him to be strong, and when he is not, Claire makes her disappointment visible and Adham feels ashamed. Actions such as cooking and cleaning are things that can be learnt. Strength, on the other hand, though possible to enhance through physical exercise, is seen as something one either has or does not. The fact that gender roles are made up both of physical ability and socially coded actions makes it even more complicated for Adham to fit in. That Adham is not strong enough to carry his own bag, exaggerates his emasculation in front of Claire.

Having carried the bag upstairs, Claire gives Adham the choice of the guestroom or her own bedroom. He chooses the guestroom, which he soon regrets. Rethinking his choice, he realises that, once again, he has not performed according to his own ideals of masculinity.

> كان عليّ أن ألحق بها، أن أواجه تحدّيها الصريح بذهابي إليها في الحال. مع ذلك بقيتُ واقفاً كالمخبول وسط الكتب والمجلات[...].[63]

> I should have followed her, faced her open challenge by going to her immediately. Despite that I remained, standing like a fool in the middle of the books and magazines [...].

Claire is, yet again, disappointed and suggests that he can always go downstairs and make himself some hot milk if he finds it difficult to fall asleep, insinuating that he is only a child. Further on in the novel, Claire expresses a view on Eastern men as being extremely virile and her disappointment with Adham's choice of bed can be understood through that comment. Not only is he weak, but he also appears disinterested in sexual activity and, as such, he means no more to her than a child. By failing to assert himself as a man and performing masculinity according to her standards, he has lost the privilege of manhood. When Claire has left, Adham wonders whether she will give him a second chance or if his choice of bed has forever spoiled his possibilities of having a relationship with her. He sees Claire as someone who only accepts the best and, in his own judgment, he has not performed masculinity at its best during his first day with her. Adham is torn between what he expects from himself in order to perform an approved version of masculinity, while at the same time he is aware that Claire has both high and different standards from himself.

The gender-based expectations that Adham and Claire place on themselves and each other position men and women into two different groups. Men are, as traditionally described, strong, virile and in charge of providing for the family, whilst women are caring and soft. Although these values seem to govern the characters, as outlined above, they constantly break them. Claire expects a man to order her around, but when Adham tries to do this, she does not listen. He expects women to look after the home, but when Claire does not, he cooks and cleans instead. By simultaneously enforcing and deflating the gendered performance expected, the novel reflects how masculinity is relational and depending on others evaluation of it. At the same time, through the characters' appropriation of behaviour coded for the other sex, it demonstrates the emptiness of the gender roles. The hegemonic masculinity sketched by Adham and Claire therefore stands out as something that is impossible to integrate in the life described in the novel but at the same time governing it in detail. Governing it in the sense that actions performed in contradiction to it leads to the enactment of female masculinity and male femininity. The hegemonic norm further governs the value of different actions and the inability to adhere to the hegemonic norm leads to marginalisation, as will be discussed in the following section. The different ways of doing masculinity that 'Ali in *Wild Mint* and Adham in *The Naked Back* perform do not derive support from the other characters, whether male or female. On the contrary, they are told to 'become men', 'toughen up' and change. Whereas the female writers create masculine characters deviating from the norm of their fictional society, they are not able to make them successful, which further reinforces the hegemonic norm of the fictional society. The accusations, and acknowledgments, of the male characters being feminine, offer an alternative reading: that of othering the male in order to forefront women's marginalisation through a hybrid character performing male femininity. This can, to some extent, be seen as the role of Farah in *Beirut 75*, who is raped and discarded by his manager and, as a result, loses his masculinity and becomes mad. While lamenting his loss of masculinity, Farah *in Beirut 75* simultaneously seems to enjoy bringing out what he sees as his feminine side. The madness can thus be read as a way of breaking free from the rules ruling those supposedly in possession of full mental health, including the narrator. Farah's deviation from the gender norms of the fictional society can be seen as a way of dealing with the fragmented and subordinated masculinities that the novel has presented. Rather than accepting the subordinated position, and constantly striving towards fulfilling an inaccessible role, breaking with the norm is an alternative option. Farah is indeed seen as mentally ill, but his position is different from when he was attempting, and failing, to perform hegemonic masculinity. In his new role, he feels free and full of hope that he can reconstruct himself. His proposed acceptance of his female sides seems to have freed him from the pressure of masculinity and made him see the city of his dreams in a clearer fashion. As such, the narrative's move from structure to chaos and from an obsession with the correct performance of masculinity to an acceptance of femininity forms a critique of the hegemonic masculinity and its hierarchical social order. By consciously or unconsciously adopting what the novel characterises as feminine behaviour, before and after his period at the mental hospital, Farah can finally step out of the circle of demands that he has been caught within since his arrival to Beirut. Although expressing a longing for his previous life and abilities, the way he describes his life, for the first time as the first-person narrator, shows that he has taken control. A similar development can be seen in *Wild Mint* where 'Ali is taken prisoner by unidentified men and forced to agree to the masculine ideals of the city. When he is set free, he has become mad and does not know what to do. He tries to find 'Alya so that she can help him, and when he is told that she has disappeared he is completely lost. When she comes back, reincarnated as an old woman, he accepts her female lead and through her, he acknowledges his roots and feminine side, and is promised a better, more complete life. By rejecting masculine restrictions and accepting their feminine side both characters are able to move on and are allowed a second chance in a life they thought was over. Farah's and 'Ali's development serves to destabilise the hegemonic norm, not by actively breaking with it or reformulating it, but by showing that, contrary to the characters' belief, the 'insane' Farah is saner than characters locked, by the norms, in a repetitive behaviour of reproducing an image of masculinity neither of them completely embraces. Rather than reinforcing the hegemonic masculinity they present, both *Beirut 75* and *Wild Mint* finally offer femininity, or an acceptance of female characteristics, as a way of breaking the hegemony. The fear of being found wanting, and the struggle to avoid being seen as weak and feminine and hence be subordinated to other performances of masculinity are counteracted by internalising femininity and denouncing the prevailing masculine norm. Notably, this is done through madness in two novels, signifying that it is not a generally accepted way of handling gender. At the same time, it suggests that what is perceived as normal might not be the ideal solution. Except for the respective main characters' madness and acceptance of femininity as a way of looking at society, the other male characters do not contest or subvert the hegemonic masculinity of the two novels. Instead, they seem trapped by the demands placed on them and are unable to change the pattern of their lives.

On the one hand, the novels seem to advocate that women can and should be able to transgress the borders created by the gender regime. On the other hand, the male characters that do the same are described as having a difficult time knowing themselves and they are not depicted as successful participants in society. The solution presented are hybrid characters who do not fit the hegemonic norms of masculinity or femininity in fictional societies. As social experiments and as way of expressing new possibilities of performing gender the characters are very successful. However, none of the characters are described as happy and content with their performance. The reflections on society offered through the novels thus deconstruct what they portray as hegemonic masculinity but do not offer a replacement. If the texts are put in the context of the gender regime they are created within, this can be assumed to show the complicity of the matter and a wish to not stray too far from the reality in which the texts are grounded. In this fashion, the texts produce gender through the narrative and create femininity and masculinity for its readers, but they do not deliver solutions.

Social Critique through the Performance of Masculinity

In *Steps in the Fog* the father is introduced as a dictatorial character through the experiences of his son Haytham. However, after some time, the reader is introduced to the father's political youth. Since there is very little information about the past in the novel as a whole, the section on the father's political ideas and previous imprisonment stands out as particularly important in the narrative. It gives the reader a better-adjusted picture of the father in opposition to the tyrant Haytham describes. It further shows how the society described, and its expectations for its participants, changed people over time. The father, once a freethinking political activist has become a man worried about reputation and tradition. Haytham goes through a similar transformation later in the novel and this makes him, towards the end of the novel, perform a comparable masculinity to that exhibited by his father. *In Storms in the Levant,* Qays's father makes a similar comment when he notes that when he was young it was enough to willingly offer oneself for one's country to be considered a man, whereas in these modern days one must have money, connections and a position.[64] Although these are comments from individual characters they reflect on the previous period of the ideological or political masculinity, where a willingness to die for one's country was part of the masculinity formation, and how those values are now seen as old fashioned.

Though very different in topics and settings, all the novels in this chapter engage with the formulation and self-perception of the performance of masculinity. In *The Naked Back,* Adham is constantly re-examining his own actions and is torn between what he thinks he should do and what he actually does. He feels the pressure from his own expectations and those of his male friends but at the same time he is not sure how to behave to please Claire, which becomes more important to him than living up to other expectations. In the views Adham expresses, he sees the male as having certain privileges over women which, in turn, means that performing masculinity means an ability to assert these privileges but also to look after a wife. His complete lack of belief in women's agency appears when he marvels, in front of Claire, at how Aliksi just gave him his wife, to which Claire pointedly adds that, she too, had a role in the events. She assures him that she could have refused him and thrown him out. This possibility does not seem to have crossed Adham's mind, despite the fact that he sometimes has quite a low opinion of himself . It is clear that he thinks that men are higher in the gender hierarchy than women, even though he tries to persuade himself of men's and women's equality.

> لكن حميّتي للعمل همدت دونما سبب، في حين سيطر عليّ شعور بخجل. حاولت أن أؤنب نفسي على هذا الشعور الخبيث مستنجداً بإيماني الراسخ بالمساواة بين الرجل والمرأة. وسعيتُ إلى طرده بأن رددتُ: هل الأعمال المنزلية التي تنهض بها المرأة هي مذلّة أساساً حتى تنتقص قيمة الرجل إذا ما قام بها؟ [...] إن كانت أعمالاً مذلّة، فلماذا يتعيّن على المرأة أن تؤديها؟[65]

> But my enthusiasm for the work faded for no reason, and feelings of embarrassment begun to take power over me. I tried to scold myself for these wicked feelings invoking for support my firm belief in the equality between men and women. I tried to drive them away by repeating: Is the housework women do humiliating in order for it to decrease the worth of a man if he performs it? [. . .] And if it was humiliating why is woman appointed to perform it?

By expecting certain things from Claire based on her sex, Adham, as a male, positions himself as the opposite. In his ideal performance of masculinity, he has the agency to act and decide and the female has the role of serving and pampering him. However, whereas Adham seems convinced that this is how things should be, he is aware that he himself is not performing accordingly. Through his internal monologues he further casts light on the formulation of masculinity and femininity and why something that is coded feminine should be seen as embarrassing for a man, thus critiquing society through his actions.

This contradiction is mirrored in his behaviour. On the one hand, he is described as a male stereotype, unable to resist a beautiful woman, spilling his whiskey because he cannot take his eyes off her. On the other hand, he is aware of what he sees as stereotypical male behaviour and avoids it. The play with gendered behaviour in the novel can be read as a critique of changing gender roles. The fact that Claire performs all the actions Adham considers masculine leaves him with no option other than to perform what he sees as feminine tasks.

Claire is definitely not excited by Adham's cooking, nor by his cleaning or willingness to serve her. Adham's inability to assert himself as the man of the house – in the eyes of Claire, himself and their friends – ultimately leads to him losing Claire and having to return home. The male femininity he performs does not lead to love and respect. His constant comparison between what he should do, and what he actually does, underlines how far he is from what he sees as hegemonic masculinity. At the same time, Claire does not perform traditional femininity either and she is not seen as a victim in the novel, on the contrary she is portrayed as happy and successful in her life.

Another possible reading is to reverse the gender roles again. Claire's actions stand out as both inconsiderate and mean, seen from Adham's perspective; at the same time Adham calls her 'the husband' and sees her behaviour as normal 'male' behaviour. Read like this, the novel plays with biological sex and expected gender roles. Conduct that is interpreted as abnormal when performed by a woman is interpreted as normal for a man. By reversing the roles, the novel chisels out the expectations brought into a relation and how, when not met, these expectations can become more important than the actual actions. The novel further emphasises the possibility of gender, especially masculinity, being performed differently than what is usually expected. Even if Adham is not successful in his quest for love, through his changes and adaptations he exemplifies that masculinity is not a fixed way of being but rather the adaption to a specific setting and specific demands.

Whether it is the norm of being an able provider, or other parts of masculinity, the expectations on the characters are internalised in a way that does not allow them to change, despite being aware of the problematic behaviour, or knowing that it is not their own fault that they cannot live up to the expectations. If they try to change, the characters are soon reminded by others of their obligations and are hence forced back to their previous attempts of living according to the norm. 'Ali, in *Wild Mint,* feels the same pressure. As a poet, he seems to have more freedom than other men do, to disregard the norms, but he is still reminded by other characters that he cannot do what he wants. His neighbours keep track of his guests, when he comes and goes and how he acts towards them, and so do his relatives and friends. Even though he would like to free himself from the expectations placed on him, as long as he lives in the city, he feels trapped by the external pressure on his conduct.

Steps in the Fog forms a circle through its events and by them critique the expectations put on masculinity performance as well as the fleetingness of the concept. Haytham is first introduced as a spoiled youngster on his way home from friends. Throughout the novel, he develops and towards the end he is seen as a man, performing the expected masculinity and treated as such by his family, employer and friends. However, in the final chapter Haytham is insulted by one of the men he works with; he overreacts and starts a fight and is subsequently told by his employer that he is still a child. The following day, when Haytham turns up for work, the police have surrounded the office and he is told his employer has been killed. The rosy future he has painted for himself is crushed and he returns home, in much a similar fashion as the novel started. Despite his development and change, Haytham proves not to be fully able to perform the expected masculinity. He fails, and dramatically loses the job that forms the basis upon which he has formed his masculinity. With no income, he cannot provide for his family and he has lost the power he had secured for a while. With this circular motion, the novel seems to suggest that the surrounding circumstances, as well as other characters, are influential in the perception and performance of masculinity. It also underlines that performing masculinity is a constant struggle of asserting oneself.

Conclusion

The quote starting the introduction suggested two ways of looking at women's construction of masculinities in novels; firstly, as the collective formulation of masculinity by male and female characters and secondly, as a relationship between society and literature. By taking these two starting points and through a comparative textual analysis of the work of Syrian female writers the different ways male characters have been formed and used in the last half of the twentieth century have been traced using Raewyn Connell's theory of hegemonic masculinity and her hierarchal levels of masculinity performance.

The masculinity formations found in the novels have been contextualised through a discussion of secondary material consisting of scholarship both on the Middle East and on masculinity in general and literary masculinity formations in particular. By putting the findings in the novels in conversation with works of sociology, anthropology and analyses of literature and film, the book has located itself within the framework of gender studies. Through the discussion of the primary material in the light of the secondary material, value systems around male and female conduct have been highlighted as well as the mechanisms of gender formation.

The book has traced the female authors' application of masculinity in the novels and shown that the characteristics and traits embodied in masculinity performance are similar during the period studied but that how and why they are evaluated has changed. The change in the perception of masculinity is shown to be connected to the female characters' participation in social life and understanding of their own roles. In the novels, masculinity is not just a way of behaving but also a way of forming a position for oneself within one's family, social group or society. In the analyses, the performance of hegemonic masculinity can be seen as ways of gaining and keeping respect and power rather than as a label for a specific masculinity. By using hegemonic masculinity in this way, the characters' perception of what hegemonic masculinity entails has been fore fronted which, in turn, has accentuated the fluidity in the concept of hegemonic masculinity.

Despite the fluidity in what masculinity involves with respect to specific traits, the concept of masculinity has been used to mean what the characters in a fictional society see as the expected, valued and normative behaviour of a grown man. This definition, in line with the theories of gender as a social construction, is applicable in various settings. The masculinity formation in the novels has been examined in connection to the novels' female characters, acknowledging Connell's idea that masculinity is formulated in contrast to femininity, as well as Judith Butler's concept of gender as a product of social interaction. The theories of masculinity studies have been used to approach the content of the novels and the actions of the fictional characters.

It is not argued that each of the novels used in this study on its own represents more than itself and no individual novel can be taken as a single example of Syrian women's writing. However, read together and compared over time they communally construct an idea of how masculinity formulations have changed since the 1950s and how they have been used since then. The change is connected to the development of women's writing from a feminist point of view. Therefore, the categorisation of the literary output into three eras is modelled on earlier divisions made by scholars of literature in Syria with focus on female character composition. The earliest period is called 'Dream Masculinity' (1959–1970), the second period 'the Political Man' (1970–1980) and the third period 'Problematic Masculinity' (1980–2000). Each period has been shown to formulate masculinity in a particular way.

In the 1950s and 1960s the analysis of a 'Dream Masculinity' explored how female characters made use of the patriarchal norms to form a better future for themselves. Rather than contesting the gender regime of their societies the female characters worked to change the ideals from within. The masculinities presented as 'Dream Masculinities' were expected to conform to the norm of society but with a greater interest in what the female characters want and need. The novels of this era do not show an outright rejection of what is presented as the hegemonic masculinity of the fictional societies but rather a suggestion for modification. The masculinities of the 1950s and 1960s are still powerful in the meaning that they are presented as having embraced the idea that women should be educated, equal partners in society and, moreover, able to marry whoever they want. The male characters advocate these ideas and treat their wives and daughters accordingly. To behave in this new way has not changed their position of power vis-à-vis other men in their fictional societies; on the contrary, their position as fathers have been used to authorise their views. They can, therefore, be interpreted as fictional experiments for how society could be if a more equal view on men and women was hegemonic.

In the 1970s, political and ideological writing became even more important, mainly due to the many political changes before and during this period. This also appears in women's novels, both as part of the plot but more importantly through the formulation of the male characters. During this era, a similar positive view of masculinity as in the period of the Dream Man can be found but, instead of focusing on personal relationships, this masculinity is used as a symbol for political and social change. Through relationships with politically engaged men, the female characters formulated a new world view connected to the masculinity performance of their man. The rhetoric of both male and female characters in this era refer to great changes, but their foundational understanding of masculinity is similar to what they reject in the older generation, for example when it comes to ideas on provision and protection. As such, the masculinity constructions in this era exemplifies a gradual change of hegemonies rather than a clear break with previous performances.

The male characters performing this political masculinity all die or disappear at an early stage from the narrative and therefore only exist as memories for the female characters. This leads to their being idolised, which further strengthens the claim that the masculinities of this period are symbols of change and ideology rather than life-like fictional characters. In this era, some of the female characters are described as studying at university and taking part in political discussions, however they never have an influence on the masculinity performance of the male characters. Like in the previous wave, the male characters have the prerogative to take decisions, educate the female characters and show others what is right or wrong.

It is not until the final wave, the Problematic Masculinity, that female characters are described to have an actual impact on the masculinities performed which, in turn, means that the powerful position of the performer of masculinity is finally shaken. The Masculinities of this last era are not just fictional experiments of good masculinity or static symbols for political ideas; instead, the focus is often on subordinate and marginalised or aggressive and brutal masculinities. In the explorations of what it means to be a man and perform masculinity some of the female writers of this era contest what it means to be a man or a woman through constructions of 'Female Masculinity and Male Femininity'. Although *Love and Mud* from the first wave touches on the idea of a woman behaving in a masculine way, it is not explored fully until the last wave, when hybrid characters or characters struggling with their gendered behaviour appears.

Final wave writers show how the application of gender-specific behaviour in an unconventional way leads to the destabilisation of the understanding of masculinity and femininity respectively. In their exploration of gender stereotypes, the authors seemingly reproduce the binary gender regime, but a closer examination shows how the characters instead break the gender boundaries and perform different versions of masculinity and femininity. The characters are aware of the distinctive roles for men and women but they prefer to behave differently and therefore create blurred concepts of what male and female means.

The acceptance or rejection of a specific masculinity is partly based on whether certain aspects are present in a man's masculinity performance but, more importantly, the characters in the novels focus on *how* these aspects are performed. Therefore, though building on the same concept in all the novels, hegemonic masculinity is proved to vary from setting to setting, sometimes even within the same novel. Women's views on these masculinities further serve to show the fluidity of the concept. By evaluating not only the action performed but also the motive behind it, the use of violence is seen to signify hegemonic masculinity at times and subordinate masculinity in other circumstances. Together, the novels therefore communicate a view of masculinity as a burden where some expectations are known, but since they can change between city and countryside, or between upper class and lower class, it is never completely certain how an acceptable form of masculinity should be performed.

The first two waves have relatively limited numbers of characters, often with a focus on the relationship between one man and one woman, where the man is more of symbol of change or hope than a character in his own right. This makes the male characters somewhat didactic, however, read as ideas for social or political change they become interesting. The final era uses more characters, furthermore characters from different backgrounds which create a web of characters that can affect, and be affected by, the masculinity formation in the novels. All the novels discussed in the book seem to agree that education, literature and art are important parts of society, but whereas the first periods focused on education only, the later periods touch on the importance of literature for social change and also the role of society in the formulation of gender.

In addition to looking at factors such as class and location, the novels of the third wave analyse how gender is shaped and formed from childhood. Many of the novels discuss how children are brought up and show, through their characters, how family members influence the understanding of what masculinity is and how it should be performed. In the case of mothers and close relatives, it is established that their own position is linked to that of their sons or husbands and it is hence important that the performance of masculinity matches the norm of the fictional society. The desire and ability to look after the family are seen as important factors in this type of masculinity formation. Through their choices, the female characters show an awareness of the patriarchal gender regime governing their societies and, by adhering to it, they further support it. The female characters are as active as the male characters in their attempts to shape and change the performance of masculinity. The analysis further demonstrates that even though the power connected to masculinity is often what attracts the young men of the novels, the female characters focus on the obligations that masculinity performance includes. They expect to be looked after and provided for by their male relatives. As such, the novels have been shown to formulate masculinity performances that are aware of the demands and expectations placed on the roles, rather than just reaping the benefits.

Through the analyses of the different themes, the book has demonstrated that women use literature as a way of both contesting and supporting masculinities. Through their descriptions and plot constructions it becomes clear what masculinity formations the novels present as positive. Through their formation of masculinity, female authors have, moreover, engaged with female gender roles as the binary opposition to, or in some cases performers of, masculinity. As such, the analyses of masculinity have contributed to the discussion of gender formation for both male and female characters. This has further shown that their view of men and the masculinity they uphold has shifted from something inherent to the characters to something that can be shaped and formed. This has, in turn, led to a change of view of the male characters, from something essential to the female characters' happiness, to something or someone that is not necessarily needed. By using this shift in focus, the balance in the gendered power relationships in the novels also changes and the female characters are no longer waiting for a man to save them but are more ready to take to action themselves.

Literature and Society

Through the examination of masculinities, the female characters' roles in the formulation of gender and their view of themselves and of femininity has also been analysed. Approaching the female-authored novels from the viewpoint of masculinity studies enhances the understanding of female-authored fiction as well as the view of society they put forward. In the introduction it was argued that masculinity construction in Syrian female-authored fiction is of interest because of the close connection between literature and social and political life in Syria,. Even though political changes can be seen in the female characters, I argue that the authors' use of male main characters has allowed them to deal with diverse topics and thus enabled them to write, for example, politically committed novels. The use of male characters has further provided a chance to explore different viewpoints and suggest how the opportunities and possibilities granted to men in patriarchal structures could be used for the greater good of society.

In novels of the first wave, written shortly before and around the time the Bath party came to power, the novels are portraying a different future with hopes of education and work, but with the change formulated within a patriarchal framework. The novels of the second wave, although engaging with political and ideological change, are also structured around a strong masculinity, symbolising social and political change. In the final wave, masculinity is no longer used as a symbol by which one can affect society through good examples or discuss political ideas; instead, in some novels, he is the result of the state's failure. Struggling masculinities are not so much a critique of the gender norms as critiques of a society where poverty is a problem and the social support is non-existent. The female authors have used struggling masculinities to pinpoint social inequalities. By showing the weakness of what is expected to be the stronger person in a gendered society and then connecting this to, for example, poverty, the authors are able to discuss both gender roles and social problems. The creation of Male Femininity can further be politically motivated by creating a male character who stands for change by accepting actions and behaviour that is coded as feminine.

It is tempting to read the changing perception of masculinity in general, and the father figure in particular, as a changing relationship between the writers and the state, or the authors and patriarchal authority, especially since Lisa Weeden has shown how the state has profited from the power of the father figure. In the earlier novels, the father was portrayed as someone who could transform his daughter's life; during the 1970s he is seen to stand for tradition and, to some extent, backwardness, but his conduct is often excused. In the final period and something that is continued in contemporary novels the father can be criticised, and his misuse of power pointed out, finally breaking the spell of patriarchal power.

The analysis ends at year 2000, but many of the female-authored novels from this period show the initial signs of what have later emerged as the twenty-first century trends of marginalised voices and very violent masculinities.

Atifa Faysal indicates that this period, spanning the end of the twentieth century and the beginning of the twenty-first, is when an awareness of women's position in society was brought into female-authored fiction in a more distinct fashion.[1] During these years, Syrian authors became more daring in their writing, a trend not exclusive to female writers. In the year 2000, when Hāfiẓ al-Asad died and his son Bashār came to power, a period named the *Damascus Spring* begun. This included promises of change: political prisoners were to be set free and censorship loosened.[2] Even though most of the changes were short-lived or never materialised, it seems like the hope for change found its way into the novel. Max Weiss asserts in an article on Syrian fiction that '[i]ndeed something very interesting has been happening in Syrian fiction writing over the past decade, which coincides with the first ten years since Bashar al-Asad acceded to power in the wake of his father's death in June 2000'.[3]

When it comes to female writers, the development towards the end of the twentieth century and the beginning of the twenty-first, though enhanced by the political changes, can also be connected to the education system. The opportunities created for women's participation in higher education during the 1960s[4] resulted in an increase in literacy with the result that more women, especially those from diverse backgrounds, were able to contribute to the literary life of their country. The increasing number of young female poets, novelists and short story writers bear witness to this change. New opportunities for publication that appeared around this time, both abroad and online, made it easier for writers without connections to distribute their work.

The beginning of the twenty-first century also saw the emergence of what was termed by Syrian critics 'the New Syrian novel'. Among its characteristics was its open preoccupation with the contemporary political situation.[5] In an article on women's writing in Syria, Buthaina al-Balkhī argues that the contemporary female novel has been able to break what she calls 'the typical style of female writing' and has instead become concerned with political, religious and philosophical thoughts.[6] Defining events in Syrian history, such as the incidents in Homs and Hama in the 1980s, were suddenly incorporated in novels, as were new readings of historical happenings, which did not faithfully follow the official state history.

Whereas social realism as a genre remained in fashion, socialism was no longer the governing ideology and only solution. The twenty-first century also features a greater variety of voices in the female-authored novel as both the number of writers and the possibility of being published increased.[7] The main characters changed from well-to-do city dwellers to inhabitants of the slum areas of the same cities, the countryside, or small towns. The focus also changed from educated journalists, doctors and upper-class women to servants, peasant women and the lower classes, groups who had previously only played minor roles in novels. Specific groups in society were put under the spotlight, such as the Bedouins in Līnā Hawyān al-Ḥasan's novels and the Alawites in Samar Yazbik's novels, something that had not previously been common in female-authored fiction. The final proof of the new awareness in political literature can be seen in the number of novels dealing openly with the ongoing conflict in Syria.[8] The multitude of voices, viewpoints and perspectives presented, at the beginning of the twenty-first century make the period distinctly different from the previous decades. The origins for these changes can be traced in the novels published at the end of the twentieth century and the foundations for some of the changes are visible in the literature of the 1990s.

Notes

Introduction

1 Ulfat al-Idlibī, *Dimashq yā basmat al-ḥuzn* (Damascus: Manshūrāt wizārat al-thaqāfa wa al-irshād al-qawmī, 1980), 162.
2 Alex Hobbs, 'Masculinity Studies and Literature' *Literature Compass* 10:4 (2013), 383.
3 Jeff Hearn, 'From Hegemonic Masculinity to the Hegemony of Men' *Feminist Theory* 5:1 (2004), 59–72.
4 See, for example, Torbjörn Forslid, *Varför män?: om manlighet i litteraturen* [*Why Men?: About Manliness in Literature*] (Stockholm: Carlsson Bokförlag, 2006). Claes Ekenstam et al (eds), *Rädd att Falla: Studier i Manlighet* [*Afraid to Fall: Studies in Manliness*] (Södertälje: Gidlunds Förlag, 1998).
5 Sarah Frantz and Katharina Rennhak (eds), *Women Constructing Men: Female Novelists and their Male Characters 1750–2000* (Lanham MD: Lexington Books, 2010), 3.
6 See, for example, Jack S Khan, *An Introduction to Masculinities* (Chichester: Wiley-Blackwell, 2009), 6. Judith Kegan Gardiner, 'Men, Masculinities and Feminist Theory' in *Handbook of Studies on Men and Masculinities*, Michael Kimmel, Jeff Hearn and RW Connell (eds) (Thousand Oaks: Sage, 2005), 36.
7 Henry Brod and Micheal Kaufman (eds), *Theorizing Masculinities* (Thousand Oaks: Sage 1994), 5.
8 Judith Butler, *Gender Trouble – Feminism and the Subversion of Identity*, 4th edn (New York and London: Routledge, 2007), xv.
9 RW Connell, *Gender in World Perspective* (Cambridge: Polity Press, 2009), 11.
10 Robyn Warhol, 'Guilty Cravings: What Feminist Narratology Can Do for Cultural Studies' in David Herman (ed.), *Narratologies: New Perspectives on Narrative Analyses* (Columbus: Ohio State University Press, 1999), 340; Ruth Page, 'Feminist Narratology? Literary and Linguistic Perspectives on Gender and Narrativity', *Literature and Language* 12(1) (2003), 43–56; Susan Lanser, *Fictions of Authority – Women Writers and Narrative Voice* (New York: Cornell University Press, 1992).
11 Warhol, 'Guilty Cravings', 342.
12 Sally Robinson, *Engendering the Subject: Gender and Self-Representation in Contemporary Women's Fiction* (Albany: SUNY Press, 1991).
13 Luc Herman and Bart Vervaeck, *Handbook of Narrative Analysis* (Lincoln and London: University of Nebraska Press, 2005), 130.

14 RW Connell, *Masculinities,* 2nd edn (Cambridge: Polity Press, 2005).

15 For a detailed discussion of the relationship between Gramsci and Connell see Richard Howson, *Challenging Hegemonic Masculinity* (London: Routledge, 2006).

16 Connell, *Masculinities*, 77.

17 Lila Abu-Lughod, *Do Muslim Women Need Saving?* (Cambridge, MA: Harvard University Press, 2013); Lila Abu-Lughod, *Remaking Women: Feminism and Modernity in the Middle East* (Princeton: Princeton University Press, 1998).

18 Connell, *Masculinities,* 76.

19 Naomi Schor, 'The Portrait of a Gentleman: Representing Men in (French) Women's Writings' *Representations 60,* University of California Press (1987), 114.

20 Stefan Horlacher (ed.), *Constructions of Masculinity in British Literature from the Middle Ages to the Present* (Basingstoke: Palgrave Macmillan, 2011), 4.

21 Samar al-Duyūb, 'Khaṣā'iṣ al-naqd al-nisā'ī: naqd al-riwāya al-sūriyya unmūdhajan' ['Specificities of Female Criticism: The Syrian Novel as an Example'], *al-Muthaqqaf 26/9-2012.*

22 Peter F. Murphy (ed.), *Fictions of Masculinity: Crossing Cultures, Crossing Sexualities* (New York and London: New York University Press, 1994), 1.

23 Samar R al-Fayṣal, *Malāmiḥ fī al-riwāya al-sūriyya* [*Features of the Syrian Novel*] (Damascus: Ittiḥād al-kuttāb al-'arab, 1979).

24 Evelyn Accad, *Sexuality and War, Literary Masks of the Middle East* (New York University Press, 1990), 5.

25 Horlacher, *Constructions of Masculinity,* 4.

26 Brian Baker, *Masculinity in Fiction and Film: Representing Men in Popular Genres 1945–2000* (London: Continuum International Publishing Group, 2006), vii.

27 Michael Kimmel, *Manhood in America: A Cultural History* (New York: The Free Press, 1997).

28 Marie Nordberg, *Jämställdhetens spjutspets?: Manliga arbetstagare i kvinnoyrken, jämställdhet, maskulinitet, femininitet och heteronormativitet* (Göteborg: Arkipelag, 2005).

29 Farah Ghannam, *Live and Die Like a Man: Gender Dynamics in Urban Egypt* (Stanford: Stanford University Press, 2013).

30 Chris Haywood and Mairtin Mac an Ghaill, *Men and Masculinities* (Buckingham: Open University Press, 2003), 152.

31 Kristina Fjelkestam, Helena Hill and David Tjeder (eds), *Kvinnorna gör mannen: maskulinitetskonstruktioner i kvinnors text och bild 1500–2000* [*Women Make the Man: Masculinity Construction in Women's Texts and Pictures, 1500–2000*] (Göteborg: Makadam, 2013), 10.

32 Elaine Showalter, *A Literature of their Own: British Women Writers from Charlotte Bronte to Doris Lessing* (London: Virago, 2009), 110.

33 Ibid., 111.
34 Ḥusām al-Khaṭīb, 'Ḥawl al-riwāya al-nisā'iyya fī sūriyā-1' ['About the Female Novel in Syria'] *al-Ma'rifa* 166 (1975), 80, 81.
35 Maysūn al-Jurf, *Binā' ṣūrat al-shakhṣiyya al-dhukūriyya fī al-riwāya al- 'arabiyya al-sūriyya* [*Building the Image of the Masculine Character in the Arabic Syrian Novel*] (Damascus: Dār al-Ṣafaḥāt, 2014), 51.
36 Muḥammad Qarānayā, 'al-Unūtha wa al-dhukūra fī riwāyat *Ḥubb fī bilād al-Shām*' ['Femininity and Masculinity in the Novel 'Love in the Levant'], *al-Mawqif al-'adabī* 43.517 (2014), 191–97.
37 For example: *Mawāqif*, *Ādāb* and *Fusūl*.
38 Yumnā al- 'Īd, *Fann al-riwāya al-'arabiyya: bayna khuṣūṣiyyat al-ḥikāya wa tamayyuz al-khiṭāb* [*The Art of the Arabic Novel: Between the Specificities of the Narrative and the Distinction of the Discourse*], (Beirut: Dār al-Ādāb, 1998), 55–56.
39 Connell, *Masculinities*. See also: Butler, *Gender Trouble*.
40 Hartmut Fähndrich, 'Fathers and Husbands: Tyrants and Victims in some Autobiographical and Semi-Autobiographical Works from the Arab World' in *Love and Sexuality in Modern Arabic Literature*, Roger Allen et al (eds) (London: Saqi Books, 1995), 115.
41 Ḥusām al-Khaṭīb, 'al-Riwāya al-tāliya fī sūriyā:3' ['The Coming Novel in Syria: 3'], *al-Ma'rifa* 168 (1976), 86.
42 Max Weiss, 'What Lies Beneath: Political Criticism in Recent Syrian Fiction' in *Syria from Reform to Revolt: Culture, Society and Religion*, ed. Christa Salamandra and Leif Stenberg (Syracuse: Syracuse University Press, 2015), 16. See also: Miriam Cooke, *Dissident Syria: Making Oppositional Arts Official* (Durham and London: Duke University Press, 2007), 20.
43 Weiss, 'What Lies Beneath' (2015), 20. See also Mohja Kahf, 'The Silences of Contemporary Syrian Literature' *World Literature Today* 75:2 (2001), 225–36.
44 Samira Aghacy, *Masculine Identity in the Fiction of the Arab East since 1967* (Syracuse: Syracuse University Press, 2009), 97.
45 Ibid.
46 See, for example, Subhi Hadidi, 'Syria' in *Arab Women Writers*. Ali Najīb Ibrahīm, *Jamāliyyāt al-riwāya: dirāsa fī al-riwāya al-wāqi'iyya al-sūriyya al-mu'āṣira* [*Aesthetics of the Novel: A Study in the Contemporary Syrian Realistic Novel*], (Damascus: Dār al-Yanābī, 1994)
47 'Adnān bin Dhurayl, 'al-riwāya al-sūriyya al-mu'āṣira' ['The Contemporary Syrian Novel'], *al-Ma'rifa* 146 (1974), 30.
48 Fayṣal Sammāq, 'al- Wāqi'iyya fī al-riwāya al-sūriyya al-mu'āṣira' ['Realism in the Contemporary Syrian Novel'], *al-Ma'rifa* 211 (1979), 176.
49 Sara Lei Sparre, 'Educated Women in Syria: Servants of the State, or Nurturers of the Family?' *Critique: Critical Middle Eastern Studies* 17:1 (2008),7.

50 Alexa Firat, 'Cultural Battles on the Literary Field: From the Syrian Writers' Collective to the Last Days of Social Realism in Syria' *Middle Eastern Literatures* 18:2 (2015), 156.
51 Available at: http://moc.gov.sy/index.php?d=48&id=189 (last accessed 14 April 2014).
52 Samar Rūḥī al-Fayṣal, *al-Riwāya al-ʿarabiyya: bināʾ wa rūʾya* [*The Arabic Novel: Construction and Vision*] (Damascus: Arab Writer's Union, 2003), 7.
53 See the introduction to *Ḥubb fī bilād al-shām* (Damascus: Ittiḥād al-kuttāb al-ʿarab, 1995).
54 See Cooke, *Dissident Syria,* 49. Saʿīd al-Barghūthī, 'al-Riwāiʾyāt al-sūriyyāt: naḥnu ṣawt al-muʿadhdhabīn' ['Syrian Female Novelists: We are the Voice of the Tormented'], Dubay al-Thaqāfiyya 3.26 (2007): 34–37.
55 Stefan G Meyer, *The Experimental Arabic Novel: Postcolonial Literary Modernism in the Levant* (Albany: State University of New York Press, 2001), 98.
56 Nabīl Sulaymān and Bū ʿAlī Yāsīn, *al-Adab wa al-idiūlūjiyya fī sūriyā: 1967–1973* (Beirut: Dār Ibn Khaldūn, 1974).
57 Ḥusayn ibn Ḥamza, 'Nabarāt jadīda fī al-riwāya al-sūriyya: al-tajrīb baʿīdan ʿan al-aydīūlūjīā' ['New Voices in the Syrian Novel: Experimenting Far from Ideology']. Available at: www.al-akhbar.com/node/86049 (last accessed 15 April 2013). See also ʿAdnān bin Dhurayl 'al-Riwāya al-sūriyya' (1974), 30. For a general discussion on realism as a genre in Syria see Samar al-Fayṣal, *al-Ittijāh al-wāqiʿī fī al-riwāya al-ʿarabiyya al-sūriyya* [*The Trend of Realism in the Arabic Syrian Novel*], (Damascus: Ittiḥād al-kuttāb al-ʿarab, 1986). And Samar al-Fayṣal, *al-Taṭawwur al-fannī li-l-ittijāh al-wāqiʿī fī al-riwāya al-ʿarabiyya al-sūriyya* [*The Artistic Development of the Trend of Realism in the Syrian Arabic Novel*] (Damascus: Dār al-Nafaʾis, 1996).
58 Zuhar Jabbūr, 'Namādhij riwāʾiyya li-kuttāb min al-lādhaqiyya' ['Examples of Novels from Lattakian Writers'], *al-Mawqif al-adabī* 42.500 (2012), 213–33.
59 Kamal Abu Deeb, *Jamāliyyāt al-tajāwur aw tashābuk al-faḍāʾāt al-ibdāʿiyya* (Beirut: Dār al-ʿilm lil-malāyīn, 1997), 231.
60 Firat, 'Cultural Battles', 153–76.
61 Aghacy, *Masculine Identity,* 56.
62 Abu Deeb, *Jamāliyyāt al-tajāwur* (1997), 231.
63 The book *al-Riwāya al-sūriyya al-muʿāsira* does, for example, only contain Nadia Khust's references to her own novels; all the other researchers and writers refer to male authors only.
64 Ḥusām al-Khaṭīb, 'Ḥawl al-riwāya al-tāliya fī sūriyā: Layla wāḥida' ['About the Coming Novel in Syria: One Night'], *al-Maʿrifa* 168 (1976): 47–60.
65 Aḥmad Jamīl al-Ḥassan, 'Naʿmat Khālid: Jarʾat al-marʾa wa al-būḥ bi-raʿashāt al-jasad' ['Naʿmat Khālid: The Courage of Woman and the Confession of the Body's Trembles'], *al-Mawqif al-adabī* 41.496 (2012), 182–87.

66 Here it is worth noting that when male Syrian writers, such as Ḥannā Mīna and 'Abd al-Salām al- 'Ujaylī draw on their personal experiences in their novels they are not criticised; on the contrary, they are described as writing in the genre of realism. See, for example, the articles in *al-riwāya al-sūriyya al-mu'āṣira: al-judhūr al-thaqāfiyya wa al-taqaniyyāt al-riwā'iyya al-jadīda* [*The Contemporary Syrian Novel, The Cultural Roots and New Novelistic Techniques*] ed. Jamāl Shuḥayyid and Heidi Toelle (Damascus: al-ma 'had al-faransī li-l-dirāsāt al-'arabiyya, 2001).

67 'Āṭifa Fayṣal, 'Taḥawwulāt al-khiṭāb al-unthawī fī al-riwāya al-niswiyya fī sūriyā' ['Changes in the Feminine Discourse in the Female Authored Novel in Syria'], *Majallat Jāmi'at Dimashq* 21.1-2 (2005), 16. See also Bouthaina Shaaban, *Voices Revealed: Arab Women Novelists 1898–2000* (London: Lynne Reiner Publishers, 2009), 37.

68 Imān al-Qāḍī, 'al-Ishām al-niswī fī al-riwāya al-'arabiyya' ['The Female Contribution to the Arabic novel'], *al-Ma'rifa* 324–25 (1990), 120.

69 Kamal Abu Deeb, 'al-Adab wa al-aydīūlūjiyya' ['Literature and Ideology'], *Fuṣūl* 5.4 (1985), 51–90.

70 Firat, 'Cultural Battles', 167.

71 Widād Sakākīnī, 'Ta'qīb 'alā dirāsat al-riwāya al-nisā'iyya fī sūriyā' [A Comment on the Study of Women's Novels in Syria'], *al-Ma'rifa* 168 (1976), 187–89.

72 Roger Allen, 'The Arabic Short Story and the Status of Women' in *Love and Sexuality in Modern Arabic Literature,* ed. Roger Allen et al. (London: Saqi Books, 1995), 77.

73 Nabīl Sulaymān, *Ḥiwāriyyat al-wāqi' wa al-khiṭāb al-riwā'ī* [*The Conversational Nature of Reality and the Discourse of the Novel*] (Latakia: Dār al-ḥiwār lil-nashr wa al-tawzī', 1999), 66.

74 Ibid.

75 Jābir 'Usfūr, *Zaman al-riwāya* (Cairo: al-Hay'a al-miṣriyya al-'āmma lil-kuttāb, 1999).

76 Fayṣal, 'Taḥawwulāt al-khiṭāb', 32.

77 *al-Mawqif al-adabī* is the monthly journal of the Arab Writers' Union in Syria. It was founded in 1971 and is primarily focused on Syrian literature.

78 *Fuṣūl* is a literary journal published in Egypt; it discusses Arabic literature from the Arab world.

79 *al-Ma'rifa* is published by the Syrian Ministry of Culture and was first established in 1962. It publishes on world literature and culture with a focus on Syria and the Arab world.

80 al-Qāḍī, 'al-Ishām al-niswī', 98.

81 Rūla Ḥasan, 'al-Mashhad al-riwā'ī al-niswī fī sūriyā' ['The Female Novelistic Scene in Syria'], *Tishrīn* (2011).

82 Fayṣal, 'Taḥawwulāt al-khiṭāb al-unthawī'.

83 Kamal Abu Deeb, 'Fī al-fikr al-naqdī wa al-fikr al-naqḍī' [On Critical Thought and Destructive Thought] (Paper presented at the conference *Arab Culture and Society on the Threshold of the 21st Century*, Granada, Spain, 1–10 May 1998).

84 Kifah Hanna, *Feminism and Avant-Garde Aesthetics in the Levantine Novel* (New York: Palgrave Macmillan), 28.

Chapter 1

1 Hiyām Nuwaylātī and Umm 'Isām, *Arṣifat al-sa'm* (Damascus: National Security Press, 1973), 299.
2 Bouthaina Shaaban, *Voices Revealed: Arab Women Novelists 1898–2000* (London: Lynne Reiner Publishers Inc, 2009) 14.
3 Different sources date the publications differently and it is unclear whether Sakākīnī's novel *al-Ḥubb al-muḥarram* (*Forbidden Love*) was published as early as 1947, as stated by Radwa Ashour in *Arab Women Writers*, 478, or if, as stated by Ḥusām al-Khaṭīb in his article 'Ḥawl al-rīwāya -1,' 82, the publication dates were 1949 for al-Ḥaffār al-Kuzbarī's *Yawmiyyāt Hāla* (*Hala's Diary*) and 1952 for Sakākīnī's *al-Ḥubb al-muḥarram* and 1950 for her other novel *Arwā bint al-khuṭūb* (*Arwa, Daughter of Upheavals*) also dated 1949.
4 al-Khaṭīb, Ḥusām, 'Ḥawl al-riwāya al-nisāi'yya fī sūriyā' ['About the Female Novel in Syria']. *al-Ma'rifa* 166 (1975): 79–94.
5 Shaaban, *Voices Revealed*, 63.
6 Khalīl al-Mūsā, 'al-Kitāba: kitābat al-ikhtilāf, kitābat al-mar'a' ['Writing: The Writing of Change, the Writing of Women'], *al-Mawqif al-adabī*, 42.500 (2012), 28.
7 Subhi Hadidi and Iman al-Qadi, 'Syria' in *Arab Women Writers: A Critical Reference Guide 1873–1999*, ed. Radwa Ashour (Cairo: the American University in Cairo Press, 2008), 64.
8 Hanna, Kifah, *Feminism and Avant-Garde Aesthetics in the Levantine Novel*. (New York: Palgrave Macmillan, 2016) 4.
9 For a discussion on the Ba'thist ideals of equality, participation in the nation state and socialism, see, for example, Sara Lei Sparre, 'Educated Women in Syria: Servants of the State, or Nurturers of the Family?' *Critique: Critical Middle Eastern Studies* 17.1 (2008), 3–20. Moshe Maoz and Joseph Ginat (eds), *Modern Syria: from Ottoman Rule to Pivotal Role in the Middle East* (Brighton: Sussex Academic Press, 1999). Lisa Wedeen, *Ambiguities of Domination: Politics, Rhetoric, and Symbols in Contemporary Syria* (Chicago: University of Chicago Press, 1999).
10 Luc Herman and Bart Vervaeck, *Handbook of Narrative Analysis* (Lincoln and London: University of Nebraska Press, 2005), 70; Mieke Bal, *Narratology: Introduction to the Theory of Narrative* (Toronto: University of Toronto Press, 1997), 146.
11 Bal, ibid, 150.
12 Shaaban, *Voices Revealed*, 39.

13 Ibid, 52.

14 Cf Lisa Wedeen for a discussion on the same rhetoric on a national level, positioning al-Asad as the father of the country.

15 Kūlīt Khūrī, *Ayyām ma'ahu* [*Days with Him*]. Beirut: al-Maktab al-tijārī lil-ṭibā'a wa al-tawzī' wa al-nashr, 1959) 144.

16 Helena Eriksson, *Husbands, Lovers and Dream Lovers: Masculinity and Female Desire in Women's Novels of the 1970s* (Stockholm: Almqvist och Wiksell, 1997), 122.

17 Ibid.

18 Raewyn Connell and James Messerschmidt, 'Hegemonic Masculinity: Rethinking the Concept', *Gender and Society* 19.6 (2005).

19 Eriksson, *Husbands,* 122.

20 Arabic for Masculinity, for a discussion of the difficulty of translating masculinity and masculinities to Arabic see Mahadeen, Ebtihal, 'Arabizing "Masculinity" *Journal of Middle Eastern Women's Studies* 12.3 (2016): 450–52.

21 Amal Jarrāḥ, *al-Riwāya al-mal'ūna* [*The Cursed Novel*] (Beirut: Dār al-Sāqī, 1968; 2010), 46.

22 Khūrī, *Days with Him,* 92.

23 Salmā al-Ḥaffār al-Kuzbarī, *'Aynān min Ishbīliya* [*Sevillan Eyes*] (Beirut: Dār al-kātib al-'arabī, 1965), 173.

24 In'ām al-Musālima, *al-Ḥubb wa al-waḥl* [*Love and Mud*] (Damascus: Dār al-thaqāfa, 1963), 8.

25 For a discussion on patriarchal dividend see Jack Khan, *An Introduction to Masculinities* (Chichester: Wiley-Blackwell, 2009*),* 27; 32.

26 Deniz Kandiyoti, 'Gender, Power and Contestation: Rethinking Bargaining with Patriarchy' in *Feminist Visions of Development: Gender Analysis and Policy,* ed. Ruth Pearson and Cecile Jackson (London: Routledge, 1998). Deniz Kandiyoti, 'Bargaining with Patriarchy', *Gender and Society* 2.3 (1988) 274–90.

27 MENA Development Report 'Gender and Development in the Middle East and North Africa- Women in the Public Sphere' (Washington: The World Bank, 2004).

28 Hiyām Nuwaylātī and Umm 'Isām, *Arṣifat al-sa'm* [*Sidewalks of Tedium*] (Damascus: National Security Press, 1973), 299.

29 Ibid, 21.

30 Khūrī, *Days with Him,* 26.

31 Sally Gallagher, *Making Do in Damascus: Navigating a Generation of Change in Family and Work* (New York: Syracuse University Press, 2012), 105.

32 Mayya al-Raḥbī, *al-Niswiyya: mafāhīm wa qaḍāyā* [*Feminism: Concepts and Issues*] (Damascus: al-Raḥba lil-nashr wa al-tawzi', 2014).

33 Kūlīt Khūrī, *Layla wāḥida* [*One Night*] (Damascus: Dār al-Fārisa, 2002; 1961), 30.

34 Ibid, 31.

35 Eriksson, *Husbands,* 129.

36 Compare how similar activities are described in *Days with Him* by Colette Khoury and also in *The Impossible Novel* by Ghada al-Samman where the main characters are seen as breaking taboos when they want to publish poetry, study and work.
37 al-Musālima, *Love and Mud*, 70.
38 Haifā' Bīṭār, Yawmiyyāt muṭalliqa [*Diaries of a Divorcing Woman*] (Algiers: Dār al-'Arabiyya li-l-'Ulūm –Nāshirūn, 2006, (1994)), 9.
39 Lanser, *Fictions of Authority*, 7.
40 Jarrāḥ, *The Cursed Novel*, 39.
41 Khūrī, *One Night*, 26.
42 al-Jurf, *bina' ṣūrat al-shakhṣiya*, 55.
43 The novel was published for the first time in 2010 but was written in 1968.
44 Khūrī, *Days with Him*, 254.
45 Ibid, 253.
46 Ibid, 109.
47 Ibid, 48.
48 Ibid, 154.
49 Ibid, 127.
50 Khūrī, *One Night*, 232
51 Ibid, 235.
52 Connell and Messerschmidt, 'Hegemonic Masculinity', 848.
53 Sarah Frantz and Katharina Rennhak (eds) *Women Constructing Men: Female Novelists and their Male Characters 1750–2000*. Langham MD: Lexington Books, 2010, 3.
54 Khūrī, *Days with Him*, 143.
55 Ibid, 36.
56 Ibid, 55.
57 Ibid, 85.
58 Ibid, 78.
59 Ibid, 81.
60 Ibid, 136.
61 Ibid, 141.
62 Ibid, 60.
63 Khūrī, *One Night*, 71.
64 Khūrī, *Days with Him*, 158.
65 Ibid, 239.
66 Ibid, 226.
67 Usayma Darwīsh, *Shajarat al-ḥubb - ghābat al-aḥzān* [*Tree of Love: Forest of Sorrows*] (Beirut: Dār al-Ādāb, 2000), 28.
68 Ibid, 11.
69 Khūrī, *Days with Him*, 129.
70 Lanser, *Fictions of Authority*, 13.

71 Khūrī, *Days with Him*, 407.
72 Ibid, 280.

Chapter 2

1 Ulfat al-Idlibī, *Dimashq yā basmat al-ḥuzn* [*Damascus, O Smile of Sadness*] (Damascus: Manshūrāt wizārat al-thaqāfa wa al-irshād al-qawmī, 1980), 207.
2 Aḥmad Mashūl, "Azmat al-baṭal al-thawrī fī al-riwāya al-'arabiyya' ['The Crisis of the Revolutionary Hero in the Arabic Novel'], *al-Ma'rifa* 277 (1985), 66.
3 Iman al-Qadi, 'Syria', in *Arab Women Writers: A Critical Reference Guide 1873–1999*, eds, Radwa Ashour et al (Cairo: the American University in Cairo Press, 2008).
4 Friederike Pannewick and Georges Khalil (eds) *Commitment and Beyond: Reflections on/of the Political in Arabic Literature since the 1940s* (Wiesbaden: Reichert Verlag, 2015), 12.
5 Ibid, 10.
6 Ḥamīda Na'na', *Man yajru' 'alā al-shawq* [*Who Dares to Long*] (Beirut: Dār al-Ādāb, 1989), 173.
7 Mieke Bal, *Narratology: Introduction to the Theory of Narrative*. 2nd edn (Toronto: University of Toronto Press 1997) 127.
8 Wilson Chacko Jacob, *Working Out Egypt: Effendi Masculinity and Subject Formation in Colonial Modernity 1870–1940* (Durham NC and London: Duke University Press, 2011).
9 Ibid.
10 See, for example, Wilson Chacko Jacob, 'The Turban, The Tarbush and the Top Hat: Masculinity, Modernity and National Identity in Interwar Egypt' *al-Raida* 21.104–5 (2004), 23–37. Joseph Massad, *Desiring Arabs* (Chicago: The University of Chicago Press, 2007).
11 Samira Aghacy, 'Masculinity and Spatial Trajectories in the Contemporary Arabic Novel' in *Cairo Papers in Social Science* 33.1, ed. Helena Rizzo (Cairo: Cairo University Press, 2010) 55.
12 'Āṭifa Fayṣal, 'Taḥawwulāt al-khiṭāb al-unthawī fī al-riwāya al-niswiyya fī sūriyā' ['Transformations in the Feminine Discourse in the Female Authored Novel in Syria']. *Majallat jāmi'at dimashq* 21.1–2 (2005): 15–41.
13 Aghacy *Masculine Identity*, 56.
14 Ibid, 57.
15 Hoda Elsadda, *Gender, Nation and the Arabic Novel: Egypt 1892–2008*. Syracuse: Syracuse University Press, 2012, xxxi.
16 Aghacy, *Masculine Identity*, 56.
17 al-Idlibī, *Damascus*, 148.
18 Ibid, 138.

19 Deniz Kandiyoti, 'The Paradoxes of Masculinity: Some Thoughts on Segregated Societies' in *Dislocating Masculinities: Comparative Ethnographies*, ed. Andrea Cornwall and Nancy Lindisfarne. (London, Routledge, 1994), 196–213.
20 al-Idlibī, *Damascus*, 72.
21 Ibid, 74.
22 Ibid, 76.
23 Na'na', *Who Dares to Long*, 197.
24 Ibid, 183.
25 Qmar Kilānī, *Bustān al-karaz* [*The Cherry Orchard*] (Damascus: Dār al-athwār lil-ṭibā'a, 1977).
26 Qamar Kilānī, *al- Dawwāma* [*The Whirlwind*] (Damascus: Manshūrāt wizārat al-thaqāfa wa al-irshād al-qawmī, 1983), 14.
27 al-Idlibī, *Damascus*, 193.
28 Ibid, 84.
29 Ibid, 72.
30 Ibid, 132.
31 Ibid, 163.
32 Ibid, 261.
33 Ibid, 195.
34 Ibid, 201.
35 Kilānī, *The Whirlwind*, 274.
36 al-Idlibī, *Damascus*, 213.
37 Ibid, 134.
38 Ibid, 11; 206.
39 Na'na', *Who Dares to Long*, 174.
40 Ibid, 184.
41 Aḥmad Mashūl, "Azmat al-baṭal al-thawrī", 66.

Chapter 3

1 Haifa Bitar, *Qabw al-'abbāsīn* [*The Abbaseen Basement*] (Damascus: Dār al-Ḥisād, 2006;1999), 16.
2 'Āṭifa Fayṣal, 'Taḥawwulāt al-khiṭāb al-unthawī fī al-riwāya al-niswiyya fī sūriyā' ['Transformations in the Feminine Discourse in the Female Authored Novel in Syria']. *Majallat jāmi'at dimashq* 21.1–2 (2005): 15–41.
3 Bouthaina Shaaban, *Voices Revealed: Arab Women Novelists 1898–2000* (London: Lynne Reiner Publishers Inc, 2009), viii.
4 Maysūn al-Jurf, *Binā' ṣūrat al-shakhṣiyya al-dhukūriyya fī al-riwāya al- 'arabiyya al-sūriyya* [*Building the Image of the Masculine Character in the Arabic Syrian Novel*] (Damascus: Dār al-Ṣafaḥāt, 2014), 176.

5 Hanadi al-Samman, *Anxiety of Erasure: Trauma, Authorship and the Diaspora in Arab Women's Writings* (New York: Syracuse University Press, 2015), 164.
6 Dalya Cohen-Mor, *Fathers and Sons in the Arab Middle East* (New York: Palgrave Macmillan, 2013), 29.
7 al-Idlibī, Ulfat. *Dimashq yā basmat al-ḥuzn* [*Damascus, O Smile of Sadness*]. (Damascus: Manshūrāt wizārat al-thaqāfa wa al-irshād al-qawmī, 1980), 12.
8 Bīṭār, *The Abbaseen Basement*, 22.
9 Lisa Wedeen, *Ambiguities of Domination: Politics, Rhetoric and Symbols in Contemporary Syria* (Chicago: University of Chicago Press, 1999).
10 Kamal Abu Deeb, 'Fī tashrīḥ al-sulṭa: al-ulūha al-ḥākimiyya al-ubūwa' ['On the Dissection of Power: Divinity, Domination and Patriarchy'], *al-Ufuq* 88:23 (1986): 42–44.
11 Hartmut Fähndrich, 'Fathers and Husbands: Tyrants and Victims in some Autobiographical and Semi-Autobiographical Works from the Arab World' in *Love and Sexuality in Modern Arabic Literature,* ed. Roger Allen et al, (London: Saqi Books, 1995) 108.
12 Ibid, 114.
13 Mayya al-Raḥbī, *Furāt* [*Euphrates*] (Damascus: al-Ahālī lil- ṭibā'a wa al-nashr wa al-tawzī', 1998), 16.
14 Malāḥa al-Khānī, *Khaṭawāt fī al-ḍabāb* [*Steps in the Fog*] (Damascus: Ittiḥād al-kuttāb al-'arab, 1984), 163.
15 Līndā 'Abdu al-Raḥman 'Abīd, *Tamthīlāt al-ab fī al-riwāya al-niswiyya al-'arabiyya al-mu'āṣira* [*Representations of the Father in the Contemporary Arabic Female Authored Novel*] (Amman: Dār Fadā'āt, 2007).
16 Ibid, 207.
17 al-Raḥbī, *Euphrates*, 138.
18 Biṭār, *The Abbaseen Basement*, 45.
19 Rebecca Joubin, 'The Politics of the Qabaday (Tough Man) and the Changing Father Figure in Syrian Television Drama' *Journal of Middle East Women's Studies* 12:1 (2016), 59.
20 Ḍiyā' Qaṣabjī, *Imra'a fī dā'irat al-khawf* [*Woman in a Circle of Fear*] (Tripoli: al-Munshā al-'āma lil-nashr wa al-tawzī' wa al-'ilān, 1985), 17.
21 Ghāda al-Sammān, *al-Riwāya al-mustaḥīla: fusayfusā' Dimashqiyya* [*The Impossible Novel: A Damascene Mosaic*] (Beirut: Manshūrāt Ghāda al-Sammān, 1997), 20.
22 Haifa Bitar, *Afrāḥ ṣaghīra afrāḥ akhīra* [*Small Joys, Final Joys*] (Beirut: Arab Scientific Publishers, Inc, 2008(1998)), 37.
23 Ibid, 36.
24 Ibid, 44.
25 Ghāliya Qabbānī, *Ṣabāḥ Imra'a* [*A Woman's Morning*] (Casablanca: al-Markaz al-thaqāfī al-'arabī, 2000), 77.

26 Ibid, 128.
27 al-Raḥbī, *Euphrates*, 61.
28 Haifā'Biṭār, *Afrāḥ ṣaghīra afrāḥ akhīra* [*Small Joys, Final Joys*] (Beirut: Arab Scientific Publishers, Inc, 2008), 87.
29 Biṭār, *The Abbaseen Basement*, 28.
30 Ibid, 29.
31 al-Jurf, *Binā' ṣūrat al-shakhṣiyya,* 61.
32 Ruth Roded, 'Alternative Images of the Prophet Muhammad's Virility' in *Islamic Masculinities,* ed. Lahoucine Ouzgane (London: Zed Books Ltd, 2006), 58.
33 Samira Aghacy, *Masculine Identity in the Fiction of the Arab East since 1967* (New York: Syracuse University Press, 2009), 19.
34 Suad Joseph and Susan Slyomovics, eds, *Women and Power in the Middle East* (Philadelphia: University of Philadelphia Press, 2001), 6.
35 Helen Nabasuta Mugambi, 'Reading Masculinities in a Feminist Text: Tsitsi Dangarembga's *Nervous Conditions*' in *Twelve Best Books by African Women: Critical Readings*, ed. Chikwenye Okonjo Ogunyemi and Tuzyline Jita Allan (Athens: Ohio University Press, 2009), 205.
36 Farah Ghannam, *Live and Die Like a Man: Gender Dynamics in Urban Egypt* (Stanford: Stanford University Press, 2013) 31.
37 Mugambi, 'Reading Masculinities in a Feminist Text', 217.

Chapter 4

1 Ghāda al-Sammān, *Bayrūt 75* [*Beirut 75*] (Beirut: Dār al-Ādāb, 1975), 22.
2 Hanna, *Feminism and Avant-Garde Aesthetics,* 29.
3 Ibid, 32
4 Laura Mulvey, 'Visual Pleasure and Narrative Cinema' *Screen* 16:3 (1975).
5 Hanrīyit, 'Abbūdī, *al-Ẓahr al-'ārī* [*The Naked Back*] (Beirut: Dār al-Ādāb, 1998), 11.
6 Ibid, 33.
7 Ibid, 25.
8 Ibid, 88.
9 al-Sammān, *Beirut 75*, 5.
10 Ghāliya Qabbānī, *Ṣabāḥ Imra'a* [*A Woman's Morning*] (Casablanca: al-Markaz al-thaqāfī al-'arabī, 2000), 116.
11 Ibid, 128.
12 Ghāda al-Sammān, *al-Riwāya al-mustaḥīla: fusayfusā' Dimashqiyya* [*The Impossible Novel: A Damascene Mosaic*] (Beirut: Manshūrāt Ghāda al-Sammān, 1997), 20.
13 Compare, with a description of the same scenario but from the female point of view, in Haifā' Bīṭār's *Afrāḥ ṣaghīra, afrāḥ akhīra,* 1998.

14 Simon Gikandi, 'Afterword' to *Masculinities in African Literary and Cultural Texts*, ed. Helen Mugambi Nabasuta and Tuzyline Jita Allan (Banbury: Ayebia Clarke Publishing Ltd, 2010), 296.

15 Showalter, *A Literature of their Own*, 112.

16 Eve Sedgwick Kosofsky, 'Gosh, Boy George, You Must be Awfully Secure in Your Masculinity' in *Constructing Masculinity*, ed. Maurice Berger, Brian Wallis and Watson Simon (New York: Routledge, 1995), 13.

17 Berthold Schoene-Harwood, *Writing Men: Literary Masculinities from Frankenstein to the New Man* (Edinburgh: Edinburgh University Press, 2000), 10.

18 Diana Wallace, 'Ventriloquizing the Male: Two Portraits of the Artist as a Young Man by May Sinclair and Edith Wharton', *Men and Masculinities* 4.4 (2002), 322–33. Sara Pearson 'Constructing Masculine Narrative: Charlotte Bronte's the Professor' in *Women Constructing Men, Female Novelists and their Male Characters 1750–2000*, ed. Sarah Frantz and Katharina Rennhak (Langham MD: Lexington Books, 2010), 83–110.

19 Abbūdī, *The Naked Back*, 145.

20 RW Connell, *Masculinities* 2nd edn (Cambridge: Polity Press, 2005), 76.

21 Robert Lang and Maher Ben Moussa, 'Choosing to Be "Not a Man": Masculine Anxiety in Nouri Bouzid's Rih Essed/Man of Ashes' in *Masculinity: Bodies, Movies, Culture*, ed. Peter Lehman (New York: Routledge, 2001), 85.

22 al-Sammān, *Beirut 75*, 52.

23 Arne Nilsson, 'Modernisering och manlig homosexualitet: Svenska storstadsmän kring mitten av 1900-talet' ['Modernising and Male Homosexuality: Swedish City Men around the Middle of the 20th Century'] in *Rädd att falla: Studier i manlighet* [*Afraid to Fall: Studies in Manliness*], ed. Claes Ekenstam et al. (Södertälje: Gidlunds förlag, 1998), 182–237.

24 Ibid, 211.

25 Michael Kimmel, ed., *Changing Men: New Directions in Research on Men and Masculinities* (Thousand Oaks: Sage Publications, 1987), 19.

26 Joseph Massad, *Desiring Arabs* (Chicago: The University of Chicago Press, 2007).

27 Marcia C Inhorn, *The New Arab Man: Emergent Masculinities, Technologies and Islam in the Middle East* (Princeton: Princeton University Press, 2012).

28 Connell, *Masculinities*, 80.

29 Ibid, 79.

30 For a further discussion of the two axes of Connell's matrix for hegemonic masculinity see Thorbjörn Forslid, *Varför män: Om manlighet i litteraturen* [*Why Men? About Manliness in Literature*] (Stockholm: Carlsson Bokförlag, 2006), 18.

31 Elizabeth Badinter, *XY: Die Identität des Mannes* (Munch, Piper, 1993) quoted in Horlacher 'Charting the Field', 6.

32 Amirhussein Vafa and Rosli Taif, 'Manhood in Crisis: Powerlessness, Homophobia and Violence in *Fightclub*', *Pertanika Journal of Humanities and Social Sciences* 19.2 (2011), 449–57.

33 Michal Kimmel, *Manhood in America: a Cultural History*, 3rd edn (Oxford: Oxford University Press, 2011).
34 Samira Aghacy, *Masculine Identity, Masculine Identity in the Fiction of the Arab East since 1967* (New York: Syracuse University Press, 2009), 4.
35 Ibid. Paul Amar 'Middle East Masculinity Studies: Discourses of "Men in Crisis" Industries of Gender Revolution' *Journal of Middle Eastern Woman's Studies* 7.3 (2011), 36–70. Sally Hayward, '(Dis)enabling Masculinities: The Word and the Body, Class Politics and Male Sexuality' in El Saadawi's *God Dies by the Nile' African Masculinities: Men in Africa from the Late Nineteenth Century to the Present.* Lahoucine Ouzgane and Robert Morrell, eds (Gordonsville: Palgrave Macmillan, 2005) 137–51.
36 Pierre Bourdieu, trans. Boel Englund, *Den manliga dominansen* [*The Male Dominance*] (Uddevalla: Daidalos AB, 1999), 65.
37 Ibid, 66.
38 Lynne Segal, 'Changing Men: Masculinities in Context', *Theory and Society* 22.5 (1993), 123.
39 miriam cooke, 'Naguib Mahfouz: Men and the Egyptian Underworld' in *Fictions of Masculinity: Crossing Cultures, Crossing Sexualities*, ed. Peter Murphy (New York and London, New York University Press, 1994), 98.
40 Aghacy, *Masculine Identity*, 130.
41 Malāḥa al-Khānī, *Khaṭawāt fī al-ḍabāb* [*Steps in the Fog*] (Damascus: Ittiḥād al-kuttāb al-'arab, 1984), 108.
42 Connell, *Masculinities*, 77.
43 Sally Gallagher, *Making Do in Damascus: Navigating a Generation of Change in Family and Work* (New York: Syracuse University Press, 2012), xiv.
44 Farah Ghannam, *Live and Die Like a Man: Gender Dynamics in Urban Egypt.* (Stanford: Stanford University Press, 2013), 6.
45 Ibid.
46 Victor J Seidler, *Transforming Masculinities: Men, Culture, Bodies, Power, Sex and Love* (London, Routledge, 2006), 96.
47 Lang and Ben Moussa, 'Choosing to Be "Not a Man"' 86
48 Inhorn, *New Arab Man*, 80, 83 and 88.
49 Aghacy, *Masculine Identity*, 21.
50 Ibid, 150.
51 Evelyn Accad, *Sexuality and War, Literary Masks of the Middle East.* New York: New York University Press, 1990.
52 al-Sammān, *Beirut 75*, 5.
53 Ibid.
54 Ibid, 108.
55 Ibid, 19.

56 muṭrib al-rujūla.
57 Aghacy, *Masculine Identity*, 76.
58 al-Sammān, *Beirut 75*, 58.
59 Ibid, 63.
60 Haifā'Bīṭār *Qabw al-'abbāsīn* [*The Abbaseen Basement*] (Damascus: Dār al-Ḥisād, 2006), 31.
61 al-Sammān, *Beirut 75*, 58.
62 al-Idlibī, *Damascus*, 242.
63 Qamar Kilānī, *al- Dawwāma* [*The Whirlwind*] (Damascus: Manshūrāt wizārat al-thaqāfa wa al-irshād al-qawmī, 1983), 325.
64 al-Sammān, *Beirut 75*, 47.
65 Ibid, 38.
66 Ibid, 87.
67 Haifa Biṭār, *Nasr bi-janāḥ wāḥid* [*A One-winged Eagle*] (Beirut: Arab Scientific Publishers, Inc, 2010 (1999)), 136.
68 al-Sammān, *Beirut 75*, 79.
69 Ibid, 66.
70 Biṭār, *A One-winged Eagle*, 146.
71 Ibid, 114.
72 Zeina Zaatari, 'Desirable Masculinity/Femininity and Nostalgia of the Anti-Modern: Bab el-Hara Television Series as a Site of Production' *Sexuality and Culture* 19 (2015), 21.
73 al-Sammān, *Beirut 75*, 81.
74 Angela Abdel-Malek, 'Masculinity as Violence in Arab Women's Fiction', *al-Raida* 21.104–5 (2004), 110.
75 al-Sammān, *Beirut 75*, 89.
76 Ibid, 89.
77 Ibid.
78 Bo Nilsson, *Maskulinitet: Representation, Ideologi och Retorik* [*Masculinity: Representation, Ideology and Rhetorics*] (Umeå: Boréa, 1999), 35.
79 With the exception of Nadya Khūst's novels which are set in the late nineteenth century and the beginning of the twentieth century.

Chapter 5

1 Hanrīyit Abbūdī, *al-Ẓahr al-'ārī* [*The Naked Back*]. (Beirut: Dār al-Ādāb, 1998), 60.
2 RW Connell, 'Globalization, Imperialism, and Masculinities' in *Handbook of Studies on Men and Masculinities*, edited by Michael Kimmel, Jeff Hearn and RW Connell (Thousand Oaks: Sage, 2005), 72.

3 The normal usage is the passive participle MuṭallAqa, emphasising the agency of the male partner. In this case, the active participle is used, accentuating the will of the female protagonist to go through with her divorce.

4 Connell, *Masculinities*, 10.

5 Candace West and Don H Zimmerman, 'Doing Gender', *Gender and Society* 1.2 (1987), 127.

6 Ibid, 134.

7 Malāḥa al-Khānī, *Khaṭawāt fī al-ḍabāb* [*Steps in the Fog*] (Damascus: Ittiḥād al-kuttāb al-'arab, 1984), 80.

8 Ibid, 161.

9 Judith Halberstam, *Female Masculinity* (Durham: Duke University Press, 1998), 2.

10 Marie Nordberg, *Jämställdhetens spjutspets? Manliga arbetstagare i kvinnoyrken, jämställdhet, maskulinitet, femininitet och heteronormativitet* [*Cutting Edge Equality? Male Employees in Female Occupations, Equality, Masculinity, Femininity and Heteronormativity*] (Göteborg: Arkipelag, 2005).

11 Marie Nordberg, 'Kvinnlig maskulinitet och manlig femininitet: en möjlighet att överskrida könsdikotomin?' ['Female Masculinity and Male Femininity: A Possibility to Bridge the Gender Dichotomy?'], *Kvinnovetenskaplig tidskrift* 1–2 (2004), 47–65.

12 Ibid.

13 Judith Halberstam, *Female Masculinity* (Durham: Duke University Press, 1998), 27.

14 al-Khānī, *Steps in the Fog*, 20.

15 Judith Butler, *Gender Trouble: Feminism and the Subversion of Identity*, 4th edn (New York and London: Routledge, 2007).

16 Connell, *Masculinities*, 71.

17 Ibid, 72.

18 Oystein Gullvåg Holter, 'Social Theories for Researching Men and Masculinities: Direct Gender Hierarchy and Structural Inequality' in *Handbook of Studies on Men*, ed. Kimmel et al., 20.

19 Michelle Adams and Scott Coltrane, 'Boys and Men in Families' in *Handbook of Studies on Men*, ed. Kimmel et al., 236.

20 Farah Ghannam, *Live and Die Like a Man: Gender Dynamics in Urban Egypt.* (Stanford: Stanford University Press, 2013).

21 Ibid, 24.

22 Nadia Zibani and Martha Braidy, 'Adolescent Boys' Response to Gender Equitable Programming in Rural Upper Egyptian Villages: Between 'Ayb' and 'Haram'' *al-Raida* 104–5 (2004), 65.

23 Samira Aghacy, *Masculine Identity in the Fiction of the Arab East since 1967* (New York: Syracuse University Press, 2009), 154.

24 Deniz Kandiyoti, 'The Paradoxes of Masculinity: Some Thoughts on Segregated Societies' in *Dislocating Masculinities: Comparative Ethnographies*, eds Andrea Cornwall and Nancy Lindisfarne (London: Routledge, 1994).

25 Adams and Coltrane, 'Boys and Men', 233.

26 Stefan Horlacher, 'Charting the Field of Masculinity Studies; or, Toward a Literary History of Masculinities' in *Constructions of Masculinity in British Literature from the Middle Ages to the Present*, ed. Stefan Horlacher (Basingstoke, Palgrave Macmillan, 2011).

27 Adams and Coltrane, 'Boys and Men', 230.

28 Bo Nilsson, *Maskulinitet: Representation, Ideologi och Retorik* [*Masculinity: Representation, Ideology and Rhetorics*] (Umeå: Boréa, 1999), 16.

29 Al-Khānī, *Steps in the Fog*, 13.

30 Ibid, 126.

31 Sally Gallagher, *Making Do in Damascus: Navigating a Generation of Change in Family and Work* (New York: Syracuse University Press, 2012), V.

32 Dalya Abudi, *Mothers and Daughters in Arab Women's Literature: The Family Front* (Leiden: Brill Academic Publishers, 2011), 47.

33 'Gender and Development in the Middle East and North Africa: Women in the Public Sphere', *MENA Development Report* (Washington: The World Bank, 2004). Bouthaina Shaaban, 'Persisting Contradictions: Muslim Women in Syria' in *Women in Muslim Societies: Diversity Within Unity*, ed. Herbert L Bodman and Nayereh Tohidi (Colorado: Lynne Rienner Publishers Inc, 1998), 101–19. Mayya al-Raḥbī, *al-Nisawiyya: mafāhīm wa qaḍāyā* [*Feminism: Concepts and Issues*] (Damascus: al-Raḥba lil-nashr wa al-tawzi', 2014). Rania Maktabi, 'Female Citizenship in Syria: Framing the 2009 Controversy over Personal Status Law' in *Syria from Reform to Revolution, vol 1*, ed. Raymond Hinnenbusch and Tina Zintl (New York: Syracuse University Press, 2015), 176–99.

34 Kristina Fjelkestam, Helena Hill and David Tjeder, eds *Kvinnorna gör mannen: maskulinitetskonstruktioner i kvinnors text och bild 1500–2000* [*Women Make the Man: Masculinity Construction in Women's Texts and Pictures, 1500–2000*]. (Göteborg: Makadam, 2013),10.

35 See Richard Collier, *Masculinity, Law and the Family* (London: Routledge, 1995) for a discussion of the relation between law and the formation of masculinity in America. For a discussion of men's feeling of a lost masculinity in response to simplified divorce proceedings for women in Egypt see Mustafa Abdalla, 'Masculinity on Shifting Grounds: Emasculation and the Rise of the Islamist Political Scene in Post-Mubarak Egypt' in *Cairo Papers in Social Science* ed. Helena Rizzo 33.1 (Cairo: Cairo University Press, 2010), 53–74.

36 Mayya al-Raḥbī, *al-Niswiyya: mafāhīm wa qaḍāyā* [*Feminism: Concepts and Issues*]. (Damascus: al-Raḥba lil-nashr wa al-tawzi', 2014), 193.

37 Ibid, 179.

38 Ghannam, *Live and Die,* 88.

39 al-Khānī, *Steps in the Fog,* 46.

40 Shawn Lisa Maurer, 'Happy Men? Mid-Eighteenth-century Women Writers and Ideal Masculinity' in *Women Constructing Men,* ed. Frantz and Rennhak, 27.

41 Zibani and Braidy, 'Adolescent Boys', 65.

42 Ibid, 66.

43 Haifa Bīṭār, *Yawmiyyāt muṭalliqa* [*Diaries of a Divorcing Woman*] (Algiers: Dār al-'Arabiyya li-l-'Ulūm –Nāshirūn, 2006 (1994)), 36.

44 David G Gilmore, *Manhood in the Making: Cultural Concepts of Masculinity* (New Haven and London: Yale University Press, 1990), 11.

45 Emma Sinclair-Webb and Mai Ghoussoub, eds, *Imagined Masculinities, Male Identity and Culture in the Modern Middle East* (London: Saqi Books, 2000).

46 Nilsson, *Maskulinitet,* 65.

47 Abdelwahab Bouhdiba and Abdu Khal, "Festivities of Violence: Circumcision and the Making of Men," in *Imagined Masculinities, Male Identity and Culture in the Modern Middle East,* ed. Emma Sinclair-Webb and Mai Ghoussoub, 19–33.

48 Ibid.

49 al-Khānī, *Steps in the Fog,* 3.

50 Ibid, 7.

51 Ibid, 8.

52 Ibid, 76.

53 Ibid, 14.

54 Ibid, 22.

55 'Abbūdī, *The Naked Back,* 43.

56 Ibid, 72.

57 Ibid, 117.

58 al-Khānī, *Steps in the Fog,* 80.

59 See, for example, John MacInnes, *The End of Masculinity: The Confusion of Sexual Genesis and Sexual Difference in Modern Society* (Buckingham: Open University Press, 1998). Alan Petersen, 'Research on Men and Masculinities: Some Implications of Recent Theory for Future Work', *Men and Masculinities* 6:1 (2003), 54–69.

60 Connell, *Masculinities,* 27.

61 Anīsa 'Abbūd, *al-Na'na' al-barrī* [*Wild Mint*] (Damascus: Dār al-Sawsan lil-nashr, 2004;1997), 430.

62 Ibid, 43.

63 Ibid, 45.

64 Nādyā Khūst, *A'āṣīr fī bilād al-shām* [*Cyclones in the Levant*] (Damascus: Ittiḥād al-kuttāb al-'arab, 1998), 177.

65 Ibid, 192.

Conclusion

1 'Āṭifa Fayṣal, 'Taḥawwulāt al-khiṭāb al-unthawī fī al-riwāya al-niswiyya fī sūriyā' [*Transformations in the Feminine Discourse in the Female Authored Novel in Syria*]. *Majallat jāmi'at dimashq* 21.1–2 (2005): 15–41 at 32.

2 Mohja Kahf, 'The Silences of Contemporary Syrian Literature' *World Literature Today* 75:2 (2001), 235. See also Max Weiss, 'Literary Transformations of Syrian Authoritarianism' in *Middle East Authoritarianisms: Governance, Contestation and Regime Resilience in Syria and Iran,* ed. Steven Heydemann and Reinoud Leenders, (Stanford: Stanford University Press, 2013), 143–69.

3 Max Weiss, 'What Lies Beneath: Political Criticism in Recent Syrian Fiction' in *Syria from Reform to Revolt: Culture, Society and Religion,* eds Christa Salamandra and Leif Stenberg (Syracuse: Syracuse University Press, 2015), 17.

4 Fayṣal, 'Taḥawwulāt al-khiṭāb', 32.

5 'Umar Qaddūr, 'al-Riwāya al-sūriyya al-jadīda: ẓāhira ibdā'iyya am ẓāhira 'ilāmiyya?' [The New Syrian Novel: A Creative Phenomenon or a Media Phenomenon?], *al-Adāb* 9-10 (2009). Available at: http://adabmag.com/node/247 (last accessed 15 December 2013).

6 Buthayna al-Balkhī, 'al-Riwā'iyya al-sūriyya istaṭā'at an tafukk quyūd al-namaṭiyya wa tulāmis al-wāqi' bi-jiddiyya' ['The Syrian Female Novelist has Managed to Break the Restraints of Form and Touch Reality with Seriousness'], 21/6-2014, *al-Watan.*

7 Nadhīr Ja'far, 'al-Khiṭāb al-riwā'ī al-niswī: 'ataba jadīda lil-takhyīl' ['The New Female Novelistic Discourse: New Thresholds for Imagination'], 27/3-2011, *Tishrīn.*

8 See, for example, Ṭāhir Sa'īd, *'Indamā tabkī al-mar'a* [*When the Woman Cries*] (Damascus: Dār Ṭlās, 2012). Ibtisām Traysī, *Mudun al-yamām* [*Cities of Doves*] (Cairo: Maktabat dār al-'arabiyya li-l- kuttāb, 2014). Mahā Ḥasan, *Ṭubūl al-ḥubb* [*Drums of Love*] (Beirut: al-Kawkab Press Service, 2013).

Bibliography

'Abbūd, Anīsa. *al-Na'na' al-barrī* [*Wild Mint*]. Damascus: Dār al-Sawsan lil-nashr, 2004. First published 1997.

'Abbūdī, Hanrīyit. *al-Ẓahr al-'ārī* [*The Naked Back*]. Beirut: Dār al-Ādāb, 1998.

Abdalla, Mustafa. 'Masculinity on Shifting Grounds: Emasculation and the Rise of the Islamist Political Scene in Post-Mubarak Egypt' in *Cairo Papers in Social Science* 33.1, edited by Helena Rizzo, 53–74. Cairo: Cairo University Press, 2010.

'Abdu al-Raḥman 'Abīd, Līndā. *Tamthīlāt al-ab fī al-riwāya al-niswiyya al-'arabiyya al-mu'āṣira* [*Representations of the Father in the Contemporary Arabic Female Authored Novel*]. Amman: Dār Fadā'āt, 2007.

Abdel-Malek, Angela. 'Masculinity as Violence in Arab Women's Fiction'. *al-Raida* 21:104–5 (2004):105–10.

Abu Deeb, Kamal. 'Fī tashrīḥ al-sulṭa: al-ulūha al-ḥākimiyya al-ubūwa' ['On the Dissection of Power: Divinity, Rulership and Patriarchy']. *al-Ufuq* 89:30 (1986): 40–44.

Abu Deeb, Kamal. 'Fī tashrīḥ al-sulṭa, al-inshā' al-'arabī wa al-dhukūriyya: Shahrazād wa al-naṣṣ al-unthawī al-muqāwam' ['On the Dissection of Power, Arabic Composition and the Patriarchal Text: Shahrazad and the Resistant Female Text']. *al-Ufuq* 88:23 (1986):42–4.

Abu Deeb, Kamal. 'Fī al-fikr al-naqdī wa al-fikr al-naqṣī' ['On Critical Thought and Destructive Thought']. Paper presented at the conference *Arab Culture and Society on the Threshold of the 21st Century*, Granada, Spain, 1–10 May 1998.

Abu Deeb, Kamal. 'al-Adab wa al-aydīūlūjiyyā' [Literature and Ideology]. *Fuṣūl* 5.4 (1985): 51–90.

Abu Deeb, Kamal. *Jamāliyyāt al-tajāwur aw tashābuk al-faḍā'āt al-ibdā'iyya* [*The Aesthetics of Contiguity or the Interlacing of Creative Spaces*]. Beirut: Dār al-'ilm lil-malāyīn, 1997.

Abu Jaber, May. 'Murder with Impunity: The Construction of Arab Masculinities and Honour Crimes' *al-Raida* 130–131.2 (2010):38–47.

Abudi, Dalya. *Mothers and Daughters in Arab Women's Literature: The Family Front.* Leiden: Brill Academic Publishers, 2011.

Abu-Lughod, Lila. *Veiled Sentiments: Honor and Poetry in a Bedouin Society.* Berkeley and Los Angeles: University of California Press, 1986.

Abu-Lughod, Lila. *Remaking Women: Feminism and Modernity in the Middle East.* Princeton: Princeton University Press, 1998.

Abu-Lughod, Lila. *Do Muslim Women Need Saving?* Cambridge, MA: Harvard University Press, 2013.

Accad, Evelyn. *Sexuality and War, Literary Masks of the Middle East*. New York: New York University Press, 1990.

Adams, Michele and Scott Coltrane. 'Boys and Men in Families: The Domestic Production of Gender, Power and Privilege' in *Handbook of Studies on Men and Masculinities*, edited by Michael Kimmel, Jeff Hearn and RW Connell, 230–49. Thousand Oaks CA: Sage, 2005.

Aghacy, Samira. 'Masculinity and Spatial Trajectories in the Contemporary Arabic Novel' in *Cairo Papers in Social Science* 33.1, edited by Helena Rizzo, 74–89. Cairo: Cairo University Press, 2010.

Aghacy, Samira. *Masculine Identity in the Fiction of the Arab East since 1967*. New York: Syracuse University Press, 2009.

Albers, Yvonne, Georges Khalil and Friederike Pannewick. 'Tracks and Traces of Literary Commitment – on Iltizām as an Ongoing Intellectual Project' in *Commitment and Beyond: Reflections on/of the Political in Arabic Literature since the 1940s, edited by* Friederike Pannewick and Georges Khalil, 9–29. Wiesbaden: Reichert Verlag, 2015.

Aldoughli, Rahaf. 'Interrogating the Constructions of Masculinist Protection and Militarism in the Syrian Constitution of 1973' *Journal of Middle Eastern Woman's Studies* 15.1 (2019): 48–74.

Allen, Roger, Hilary Kilpatrick and Ed de Moor, eds, *Love and Sexuality in Modern Arabic Literature*. London: Saqi Books, 1995.

Allen, Roger. 'The Arabic Short Story and the Status of Women' in *Love and Sexuality in Modern Arabic Literature,* edited by Roger Allen, Hilary Kilpatrick and Ed de Moor, 77–91. London: Saqi Books, 1995.

Allen, Roger. *The Arabic Novel: An Historical and Critical Introduction*. New York: Syracuse University Press, 1982.

Alsop, Rachel, Annette Fitzsimons and Kathleen Lenno. *Theorizing Gender: An Introduction*. Cambridge: Polity Press, 2002.

Amar, Paul. 'Middle East Masculinity Studies: Discourses of "Men in Crisis" Industries of Gender Revolution' *Journal of Middle Eastern Woman's Studies* 7.3 (2011): 36–70.

Ashour, Radwa, Ferial Ghazoul and Hasna reda-mekdashi, eds, *Arab Women Writers: A Critical Reference Guide 1873–1999*. Cairo: the American University in Cairo Press, 2008.

Badran, Margot and miriam cooke, eds, *Opening the Gates – An Anthology of Arab Feminist Writing*. 2nd edn Bloomington: Indiana University Press, 2004.

Bahoora, Haytham. 'The Figure of the Prostitute: Tajdid, and Masculinity in Anticolonial Literature of Iraq' *Journal of Middle Eastern Women's Studies* 11:1 (2015): 42–62.

Baker, Brian. *Masculinity in Fiction and Film: Representing Men in Popular Genres 1945-2000*. London: Continuum International Publishing Group, 2006.

Bal, Mieke. *Narratology: Introduction to the Theory of Narrative*. 2nd edn. Toronto: University of Toronto Press 1997.

al-Balkhī, Buthayna. 'al-Riwā'iyya al-sūriyya istaṭā'at an tafukk quyūd al-namaṭiyya wa tulāmis al-wāqiʻ bi-jiddiyya' ['The Syrian Female Novelist has managed to Break the Restraints of Form and Touch Reality with Seriousness']. 21/6-2014, al-Watan.

Barakat, Halim. *The Arab World: Society, Culture and State*. Berkeley CA: University of California Press, 1993.

al-Barghūthī, Saʻīd. 'al-Riwā'iyyāt al-sūriyyāt: naḥnu ṣawt al-muʻadhdhabīn' ['Syrian Female Novelists: We are the Voice of the Tormented']. *Dubay al-Thaqāfiyya* 3.26 (2007):34–37.

Beasley, Christine. 'Rethinking Hegemonic Masculinity in a Globalizing World' *Men and Masculinities*. 11.1 (2008): 86–103.

Berger, Maurice, Brian Wallis and Watson Simon, eds, *Constructing Masculinity*. New York: Routledge, 1995.

Beynon, John. *Masculinities and Culture*. Buckingham: Open University Press, 2002.

Birenbaum-Carmeli, Daphna and Maria Inhorn. 'Masculinity and Marginality: Palestinian Men's Struggles with Infertility in Israel and Lebanon' *Journal of Middle Eastern Women's Studies* 5.2 (2009): 23–52.

Bīṭār, Haifāʼ. *Yawmiyyāt muṭalliqa* [*Diaries of a Divorcing Woman*]. Algiers: Dār al-ʻArabiyya li-l-ʻUlūm –Nāshirūn, 2006. First published 1994.

Bīṭār, Haifāʼ. *Qabw al-ʻabbāsīn* [*The Abbaseen Basement*]. Damascus: Dār al-Ḥisād, 2006. First published 1995.

Bīṭār, Haifāʼ. *Afrāḥ ṣaghīra afrāḥ akhīra* [*Small Joys, Final Joys*]. Beirut: Arab Scientific Publishers Inc, 2008. First published 1998.

Bīṭār, Haifāʼ. *Nasr bi-janāḥ wāḥid* [*A One-winged Eagle*]. Beirut. Arab Scientific Publishers Inc, 2010. First published 1999.

Bourdieu, Pierre. *Den manliga dominansen* [*The Male Dominance*]. Translated by Boel Englund. Uddevalla: Daidalos AB, 1999.

Bonvillain, Nancy. *Women and Men: Cultural Constructs of Gender*. 4th edn Upper Saddle River: Pearson Prentice Hall, 2007.

Bouhdiba, Abdelwahab and Abdu Khal. 'Festivities of Violence: Circumcision and the Making of Men' in *Imagined Masculinities, Male Identity and Culture in the Modern Middle East*, edited by Emma Sinclair-Webb and Mai Ghoussoub, 19–33. London: Saqi Books, 2000.

Brod, Henry and Micheal Kaufman, eds, *Theorizing Masculinities*. Thousand Oaks CA: Sage, 1994.

Bulbeck, Chilla. *Re-Orienting Western Feminisms: Women's Diversity in a Postcolonial World*. Cambridge: Cambridge University Press, 1998.

Butler, Judith. *Gender Trouble – Feminism and the Subversion of Identity*. 4th edn, New York and London: Routledge, 2007.

Cohen-Mor, Dalya. *Fathers and Sons in the Arab Middle East*. New York: Palgrave Macmillan, 2013.

Clatterbaugh, Kenneth. 'What is Problematic about Masculinities' in *Feminism and Masculinities*, edited by Peter Murphy, 200–14. Oxford: Oxford University Press, 2004.

Collier, Richard. *Masculinity, Law and the Family*. London: Routledge, 1995.

Connell, RW *Gender and Power*. Stanford CA: Stanford University Press, 1987.

Connell, RW 'The Big Picture: Masculinities in Recent World History' *Theory and Society* 22.5 (1993): 597–623.

Connell, RW *Masculinities*. 2nd edn Cambridge: Polity Press, 2005.

Connell, RW 'Globalization, Imperialism, and Masculinities' in *Handbook of Studies on Men and Masculinities*, edited by Michael Kimmel, Jeff Hearn and RW Connell. Thousand Oaks CA: Sage, 2005. 71–90.

Connell, RW *Gender in World Perspective*. Cambridge: Polity Press, 2009.

Connell, RW and James W Messerschmidt. 'Hegemonic Masculinity: Rethinking the Concept' *Gender and Society* 19.6 (2005):829–59.

cooke, miriam. *War's Other Voices: Women Writers on the Lebanese Civil War*. New York: Syracuse University Press, 1987.

cooke, miriam. *Dissident Syria: Making Oppositional Arts Official*. Durham and London: Duke University Press, 2007.

cooke, miriam. 'Naguib Mahfouz: Men, and the Egyptian Underworld' in *Fictions of Masculinity: Crossing Cultures, Crossing Sexualities* edited by Peter Murphy, 96–120. New York and London: New York University Press, 1994.

Darvishpour, Mehrdad. 'Jämställdhet och invandrarmän' [Equality and Immigrant Men] in *Migration och etnicitet: Perspektiv på ett mångkulturellt Sverige* [*Migration and Ethnicity: Perspectives on a Multicultural Sweden*], edited by Mehrdad Darvishpour and Charles Westin, 395–419. Lund: Studentlitteratur AB, 2015.

Darwīsh, Usayma. *Shajarat al-ḥubb – ghābat al-aḥzān* [*Forest of Love: Tree of Sorrows*]. Beirut: Dār al-Ādāb, 2000.

Deebo, Mohammed. 'al-Būḥ al-jinsī fī al-riwāya al-sūriyya' [*The Sexual Confession in the Syrian Novel*]. Available at: www.aleftoday.info/node/5462, 1/4 –2013.

Deheuvels, Luc, Barbara Michalak-Pikulska and Paul Starkey, eds, *Intertextuality in Modern Arabic Literature since 1967: A Selection*. Manchester: Manchester University Press, 2006.

Demetriou, Demetrakis, Z. 'Connell's Concept of Hegemonic Masculinity: A Critique' *Theory and Society* 3.30 (2001): 337–61.

De Sondy, Amanullah. *The Crisis of Islamic Masculinity*. London: Bloomsbury, 2013.

bin Dhurayl, 'Adnān. 'al-Riwāya al-sūriyya al-mu'āṣira' ['The Contemporary Syrian Novel']. *al-Ma'rifa* 146 (1974): 23–50.

Donaldson, Mike. 'What is Hegemonic Masculinity?' *Theory and Society* 22.5 (1993):643–57.

Downing, John. 'Masculinity in Selected North African Films: An Exploration' in *Masculinity in African Literary and Cultural Texts,* edited by Helen Nabasuta Mugambi and Tuzyline Allan Jita, 116–29. Banbury: Ayebia Clarke Publishing Ltd, 2010.

al-Duyoob, Samar. 'Khaṣā'iṣ al-naqd al-nisā'ī: naqd al-riwāya fī sūriyā unmūdhajan' ['Specificities of Female Criticism: The Syrian Novel as an Example']. *al-Muthaqqaf* no 2226 26/9-2012. Available at: http://almothaqaf.com/index.php/araaa/67353.html (last accessed 1 January 2014).

Ekenstam, Claes, Jonas Frykman, Thomas Johansson, Jari Kuosmanen, Jens Ljunggren and Arne Nilsson, eds, *Rädd att Falla: Studier i Manlighet* [*Afraid to Fall: Studies in Manliness*]. Södertälje: Gidlunds Förlag, 1998.

Elad, Ami, ed. *Writer, Culture, Text: Studies in Modern Arabic Literature*. Fredericton: York Press Ltd, 1993.

El Feeki, Shereen. *Sex and the Citadel - Intimate Life in a Changing Arab World*. London: Chatto and Windus, 2013.

Elsadda, Hoda. *Gender, Nation and the Arabic Novel: Egypt 1892–2008*. New York: Syracuse University Press, 2012.

Elsadda, Hoda. 'Imagining the "New Man": Gender and Nation in Arab Literary Narratives in the Early Twentieth Century' *Journal of Middle Eastern Women's Studies* 3.2 (2007): 31–55.

Eriksson, Helena. *Husbands, Lovers and Dream Lovers: Masculinity and Female Desire in Women's Novels of the 1970s*. Stockholm: Almqvist och Wiksell, 1997.

Evans, Mary. *Gender: The Key Concepts*. Abingdon: Routledge, 2012.

Faqir, Fadia, ed. *In the House of Silence - Autobiographical Essays by Arab Women Writers*. Reading: Garnet Publishing Ltd, 1998.

Fatū, 'Isā. *'Adabiyyāt 'arabiyyāt: siyar wa dirāsāt* [*Arabic Female Writers: Bibliographies and Studies*]. Damascus: Manshūrāt jama'iyyat al-nadwa al-thaqāfiyya al-nisā'iyya, 1994.

Fayṣal, 'Āṭifa. 'Taḥawwulāt al-khiṭāb al-unthawī fī al-riwāya al-niswiyya fī sūriyā' [Transformations in the Feminine Discourse in the Female Authored Novel in Syria]. *Majallat jāmi'at dimashq* 21.1–2 (2005): 15–41.

Fayṣal, 'Āṭifa. 'al-Mādda al-ḥikā'iyya fī al-qiṣṣa al-qaṣīra fī sūriyā' ['The Narrative Material in the Short Story in Syria']. *Majallat jāmi'at dimashq* 23:2 (2007): 17–49.

al-Fayṣal, Samar, R. *Malāmiḥ fī al-riwāya al-sūriyya* [*Features of the Syrian Novel*]. Damascus: Ittiḥād al-kuttāb al-'arab, 1979.

al-Fayṣal, Samar, R. *Tajrubat al-riwāya al-sūriyya* [*The Experiment of the Syrian Novel*]. Damascus, Ittiḥād al-kuttāb al-'arab, 1985.

al-Fayṣal, Samar, R. *al-Ittijāh al-wāqi'ī fī al-riwāya al-'arabiyya al-sūriyya* [*The Trend of Realism in the Arabic Syrian Novel*]. Damascus: Ittiḥād al-kuttāb al-'arab, 1986.

al-Fayṣal, Samar, R. *Binā' al-riwāya al-'arabiyya al-sūriyya 1980-1990* [*The Construction of the Syrian Arabic Novel 1980–1990*]. Damascus: Ittiḥād al-kuttāb al-'arab, 1995.

al-Fayṣal, Samar, R. *Mu'jam al-qāṣṣāt wa al-riwā'iyyāt al-'arabiyyāt* [*Lexicon of Arabic Female Short Story Writers and Novelists*]. Tripoli: Jarus Bars, 1995.

al-Fayṣal, Samar, R. *al-Taṭawwur al-fannī li-l-ittijāh al-wāqi'ī fī al-riwāya al-'arabiyya al-sūriyya* [*The Artistic Development of the Trend of Realism in the Syrian Arabic Novel*]. Damascus: Dār al-Nafa'is, 1996.

al-Fayṣal, Samar, R. *al-Riwāya al-'arabiyya: binā' wa rū'ya* [*The Arabic Novel: Construction and Vision*]. Damascus: Ittiḥād al-kuttāb al-'arab, 2003.

Fernea, Robert. 'Gender, Sexuality and Patriarchy in Modern Egypt' *Critique: Critical Middle Eastern Studies* 12:2 (2003): 141–53.

Firat, Alexa. 'Cultural Battles on the Literary Field: From the Syrian Writers' Collective to the Last Days of Social Realism in Syria' *Middle Eastern Literatures* 18.2 (2015):153–76.

Fjelkestam, Kristina, Helena Hill and David Tjeder, eds, *Kvinnorna gör mannen: maskulinitetskonstruktioner i kvinnors text och bild 1500-2000* [*Women Make the Man: Masculinity Construction in Women's Texts and Pictures, 1500–2000*]. Göteborg: Makadam, 2013.

Fjellestad, Danuta. *Eros, Logos and (Fictional) Masculinity*. Uppsala: Acta Universitatis Upsaliensis, Studia Anglistica Upsaliensia, 1998.

Forslid, Torbjörn. *Varför män? om manlighet i litteraturen* [*Why Men? About Manliness in Literature*]. Stockholm: Carlsson Bokförlag, 2006.

Frantz, Sarah and Katharina Rennhak, eds, *Women Constructing Men: Female Novelists and their Male Characters 1750–2000*. Lanham MD: Lexington Books, 2010.

Fähndrich, Hartmut. 'Fathers and Husbands: Tyrants and Victims in some Autobiographical and Semi-Autobiographical Works from the Arab World' in *Love and Sexuality in Modern Arabic Literature,* edited by Ed de Moor, Hilary Kilpatrick and Roger Allen 106–16. London: Saqi Books, 1995.

Gallagher, Sally. *Making Do in Damascus: Navigating a Generation of Change in Family and Work*. New York: Syracuse University Press, 2012.

Gerami, Shahin. 'Islamist Masculinity and Muslim Masculinities' in *Handbook of Studies on Men and Masculinities*, edited by Michael Kimmel, Jeff Hearn and RW Connell, 448–58. Thousand Oaks CA: Sage, 2005.

Ghannam, Farah. *Live and Die Like a Man: Gender Dynamics in Urban Egypt*. Stanford: Stanford University Press, 2013.

Gilmore, David, G. *Manhood in the Making: Cultural Concepts of Masculinity*. New Haven and London: Yale University Press, 1990.

Gullvåg Holter, Oystein. 'Social Theories for Researching Men and Masculinities: Direct Gender Hierarchy and Structural Inequality' in *Handbook of Studies on Men and Masculinities*, edited by Michael Kimmel, Jeff Hearn and RW Connell, 15–35. Thousand Oaks CA: Sage, 2005.

Hadidi, Subhi and Iman al-Qadi. 'Syria', in *Arab Women Writers: A Critical Reference Guide 1873–1999*, ed. Radwa Ashour, Ferial Ghazoul and Hasna Reda-Mekdashi (Cairo: the American University in Cairo Press, 2008), 60–98.

Haddad, Jumana. *Sūbermān 'Arabī* [*Superman is an Arab*]. Beirut: Dār al-Sāqī, 2014.

Hadeed, Khalid. 'Homosexuality and Epistemic Closure in Modern Arabic Literature' *IJMES* 45:2 (2013): 271–91.

Hafez, Sabry. *The Genesis of Arabic Narrative Discourse: A Study in the Sociology of Modern Arabic Literature*. London: Saqi Books, 1993.

al-Ḥaffār al-Kuzbarī, Salmā. *'Aynān min Ishbīliya* [*Sevillan Eyes*]. Beirut: Dār al-kātib al-'arabī, 1965.

Halberstam, Judith. *Female Masculinity*. Durham: Duke University Press, 1998.

ibn Ḥamza, Ḥusayn. 'Nabrāt jadīda fī al-riwāya al-sūriyyā: al-tajrīb ba'īdan 'an al-aydīūlūjīā' [*New Tones in the Syrian Novel: Experimenting Far from Ideology*]. Available at: www.al-akhbar.com/node/86049 (last accessed 15 April 2013).

Hanna, Kifah. *Feminism and Avant-Garde Aesthetics in the Levantine Novel*. New York: Palgrave Macmillan, 2016.

al-Ḥasan, Ahmad Jamīl. 'Na'mat Khālid: Jar'at al-mar'a wa al-būḥ bi-ra'ashāt al-jasad' ['Na'mat Khālid: The Courage of Woman and the Confession of the Body's Trembles']. *al-Mawqif al-adabī* 41.496 (2012): 182–87.

Ḥasan, Rūla. A Series of 38 Articles on Women Writers in Syria, 'al-mashhad al-riwā'ī al-niswī fī sūriya'. ['The Female Novelistic Scene in Syria'] Tishrīn Newspaper 2011–2012.

Hayward, Sally. '(Dis)enabeling Masculinities: The Word and the Body, Class Politics and Male Sexuality in El Saadawi's *God Dies by the Nile*' in *African Masculinities: Men in Africa from the Late Nineteenth Century to the Present*. Lahoucine Ouzgane and Robert Morrell, eds, Gordonsville: Palgrave Macmillan, 2005. 137–51.

Haywood, Chris and Mairtin Mac an Ghaill. *Men and Masculinities: Theory, Research and Social Practice*. Buckingham: Open University Press, 2003.

Hearn, Jeff. 'From Hegemonic Masculinity to the Hegemony of Men' *Feminist Theory* 5:1 (2004): 49–72.

Herman, Luc and Bart Vervaeck. *Handbook of Narrative Analysis*. Lincoln and London: University of Nebraska Press, 2005.

Hinnebusch, Raymond, A. *Syria: Revolution from Above*. New York: Routledge, 2001.

Hinnebusch, Raymond, A. and Tina Zintl, eds, *Syria: From Revolution to Revolt*. vol 1. New York: Syracuse University Press, 2015.

Hobbs, Alex. 'Masculinity Studies and Literature' *Literature Compass* 10:4 (2013): 383–95.

Horlacher, Stefan, ed., *Constructions of Masculinity in British Literature from the Middle Ages to the Present*. Basingstoke: Palgrave Macmillan, 2011.

Horlacher, Stefan, ed. *Configuring Masculinity in Theory and Literary Practice*. Lieden: Brill, 2015.

Howson, Richard. *Challenging Hegemonic Masculinity*. London: Routledge, 2006.

Ibrahīm, Ali Najīb. *Jamāliyyāt al-riwāya: dirāsa fī al-riwāya al-wāqi'iyya al-sūriyya al-mu'āṣira* [Aesthetics of the Novel: A Study in the Contemporary Syrian Realistic Novel]. Damascus: Dār al-Yanābī, 1994.

al-'Īd, Yumnā. *Fann al-riwāya al-'arabiyya: bayn khuṣūṣiyyat al-ḥikāya wa tamayyuz al-khiṭāb* [The Art of the Arabic Novel: Between the Specificities of the Narrative and the Distinction of the Discourse]. Beirut: Dār al-Adāb, 1998.

al-Idlibī, Ulfat. *Dimashq yā basmat al-ḥuzn* [*Damascus, O Smile of Sadness*]. Damascus: Manshūrāt wizārat al-thaqāfa wa al-irshād al-qawmī, 1980.

al-Idlibī, Ulfat. *Ḥikāyat jaddī* [*My Grandfather's Tale*]. Damascus: Dār al-Ṭalās, 1999. First published 1990.

Inhorn, Marcia, C. *The New Arab Man: Emergent Masculinities, Technologies and Islam in the Middle East*. Princeton CT: Princeton University Press, 2012.

Jabbūr, Zuhar. 'Namādhij riwā'iyya li-kuttāb min al-lādhaqiyya' ['Examples of Novels from Lattakian Writers']. *al-Mawqif al-adabī* 42.500 (2012): 213–23.

Jacob, Wilson Chacko. 'The Turban, The Tarbush and the Top Hat: Masculinity, Modernity and National Identity in Interwar Egypt' *al-Raida* 21:104–5 (2004): 23–37.

Jacob, Wilson Chacko. *Working Out Egypt: Effendi Masculinity and Subject Formation in Colonial Modernity 1870–1940*. Durham and London: Duke University Press, 2011.

Ja'far, Nadhīr. 'al-Khiṭāb al-riwā'ī al-niswī: 'ataba jadīda lil-takhyīl' ['The New Female Novelistic Discourse: New Thresholds for Imagination']. 27/3-2011, *Tishrīn*.

Jarrāḥ, Amal. *al-Riwāya al-mal'ūna* [*The Cursed Novel*]. Beirut: Dār al-Sāqī, 2010. First published 1968.

Joubin, Rebecca. *The Politics of Love: Sexuality, Gender, and Marriage in Syrian Television Drama*. Lanham MD: Lexington Books, 2013.

Joubin, Rebecca. 'The Politics of the Qabaday (Tough Man) and the Changing Father Figure in Syrian Television Drama' *Journal of Middle Eastern Women's Studies* 12.1 (2016): 50–67.

Joseph, Suad. 'Thinking Intentionality: Arab Women's Subjectivity and its Discontents' *Journal of Middle Eastern Women's Studies* 8.2 (2012): 1–25.

Joseph, Suad and Susan Slyomovics, eds, *Women and Power in the Middle East*. Philadelphia PA: University of Philadelphia Press, 2001.

al-Jurf, Maysūn. *Binā' ṣūrat al-shakhṣiyya al-dhukūriyya fī al-riwāya al- 'arabiyya al-sūriyya* [*Building the Image of the Masculine Character in the Arabic Syrian Novel*]. Damascus: Dār al-Ṣafaḥāt, 2014.

Kahf, Mohja. 'The Silences of Contemporary Syrian Literature' *World Literature Today*. 75:2 (2001): 225–36.

Kandiyoti, Deniz. 'Bargaining with Patriarchy' *Gender and Society* 2:3 (1988): 274–90.

Kandiyoti, Deniz. 'Islam and Patriarchy: A Comparative Perspective' in *Women in Middle Eastern History: Shifting Boundaries in Sex and Gender*, edited by Beth Baron and Nikki R Keddie, 23–43. New Haven CT: Yale University Press, 1991.

Kandiyoti, Deniz. 'The Paradoxes of Masculinity: Some Thoughts on Segregated Societies' in *Dislocating Masculinities: Comparative Ethnographies*, edited by Andrea Cornwall and Nancy Lindisfarne, 196–213. London: Routledge, 1994.

Kandiyoti, Deniz. ed. *Gendering the Middle East: Emerging Perspectives* New York: Syracuse University Press, 1996.

Kandiyoti, Deniz. 'Gender, Power and Contestation: Rethinking Bargaining with Patriarchy' in *Feminist Visions of Development: Gender Analysis and Policy*, edited by Ruth Pearson and Cecile Jackson, 135–53. Abingdon: Routledge, 1998. 135–53.

Kegan Gardiner, Judith. 'Men, Masculinities, and Feminist Theory' in *Handbook of Studies on Men and Masculinities*, edited by Michael Kimmel, Jeff Hearn and RW Connell, 35–51. Thousand Oaks CA: Sage, 2005.

Khan, Jack, S. *An Introduction to Masculinities*. Chichester: Wiley-Blackwell, 2009.
al-Khānī, Malāḥa. *Khaṭawāt fī al-ḍabāb* [*Steps in the Fog*]. Damascus: Ittiḥād al-kuttāb al-ʿarab, 1984.
al-Khānī, Malāḥa. *Banāt ḥāratina* [*The Girls of Our Neighbourhood*]. Damascus: Ittiḥād al-kuttāb al-ʿarab, 1998.
al-Khaṭīb, Ḥusām. 'Ḥawl al-riwāya al-nisāi'yya fī sūriyā' ['About the Female Novel in Syria']. *al-Maʿrifa* 166 (1975):79–94.
al-Khaṭīb, Ḥusām. 'Ḥawl al-riwāya al-tāliya fī sūriyā: *Layla wāḥida*' ['About the Coming Novel in Syria: *Layla wāḥida*']. *al-Maʿrifa* 168 (1976): 47–60.
al-Khaṭīb, Ḥusām. 'al-Riwāya al-tāliya fī sūriyā:3' ['The Coming Novel in Syria: 3']. *al-Maʿrifa* 169 (1976): 77–89.
al-Khush, Umayma. *al-Tawq* [*Longing*]. Beirut: Dār al-kunūz al-ʿarabiyya, 1997.
Khūrī, Kūlīt. *Ayyām maʿahu* [*Days with Him*]. Beirut: al-Maktab al-tijārī lil-ṭibāʾa wa al-tawzīʿ wa al-nashr, 1959.
Khūrī, Kūlīt. *Layla wāḥida* [*One Night*]. Damascus: Dār al-Fārisa, 2002. First published 1961.
Khūst, Nadya. *Ḥubb fī bilād al-shām* [*Love in the Levant*]. Damascus: Ittiḥād al-kuttāb al-ʿarab, 1995.
Khūst, Nadya. *Aʿāṣīr fī bilād al-shām* [*Cyclones in the Levant*]. Damascus: Ittiḥād al-kuttāb al-ʿarab, 1998.
Khūst, Nadya. *Shuhadāʾ wa ʿushshāq fī bilād al-shām* [*Martyrs and Lovers in the Levant*]. Damascus: Ittiḥād al-kuttāb al-ʿarab, 2000.
Kilānī, Qamar. *Bustān al-karaz* [*The Cherry Orchard*]. Damascus: Dār al-athwār lil-ṭibāʾa, 1977.
Kilānī, Qamar. *al- Dawwāma* [*The Whirlwind*]. Damascus: Manshūrāt wizārat al-thaqāfa wa al-irshād al-qawmī, 1983.
Kimmel, Michael, ed. *Changing Men: New Directions in Research on Men and Masculinities*. Thousand Oaks CA: Sage Publications, 1987.
Kimmel, Michael, ed. *History of Men: Essays on the History of American and British Masculinities*. Ithaca: State University of New York Press, 2005.
Kimmel, Michael, ed. *Misframing Men: The Politics of Contemporary Masculinities*. Piscataway: Rutgers University Press, 2010.
Kimmel, Michael, ed. *Manhood in America: A Cultural History*. 3rd edn. Oxford: Oxford University Press, 2011.
Kimmel, Michael, Jeff Hearn and RW Connell, eds, *Handbook of Studies on Men and Masculinities*. Thousand Oaks CA: Sage, 2005.
Kirām, Zuhūr. *al-Sard al-nisāʾī al-ʿarabī: muqāraba fī al-mafhūm wa al-khiṭāb* [*Female Arabic Narration: A View on Concepts and Discourse*]. Casa Blanca: Sharikat al-nashr wa al-tawzīʾ al-madāris, 2004.
Knights, Ben. *Writing Masculinities: Male Narratives in Twentieth Century Fiction*. London: Macmillan, 1999.
Kuosmanen, Jari. Männens resor i det moderna [Men's Travels in Modernity]. In *Rädd att Falla: Studier i Manlighet* [*Afraid to Fall: Studies in Manliness*], edited by Claes

Ekenstam Thomas Johansson and Jari Kuosmanen, 237–44. Södertälje: Gidlunds Förlag, 1998.

Lagrange, Frédéric. 'Male Homosexuality in Modern Arabic Literature' in *Imagined Masculinities: Male Identity and Culture in the Modern Middle East*, edited by Mai Ghoussoub and Emma Sinclair-Webb. 169–99. London: Saqi Books, 2000.

Lang, Robert and Maher Ben Moussa. 'Choosing to Be "Not a Man": Masculine Anxiety in Nouri Bouzid's *Rih Essed/Man of Ashes*' in *Masculinity: Bodies, Movies, Culture*, edited by Peter Lehman, 81–95, New York: Routledge, 2001.

Lanser, Susan. *Fictions of Authority – Women Writers and Narrative Voice*. New York: Cornell University Press, 1992.

Lawson, Fred, ed. *Demystifying Syria*. London: Saqi Books, 2009.

Lehman, Peter. *Running Scared: Masculinity and the Representation of the Male Body*. Philadelphia: Temple University Press, 1993.

Lehman, Peter. ed. *Masculinity: Bodies, Movies, Culture*. New York: Routledge, 2001.

Lei Sparre, Sara. 'Educated Women in Syria: Servants of the State, or Nurturers of the Family?' *Critique: Critical Middle Eastern Studies* 17:1 (2008): 3–20.

Lesch, David, W. *The New Lion of Damascus: Bashar al-Assad and Modern Syria*. New Haven CT: Yale University Press, 2005.

Lindisfarne, Nancy. 'Variant Masculinities, Variant Virginities: Rethinking Honour and Shame' in *Dislocating Masculinities: Comparative Ethnographies*, edited by Andrea Cornwall and Nancy Lindisfarne, 82–97. London: Routledge, 1994.

Lukacs, George. *Realismens seger: litteraturkritiska essäer* [*The Victory of Realism: Essays on Literary Criticism*]. Lund: Arkiv, 1983.

Mac an Ghaill, Mairtin. *The Making of Men: Masculinities, Sexualities and Schooling*. Buckingham: Open University Press, 1994.

Mac an Ghaill, Mairtin. *Understanding Masculinities: Social Relations and Cultural Arenas*. Buckingham: Open University Press, 1996.

MacInnes, John. *The End of Masculinity: The Confusion of Sexual Genesis and Sexual Difference in Modern Society*. Buckingham: Open University Press, 1998.

Mahadeen, Ebtihal. 'Arabizing "Masculinity"' *Journal of Middle Eastern Women's Studies* 12.3 (2016): 450–52.

al-Mahūs, Manṣūr. 'Ṣūrat al-rajul fī al-kitāba al-niswiyya al-ṣaʿudiyya' ['The Image of Man in Saudi Women's Writing']. PhD dissertation, University of Alexandria, 2015.

Majaj Suheir, Lisa, Paula Sunderman and Therese Saliba, eds, *Intersections: Gender, Nation, and Community in Arab Women's Novels*. New York: Syracuse University Press, 2002.

Maktabi, Rania. 'Female Citizenship in Syria: Framing the 2009 Controversy over Personal Status Law' in *Syria from Reform to Revolution*, vol 1, edited by Raymond Hinnenbusch and Tina Zintl, 176–99. New York: Syracuse University Press, 2015.

Maktabi, Rania. 'Gender, Family Law and Citizenship in Syria' *Citizenship Studies* 14:5 (2010): 557–72.

Maoz, Moshe and Joseph Ginat, eds, *Modern Syria: From Ottoman Rule to Pivotal Role in the Middle East*. Brighton: Sussex Academic Press, 1999.

Marsiglio, William and Joseph H Pleck. 'Fatherhood and Masculinities' in *Handbook of Studies on Men and Masculinities*, edited by Michael Kimmel, Jeff Hearn and RW Connell, 249–70. Thousand Oaks CA: Sage, 2005.

Mashūl, Ahmad. 'Azmat al-baṭal al-thawrī fī al-riwāya al-'arabiyya' ['The Crisis of the Revolutionary Hero in the Arabic Novel']. *al-Ma'rifa* 277 (1985): 66–92.

Massad, Joseph. *Desiring Arabs*. Chicago: The University of Chicago Press, 2007.

Maurer, Shawn Lisa. 'Happy Men?: Mid-Eighteenth Century Women Writers and Ideal Masculinity' in *Women Constructing Men: Female Novelists and Their Male Characters 1750–2000*, edited by Sarah Frantz and Katharina Rennhak, 11–31. Lanham MD: Lexington Books, 2011.

MENA Development Report. 'Gender and Development in the Middle East and North Africa – Women in the Public Sphere' Washington: The World Bank, 2004.

Mernissi, Fatima. *Beyond the Veil: Male–Female Dynamics in Muslim Society.* London: Saqi Books, 2011.

Meyer, Stefan, G. *The Experimental Arabic Novel – Postcolonial Literary Modernism in the Levant*. Albany: State University of New York Press, 2001.

Morgan, David. *Discovering Men: Critical Studies on Men and Masculinities*. New York: Routledge, 1992.

Mugambi Nabasuta, Helen and Tuzyline Allan Jita, eds, *Masculinities in African Literary and Cultural Texts*. Banbury: Ayebia Clarke Publishing Ltd, 2010.

Mugambi Nabasuta, Helen and Tuzyline Allan Jita, eds, 'Reading Masculinities in a Feminist Text: Tsitsi Dangarembga's *Nervous Conditions*' in *Twelve Best Books by African Women: Critical Readings*, edited by Chikwenye Okonjo Ogunyemi and Tuzyline Jita Allan, 199–220. Athens: Ohio University Press, 2009.

Muhsin, Yousef. 'Ṣinā'at al-rujūla al-mutakhayyila fī mujtama'āt al-sharq al-awsaṭ' ['The Construction of Imaginary Masculinity in the Societies of the Middle East']. Available at: www.qadita.net/2012/11/04/manhood/ (last accessed 6 July 2013).

Mulry, David. 'Lost in the Haze: Joseph Conrad, the Ruined Maid and the Male Gaze' *South Central Review* 31.1 (2014): 74–98.

Mulvey, Laura. 'Visual Pleasure and Narrative Cinema' *Screen* 16.3 (1975): 6–18.

Mulvey, Laura. Afterthoughts on "Visual Pleasure and Narrative Cinema" inspired by King Vidor's Duel in the Sun' in *Visual and other Pleasures*, edited by Laura Mulvey, 29–38. Gordonsville: Palgrave Macmillan, 1989.

Murphy, Peter, ed. *Fictions of Masculinity: Crossing Cultures, Crossing Sexualities*. New York and London: New York University Press, 1994.

Murphy, Peter, ed.*Feminism and Masculinities*. Oxford: Oxford University Press Inc, 2004.

al-Mūsā, Khalīl. 'al-Kitāba: kitābat al-ikhtilāf, kitābat al-mar'a' ['Writing: The Writing of Difference, the Writing of Women']. *al-Mawqif al-adabī* 42.500 (2012): 17–31.

al-Musālima, In'ām. *al-Ḥubb wa al-waḥl* [*Love and Mud*]. Damascus: Dār al-thaqāfa, 1963.

al-Musawi, Muhsin. *The Postcolonial Arabic Novel: Debating Ambivalence*. Leiden: Brill, 2003.

Na'na', Ḥamīda. *al-Waṭan fī al-'aynayn* [*The Homeland in a Pair of Eyes*]. Beirut: Dār al-Ādāb, 1979.

Na'na', Ḥamīda. *Man yajru' 'alā al-shawq* [*Who Dares to Long*]. Beirut: Dār al-Ādāb, 1989.

Neuwirth, Angelika, Andreas Pflitsch and Barbara Winckler, eds, *Arabic Literature: Postmodern Perspectives*. London: Saqi Books, 2010.

Nuwaylātī, Hiyām and Umm 'Isām. *Arṣifat al-sa'm* [*Sidewalks of Tedium*]. Damascus: National Security Press, 1973.

Nilsson, Arne. 'Modernisering och manlig homosexualitet: Svenska storstadsmän kring mitten av 1900-talet' [Modernising and Male Homosexuality: Swedish City Men Around the Middle of the 20th Century]. In *Rädd att falla: Studier i manlighet* [*Afraid to Fall: Studies in Manliness*], Claes Ekenstam 183–237. Södertälje: Gidlunds förlag, 1998.

Nilsson, Bo. *Maskulinitet: Representation, Ideologi och Retorik* [*Masculinity: Representation, Ideology and Rhetorics*]. Umeå: Boréa, 1999.

Nordberg, Marie. 'Kvinnlig maskulinitet och manlig femininitet: en möjlighet att överskrida könsdikotomin?' ['Female Masculinity and Male Femininity: A Possibility to Bridge the Gender Dichotomy?']. *Kvinnovetenskaplig tidskrift* 1–2 (2004): 47–65.

Nordberg, Marie. *Jämställdhetens spjutspets?: Manliga arbetstagare i kvinnoyrken, jämställdhet, maskulinitet, femininitet och heteronormativitet* [*Cutting Edge Equality? Male Employees in Female Occupations, Equality, Masculinity, Femininity and Heteronormativity*]. Göteborg: Arkipelag, 2005.

Ouzgane, Lahoucine, ed. *Islamic Masculinities*. London: Zed Books Ltd, 2006.

Ouzgane, Lahoucine and Robert Morrell, eds, *African Masculinities: Men in Africa from the Late Nineteenth Century to the Present*. Gordonsville: Palgrave Macmillan, 2005.

Ouyang, Wen-chin. *Poetics of Love in the Arabic Novel: Nation-State, Modernity and Tradition*. Edinburgh: Edinburgh University Press, 2012.

Page, Ruth. 'Feminist Narratology? Literary and Linguistic Perspectives on Gender and Narrativity' *Literature and Language* 12.1 (2003): 43–56.

Page, Ruth. '*Literary and Linguistic Approaches to Feminist Narratology*. Basingstoke: Palgrave Macmillan, 2006.

Pannewick, Friederike and Georges Khalil, eds, *Commitment and Beyond: Reflections on/of the Political in Arabic Literature since the 1940s*. Wiesbaden: Reichert Verlag, 2015.

Pearce, Margaret. 'Morpho Eugenia: Problems with the Male Gaze' *Critique Studies in Contemporary Fiction* 40:4 (1999): 399–411.

Pearson, Sara. 'Constructing Masculine Narrative: Charlotte Bronte's the Professor' in *Women Constructing Men, Female Novelists and their Male Characters 1750–2000*, edited by Sarah Frantz, and Katharina Rennhak, 83–110. Lanham MD: Lexington Books, 2010.

Petersen, Alan. 'Research on Men and Masculinities: Some Implications of Recent Theory for Future Work' *Men and Masculinities* 6:1 (2003): 54–69.

Pringle, Keith, Michael Flood, Judith Kegan Gardiner and Bob Pease, eds, *International Encyclopaedia of Men and Masculinities*. London: Taylor and Francis, 2007.

Qabbānī, Ghāliya. *Ṣabāḥ Imra'a* [*A Woman's Morning*]. Casablanca: al-Markaz al-thaqāfī al-'arabī, 2000.

Qaddūr, 'Umar. 'al-Riwāya al-sūriyya al-jadīda: ẓāhira ibdā 'iyya am ẓāhira 'ilāmiyya?' [The New Syrian Novel: A Creative Phenomenon or a Media Phenomenon?]. *al-Adāb* vol 9-10 (2009). Available at: http://adabmag.com/node/247 (last accessed 15 December 2013).

al-Qāḍī, Imān. 'al-Ishām al-niswī fī al-riwāya al-'arabiyya' ['Feminine Contribution in the Arabic Novel']. *al-Ma'rifa*, nos. 324–25. (1990): 76–124.

al-Qāḍī, Imān. *al-riwaya al-niswiyya fī bilād al-Shām: al-simāt al-nafsiyya wa al-fanniyya 1950–1985* [*The Female Novel in the Levant: Psychological and Artistic Characteristics 1950–1985*]. Damascus: Dār al-ahālī lil-ṭibā'a wa al-nashr wa al-tawzī', 1991.

al-Qāḍī, Imān. 'al-riwaya al-niswiyya al-sūriyya fī saba'at 'uqūd': jadaliyyat al-khāṣ wa al-'ām ['The Syrian Female Novel in Seven Decades: The Argument between the Personal and the Public']. al-Kalima, no 156. (2020):np.

Qarānayā, Muḥammad. 'al-Unūtha wa al-dhukūra fī riwāyat *Ḥubb fī bilād al-shām*' ['Femininity and Masculinity in the Novel *Love in the Levant*']. *al-Mawqif al-adabī* 43.517 (2014): 191–97.

Qaṣabjī, Ḍiyā'. *Imra'a fī dā'irat al-khawf* [*Woman in a Circle of Fear*]. Tripoli: al-Munshā al-'āma lil-nashr wa al-tawzī' wa al-'ilān, 1985.

Quataert, Donald, and Richard Antoun, eds, *Syria: Society, Culture, and Polity*. Albany: State University of New York Press, 1991.

al-Raḥbī, Mayya. *Furāt* [*Euphrates*]. Damascus: al-Ahālī lil- ṭibā'a wa al-nashr wa al-tawzī', 1998.

al-Raḥbī, Mayya. *al-Niswiyya: mafāhīm wa qaḍāyā* [*Feminism: Concepts and Issues*]. Damascus: al-Raḥba lil-nashr wa al-tawzi', 2014.

al-Raida. Special Issue on Masculinity in the Middle East. Lebanese American University, XXI: 104-105 (2004).

al-Raida. Special Issue on Gender Based Violence in the Arab World. Lebanese American University. 131–32 (2010).

al-Rasheed, Madawi. *A Most Masculine State: Gender, Politics and Religion in Saudi Arabia*. New York: Cambridge University Press, 2013.

Rashū, Mārī. *Harwala fawqa saqī' tūlīdū* [*Hurrying over the Frost of Toledo*]. Damascus: D A L lil-nashr wa al-tawzī', 2011. First published 1993.

Rizzo, Helen, ed. 'Masculinities in Egypt and the Arab World: Historical, Literary and Social Sciences Perspectives' *Cairo Papers in Social Sciences* 33.1 (2010).

Robinson, Sally. *Engendering the Subject: Gender and Self-Representation in Contemporary Women's Fiction*. Albany: SUNY press, 1991.

Roded, Ruth. 'Alternative Images of the Prophet Muhammad's Virility' *Islamic Masculinities*. Lahoucine Ouzgane, ed. 57–72, London: Zed Books Ltd, 2006.

Rogoff, Irit, and David van Leer. 'Afterthoughts: A Dossier on Masculinities' *Theory and Society* 22.5 (1993): 739–62.

Rosen, David. *The Changing Fictions of Masculinity*. Chicago IL: University of Illinois Press, 1993.

El-Rouayheb, Khaled. *Before Homosexuality in the Arab–Islamic World: 1500–1800*. Chicago: University of Chicago Press, 2005.

Rowland, Antony, Emma Liggins and Eriks Uskalis, eds, *Signs of Masculinity: Men in Literature 1700 to the Present*. Amsterdam: Rodopi, 1998.

al-Saʿāfīn, Ibrahīm. *Taṭawwur al-riwāya al- ʿarabiyya al-ḥadītha fī bilād al-shām 1870–1967* [*The Development of the Modern Arabic Novel in the Levant 1870–1967*]. 2nd edn. Beirut: Dār al-Manāhil, 1987.

Said, Edward. *The World, the Text and the Critic*. Cambridge MA: Harvard University Press, 1983.

Said, Edward. *Culture and Imperialism*. London: Chatto and Windus, 1993.

Sakākīnī, Widād. 'Taʿqīb ʿalā dirāsat al-riwāya al-nisāʾiyya fī sūriyā' ['A Commentary on the Study of Women's Novels in Syria']. *al-Maʿrifa* 168 (1976): 187–89.

Salamandra, Christa. *A New Old Damascus: Authenticity and Distinction in Urban Syria*. Bloomington: Indiana, 2004.

Salamandra, Christa. and Leif Stenberg, eds, *Syria from Reform to Revolt: Culture, Society and Religion*. New York: Syracuse University Press, 2015.

Ṣalih, Nidal. *al-Qiṣṣa al-qaṣīra fī sūriyā: qiṣaṣ al-tisʿīniyāt* [*The Short Story in Syria: The Stories of the Nineties*]. Damascus, Ittiḥād al-kuttāb al-ʿArab, 2005.

al-Sammān, Ghāda. *Bayrūt 75* [*Beirut 75*]. Beirut: Dār al-Ādāb, 1975.

al-Sammān, Ghāda. *Kawābīs Bayrūt* [*Beirut Nightmares*]. Beirut: Dār al-Ādāb, 1976.

al-Sammān, Ghāda. *al-Riwāya al-mustaḥīla: fusayfusāʾ Dimashqiyya* [*The Impossible Novel: A Damascene Mosaic*]. Beirut: Manshūrāt Ghāda al-Sammān, 1997.

al-Samman, Hanadi. 'Out of the Closet: Representation of Homosexuals and Lesbians in Contemporary Arabic Literature' *Journal of Arabic Literature* 39.2 (2008): 270–310.

al-Samman, Hanadi. *Anxiety of Erasure: Trauma, Authorship and the Diaspora in Arab Women's Writings*. New York: Syracuse University Press, 2015.

Sammāq, Fayṣal. 'al- Wāqiʿiyya fī al-riwāya al-sūriyya al-muʿāṣira' ['Realism in the Contemporary Syrian Novel']. *al-Maʿrifa* 211 (1979): 159–77.

Schoene-Harwood, Berthold. *Writing Men: Literary Masculinities from Frankenstein to the New Man*. Edinburgh: Edinburgh University Press, 1999.

Schor, Naomi. 'The Portrait of a Gentleman: Representing Men in (French) Women's Writings', *Representations* vol. 20, Fall (1987):113–33.

Sedgwick Kosofsky, Eve. 'Gosh, Boy George, You Must be Awfully Secure in Your Masculinity' in *Constructing Masculinity,* edited by Maurice Berger, Brian Wallis and Simon Watson, 11–20. New York: Routledge, 1995.

Seidler, Victor, J. *Transforming Masculinities: Men, Culture, Bodies, Power, Sex and Love.* Abingdon: Routledge, 2006.

Segal, Lynne. 'Changing Men: Masculinities in Context' *Theory and Society* 22.5 (1993): 625–41.

Shaaban, Bouthaina. 'Persisting Contradictions: Muslim Women in Syria' in *Women in Muslim Societies: Diversity within Unity*, edited by Herbert L Bodman and Nayereh Tohidi, 101–19. Colorado: Lynne Rienner Publishers Inc, 1998.

Shaaban, Bouthaina. *Voices Revealed: Arab Women Novelists 1898–2000.* London: Lynne Reiner Publishers Inc, 2009.

Sharābī, Hishām. *al-Naqd al-ḥaḍārī lil-mujtama ʿal- ʿarabī fī nihāyat al-qarn al-ʿashrīn* [*Social Criticism of the Arabic Society at the end of the 20th century*]. Beirut: Markaz dirasāt al-wahda al-Arabiyya, 1999.

al-Shimālī, Sāmir Anwar. *Wujūh wa muwājahāt min al-qiṣṣa al-qaṣīra al-sūriyya fī al-ʿaqd al-awwal min al-qarn al-ḥādī wa al-ʿashrīn* [*Faces and Encounters in the Syrian Short Story in the First Decennium of the 21st Century*]. Damascus: Ittiḥād al-kuttāb al-ʿarab, 2011.

Showalter, Elaine. *A Literature of their Own: British Women Writers from Charlotte Bronte to Doris Lessing.* London: Virago, 2009.

Shuḥayyid, Jamāl and Heidi Toelle. al-riwāya al-sūriyya al-muʿāṣira: al-judhūr al-thaqāfiyya wa al-taqaniyyāt al-riwā'iyya al-jadīda[*The Contemporary Syrian Novel, the Cultural Roots and New Novelistic Techniques*]. Damascus: al-ma ʿhad al-faransī li-l-dirāsāt al-ʿarabiyya, 2001.

Sinclair-Webb, Emma and Mai Ghoussoub, eds, *Imagined Masculinities: Male Identity and Culture in the Modern Middle East.* London: Saqi Books, 2000.

Sirees, Nihad: *al-Riwāya al-sūriyya: injāzātuhā wa maṣā'ib allati qad taqif fī wajhiha* ['The Syrian Novel: Its Achievements and the Problems Standing in its Way']. Available at: http://nihadsirees.com/2012-07-02-08-08-28/55-2012-07-03-12-34-55.html (last accessed 20 December 2013).

Snow, Edward. 'Theorizing the Male Gaze: Some Problems' *Representations* no 25. (Winter, 1989): 30–41.

Starkey, Paul. *Modern Arabic Literature.* Washington DC: Georgetown University Press, 2006.

Sulaymān, Nabīl. 'al-Riwāya al-ʿarabiyya wa al-mujtamaʿ al-madanī' ['The Arabic Novel and Civic Society']. *ʿAlāmāt*, 23, nd.

Sulaymān, Nabīl. *Fī al-'ibdāʿ wa al-naqd* [*On Creativity and Criticism*]. Latakia: Dār al-ḥiwār, 1989.

Sulaymān, Nabīl. *Ḥiwāriyyat al-wāqiʿ wa al-khiṭāb al-riwā'ī* [*The Conversational Nature of Reality and the Discourse of the Novel*]. 2nd edn Lataqia: Dār al-Ḥiwār, 1999.

Sulaymān, Nabīl. *al-musāhama al-riwā'iyya lil-kātiba al- 'arabiyya* [*The Novelistic Contribution the Arabic Female Writer*]. Lataqia: Dār al-Ḥiwār, 2013.

Sulaymān, Nabīl and Bū Ali Yāsīn. *al-Adab wa al-aydīūlūjiyya fī sūriyā: 1968-1973* [*Literature and Ideology in Syria: 1968–1973*]. Beirut: Dār Ibn Khaldūn, 1974.

Svedjedal, Johan, ed. *Litteratursociologi: Texter om litteratur och samhälle* [*Sociology of Literature: Texts about Literature and Society*]. Lund: Studentlitteratur, 2012.

Taqī al-Dīn, Nawāl. *Shams khalfa al-ḍabāb* [*A Sun Behind the Fog*]. Damascus: Dār al-kātib al-'arabī, 1986.

Ṭarābīshī, Jūrj. *Sharq, gharb, rujūla, unūtha* [*East, West, Masculinity, Femininity*]. Beirut: Dār al-Ṭalī'a, 1977.

Thompson, Elizabeth. *Colonial Citizens: Republican Right, Paternal Privilege, and Gender in French Syria and Lebanon*. New York: Columbia University Press, 2001.

Tijani, Ishaq. *Male Domination, Female Revolt: Race, Class, and Gender in Kuwaiti Women's Fiction* Leiden: Brill Academic Publishers, 2009.

Todd, Janet, ed. *Men by Women*. New York: Holmes and Meier, 1981.

Totah, Faedah. 'The Memory Keeper: Gender, Nation and Remembering in Syria' *Journal of Middle Eastern Women's Studies* 9.1 (2013): 1–29.

Travis, Jennifer. *Wounded Hearts: Masculinity, Law, and Literature in American Culture*. Chapel Hill: University of North Carolina Press, 2005.

al-'Udwānī, Ahmad. *Bidāyat al-naṣṣ al-riwā'ī: muqāraba li-'āliyāt tashakkul al-dalāla* [*The Beginning of the Novelistic Text: Approaching the Mechanisms of Formulation of Meaning*]. Casa Blanca: al-nādī al-adabī b-al-riyāḍ wa al-markaz al-thaqāfī al-'arabī, 2011.

al-'Ujaylī, Shahlā. *al-Riwāya al-sūriyya: al-tajriba wa al-maqūlāt al-naẓariyya* [*The Syrian Novel: The Experience and Theoretical Statements*]. Dar al-Farqaan, 2008.

al-'Ujaylī, Shahlā. *al-Khuṣūsiyya al-thaqāfiyya fī al-riwāya al-'arabiyya* [*The Cultural Specificities of the Arabic Novel*]. Dar al-Miṣriyya al-Lubnāniyya, 2011.

'Usfūr, Jābir. *Zaman al-riwāya* [*The Time of the Novel*]. Cairo: al-Hayy'a al-miṣriyya al-'āma lil-kuttāb, 1999.

Vafa, Amirhussein and Rosli Taif. 'Manhood in Crisis: Powerlessness, Homophobia and Violence in "Fightclub"' *Pertanika Journal of Humanities and Social Sciences* 19.2 (2011): 449–57.

Valassopoulos, Anastasia. *Contemporary Arab Women Writers: Cultural Expression in Context*. Abingdon: Routledge, 2007.

Wallace, Diana. 'Ventriloquizing the Male: Two Portraits of the Artist as a Young Man by May Sinclair and Edith Wharton' *Men and Masculinities* 4.4 (2002): 322–33.

Warhol, Robyn. 'Guilty Cravings: What Feminist Narratology can do for Cultural Studies' in *Narratologies: New Perspectives on Narrative Analyses*, edited by David Herman, 340–57. Columbus: Ohio State University Press, 1999.

Watār, Muḥammad Riyāḍ. *Shakhṣiyyat al-muthaqqaf fī al-riwāya al-'arabiyya al-sūriyya* [*The Cultural Character in the Arabic Syrian Novel*]. Damascus: Ittiḥād al-kuttāb al-'arab, 1999.

West, Candace, and Don H Zimmerman. 'Doing Gender' *Gender and Society* 1.2 (1987): 125–51.

Wedeen, Lisa. 'Acting "As If": Symbolic Politics and Social Control in Syria' *Comparative Studies in Society and History* 40.3 (1998): 503–23.

Wedeen, Lisa. '*Ambiguities of Domination: Politics, Rhetoric, and Symbols in Contemporary Syria*. Chicago: University of Chicago Press, 1999.

Weiss, Max. 'Who Laughs Last: Literary Transformations of Syrian Authoritarianism' In *Middle East Authoritarianisms: Governance, Contestation and Regime Resilience in Syria and Iran*, edited by Steven Heydemann and Reinoud Leenders, 143–69. Stanford CA: Stanford University Press, 2013.

Weiss, Max. 'What Lies Beneath: Political Criticism in Recent Syrian Fiction' in *Syria from Reform to Revolt: Culture, Society and Religion*, edited by Christa Salamandra and Leif Stenberg, 16–36. New York: Syracuse University Press, 2015.

Wieland, Carsten. *Syria at Bay: Secularism, Islamism and 'Pax Americana'*. London: C Hurst and Co Ltd, 2006.

al-Yabūrī, Ahmad. *Fī al-riwāya al- 'arabiyya: al-takawwun wa al-ishtighāl* [*On the Arabic Novel: Formulation and Work*]. Casablanca: Sharikat al-nashr wa al-tawzī' wa al-madāris, 2000.

al-Yāfī, Laylā. *Thulūj taḥta al-shams* [*Snow Under the Sun*]. Cairo: Dār al-fikr al- 'arabī, 1961.

Yaqṭīn, Sa'īd. *Taḥlīl al-khiṭāb al-riwā'ī: al-zaman, al-sard al-ta'bīr* [*Analysis of the Novelistic Discourse: The Time, the Narration, the Expression*]. 4th edn, Casablanca: al-Markaz al-thaqāfī al-'arabī, 2005.

Zaatari, Zeina. 'Desirable Masculinity/Femininity and Nostalgia of the Anti-Modern: Bab el-Hara Television Series as a Site of Production' *Sexuality and Culture* 19 (2015): 16–36.

al-Zayyat, Latifa. 'Testimonial of a Creative Woman' in *Opening the Gates: An Anthology of Arab Feminist Writing*, edited by Margot Badran and miriam cooke, 411–16. 2nd edn, Bloomington: Indiana University Press, 2004.

al-Zayn, Hudā. *al-Adab al-nisā'ī al-mu'āṣir fī sūriyā wa lubnān* [*Contemporary Female Fiction in Syria and Lebanon*]. Cairo: al-Hay'a al-Maṣriyya al-'āma lil-kitāb, 2007.

Zeidan, Joseph. *Arab Women Novelists: The Formative Years and Beyond*. Albany: State University of New York Press, 1995.

Zibani, Nadia and Martha Braidy. 'Adolescent Boys' Response to Gender Equitable Programming in Rural Upper Egyptian Villages: Between 'Ayb' and 'Haram" *al-Raida* 104–5 (2004): 64–69.

Zisser, Eyal. 'Clues to the Syrian Puzzle' *The Washington Quarterly* 23.2 (2000): 79–90. 104–5 (2004): 64–69.

Zisser, Eyal. *Commanding Syria: Bashar al-Assad and the First Years in Power*. London: IB Tauris, 2007.

Zuhur, Sherifa. 'Building a Man on Stage: Masculinity, Romance and Performance According to Farid al-Atrash' *Men and Masculinities* 5.3 (2003): 275–94.

Biographical Appendix

'Abbūd, Anīsa (1958–) was born in Jabla in the coastal region of Syria, she studied agricultural engineering at university. She has published short story collections, for example *Ḥina tunza' al-aqni'a* [*When the Masks are Removed*] (1991), poetry collections, for example *Qamīṣ al-as'ila* [The Shirt of Questions] (1999) and novels, among others al-*Na'na' al-barrī* [Wild Mint] (1997) and *Bāb al-ḥīra* [*The Door of Confusion*] (2002).

'Abbūdī, Hanrīyit (nd) has worked as a literary translator. She has published several novels and collections of short stories, among others *al-Ẓahr al-'ārī* [*The Naked Back*] (1996) and *al-Dumiya al-rūsiyya* [*The Russian Doll*] (2005).

Bīṭār, Haifā'(1958–) was born in Latakia. Bīṭār is an ophthalmologist by training and began publishing novels and short stories in addition to her day-time work. She is a very productive writer and among her short story collections are *Wurūd lan tamūt* [*Roses Do Not Die*] (1992) and *Mawt al-baja'a* [*The Death of the Swan*] (1997) and among her novels are *Nasr bi-janāḥ wāḥid* [*A One Winged Eagle*] (1998) and *Afrāḥ ṣaghīra afrāḥ akhīra* [*Small Joys, Final Joys*] (1998).

Darwīsh, Usayma (1939–2017) was born in Damascus and studied Arabic at university. She has published one novel, *Shajarat al-ḥubb –ghābat al-aḥzān* [*Tree of Love – Forest of Sorrows*] (2000) and non-fictional work on literature.

al-Ḥaffār al-Kuzbarī, Salmā (1923–2006) was born in Damascus and studied political science by correspondence. Al-Ḥaffār al-Kuzbarī lived parts of her life in Spain and in Egypt. She was a prolific writer who published novels in addition to biographies, translations, poetry and short stories. Among her novels are *Yawmiyyāt Hāla* [*Haāla's Diary*] (1950) and *'Aynan min Ishbīliya* [*Sevillan Eyes*] (1965) and her short story collections include *Ḥuzn al-ashjār* [*The Sorrows of Trees*] (1986) and *Zawāya* [*Corners*] (1955).

al-Idlibi, Ulfat (1912–2007) was born in Damascus. She began her literary career in 1947 by writing and publishing short stories. In addition to several short story collections, she has published non-fictional work on the history and culture of Damascus and two novels. Among her short story collections are *Qiṣaṣ shāmiyya* (1954) and *Ma wara' al-ashya' al-jamīla* [*What Lies Behind the Pretty Things*] (1993) and her novels are *Dimashq ya baṣmat al-ḥuzn* [*Damascus O Smile of Sadness*] (1980) and *Ḥikayat jaddi* [*My Grandfather's Tale*] (1991).

Jarrāḥ, Amal (1945–2004) was born in Lebanon to Syrian parents, during the war in 1948 the family moved to Syria. Jarrāḥ was a poet and journalist. Her only novel, *al-Riwāya al-Mala'ūna* [*The Naughty Novel*] (1968/2010), was published posthumously in accordance with her wishes. Among her poetry collections are; *Rasā'il imra'a Dimashqiyya* [*Letters of a Damascene Woman*] (1970), *Ṣafṣāfa taktubu ismaha* [*A Willow Writing Its Name*] (1986) and *Imra'a min shama'a wa shams wa qamar* [*A Woman of Wax and Sun and Moon*] (1992).

al-Khānī, Malāḥa (1935–2003) was born in Damascus and worked as a TV presenter and editor. She was a novelist and short story writer and among her publications are *Kayfa nashtarī al-shams?* [*How Do we Buy the Sun?*] (Short Stories, 1978) and the two novels *Khaṭawāt fi al-ḍabāb* [*Steps in the Fog*] (1984) and *Banāt ḥāratina* [*The Girls of Our Neighbourhood*] (1998).

al-Khush, Umayma (1948–2019) was born in Misyaf on the Syrian coast, she has studied, and later taught, Arabic at Damascus University. She writes both novels and short stories and among her published work is *Da'wa' ila al-raqṣ* [*An Invitation to Dance*] (Short Stories, 1991) and the two novels *Zahrat al-Lutūs* [*The Lotus Flower*] (1993) and *al-Tawq* [*Longing*] (1997).

Khūrī, Kūlīt (1936–) was born in Damascus. She has worked as a lecturer at Damascus University and also been politically active. In addition to poetry, short stories and novels she has published biographical work on her grandfather's life and theatre plays. Among her short story collections are; *Dimashq baytī al-kabīr* [*Damascus is My Big Home*] (1969) and *Qiṣṣatan* [*Two Stories*] (1972) and among her novels are *Ayyām ma'ahu* [*Days with Him*] (1959) and *Layla wāḥida* [*One Night*] (1961).

Khūst, Nadya (1935–) was born in Damascus. She studied in Russia and obtained her PhD in comparative literature from Moscow University. She has worked in the media industry and has been active in the preservation of the old city in Damascus. In addition to her fictional work, she has written literary criticism and on identity and culture in the Arab world. Among her short story collections are *Uḥibbu al-Shām* (1967) and *La makān li-l-gharīb* [*No Place for the Stranger*] (1990) and among her novels are *Ḥubb fī bilād al-Shām* [*Love in the Levant*] (1996) and *A'āṣīr fī bilād al-Shām* [*Cyclones in the Levant*] (1998).

Kilānī, Qamar (1932–2011) was born in Damascus. She worked as a teacher both at schools and at the teacher training academy and wrote regularly for the Arabic press. In addition to her fictional works of short stories and novels she has written biographies and on Sufism. Among her short story collections are *'Ālam bi-la ḥudūd* [*A World without Borders*] (1972) and *Ḥulm 'alā jidrān al-sujūn* [*A Dream on Prison Walls*] (1985) and among the novels are *Bustān al-karaz* [*The Cherry Orchard*] (1977) and *al-Dawwāma* [*The Whirlwind*] (1987).

al-Musālima, In'ām (1938–) was born in Dar'a, she studied medicine in Damascus and London and has worked as a surgeon and dentist in Syria. She has published her work in newspapers and magazines and has one novel, *al-Ḥubb wa al-waḥl* [*Love and Mud*] (1963) and one short story collection, *al-Kahf* [*The Cave*] (1973).

Na'na', Ḥamīda (1946–) was born in Idlib, in northern Syria, and completed her university studies in Damascus. Na'na' is a journalist based in Paris and in addition to her two novels, *al-Watan fī al-'aynayn* [*The Homeland in a Pair of Eyes*] (1979) and

Man yajru' 'alā al-shawq [*Who Dares to Long*] (1989), she has published poetry and critical and political works.

Nuwaylātī, Hiyām (1932–1977) was born in Damascus. Nuwaylātī obtained and MA in philosophy from Cairo University. She is mostly known for her numerous poetry collections, but she also published two novels, one in co-operation with Um 'Isām. Among her poetry collections are *al-Qaḍiya* [*The Issue*] (1973), *Madīnat al-salām* [*City of Peace*] (1974) and *Yā Shām* [*O Damascus*] (1977) and her novels are *Fī al-layl* [*At Night*] (1959) and *Arṣifat al-sa'am* [*Sidewalks of Tedium*] (1973).

Qabbānī, Ghāliya (nd) was born in Aleppo. She moved with her family to Kuwait where she completed her university studies, she now lives in London. She is a novelist and short story writer and works in journalism. Among other things she has published a short story collection *Hālunā wa ḥāl hadhā al- 'abd* [*Our Situation and the Situation of this Slave*] (1992) and the novel *Asrār wa akādhīb* [*Secrets and Lies*] (2012).

Qaṣabjī, Ḍiyā'(1939–) was born in Aleppo. She studied law at university then taught Arabic for a while in Algeria before spending time in Saudi Arabia. In addition to her novel *Imra'a fī da'irat al-khauf* [*A Woman in a Circle of Fear*] (1985) she has published a number of short story collections among others *al-'Ālam bayna qawsayn* [*The World between Parentheses*] (1973), *Antum yā man uḥibbukum* [*You Whom I Love*] (1981) and *Thulūj dāfi'a* [*Warm Snow*] (1992).

al-Raḥbī, Mayya (1954–) has a PhD in medicine. She writes on medicine, literature and feminism for Syrian and Arab newspapers. She has published one novel, *Furāt* [*Euphratis*] (1998) and a collection of short stories in 1995.

Rashū, Mārī (1942–) was born in Latakia. She is a productive novelist and among her novels are *Harwala fawqa ṣaqī' Tūlīdū* [*Hurrying of the Frost of Toledo*] (1993) and *al-Ḥubb fī sā 'at ghaḍab* [*Love in a Time of Anger*] (1998). She has also written short stories and her collections include *Wajh wa ughniyya* [*A Face and a Song*] (1989).

al-Sammān, Ghāda (1942–) was born in Damascus. She studied English literature at the university and after her graduation she moved to Lebanon to complete her MA. She lived for a long period of time in Beirut working as a writer and journalist before moving to France and then back to Beirut. Al-Sammān has her own publishing house and has published a large number of publications including poetry, essays, novels and shorts stories. Among her novels are *Bayrūt 75* [*Beirut 75*] (1975), *Kawābīs Bayrūt* [*Beirut Nightmares*] (1976) and *Laylat al-milyār* [*The Night of a Million*] (1986). Her short story collections include *La baḥr fī Bayrūt* [*There is no Sea in Beirut*] (1963) and *al-Qamar al-Murabba'* [*The Square Moon*] (1994).

Taqī al-Dīn, Nawāl (1942–2020) was born in Damascus. She studied philosophy and psychology at Damascus University and worked as a journalist. She published two novels, *Shams khalfa al-ḍabāb* [*A Sun behind the Fog*] (1986) and *Fajr al-Ḥubb* [*The Dawn of Love*] (1995).

Umm 'Isām (Khadija al-Jarraḥ al-Nashawātī) (1923–2000) was born in Damascus. She wrote articles and short stories and TV scripts in addition to a novel together with

Hiyām Nuwaylātī. Among her short story collections are *Dhākir, yā turā?* [*Do you Remember, I Wonder?*] (1960) and *Ilayka* [*To You*] (1970) and her novel is called *Arṣifat al-Sa'am* [*Sidewalks of Tedium*] (1973).

al-Yāfī, Laylā (nd) was born in Damascus. She has published poetry and novels. Her two novels are *Thulūj taḥta al-shams* [*Snow under the Sun*] (1960) and *al-Wāḥa* [*The Oasis*] (1982).

Index

'Aynān min ishbīliya (Sevillan Eyes) (al-Haffar al-Kuzbari) 21, 26–7, 37, 41
A One-Winged Eagle (Nasr bi-janāḥ waḥīd)(Bitar) 96, 103, 106, 109, 112, 119–21
A'āṣīr fī bilād al-shām (Cyclones in the Levant) (Khust) 128, 130, 134–5, 140, 143, 148
Abbaseen Basement, The (Qabw al-'abbāsīn)(Bitar) 79, 85, 87, 90, 91, 116, 118
Abbud, Anisa 76–78, 86, 91, 128, 130
Abbudi, Hanriyit 126, 129–130
Afrāḥ ṣaghīra afrāḥ akhīra (Small Joys, Final Joys) (Bitar) 79, 87, 89, 113
Aghacy, Samira 10, 13, 60–1, 92, 108–9, 114–15
Allen, Roger 15
Arṣifat al-sa'm (Sidewalks of Tedium) (Nuwaylati) 22–3, 27, 31, 33, 42, 46–7
Asad 165
authorisation 37, 80–2, 105, 111
Ayyām ma'ahu (Days with Him) (Khury) 19, 24–9, 42, 46–7

Banāt ḥāratina (Girls of our Neighbourhood)(al-Khani) 122, 135, 136, 142
Bayrūt 75 (Beirut 75) (al-Samman) 95,98, 104, 107, 109, 112–18, 153
Beirut Nightmares (Kawābīs Bayrūt) (al-Samman) 12, 42, 53–4, 57, 64
Bitar, Haifa 16, 32, 79, 81, 85, 96, 116, 118, 129, 139
Bourdieu, Pierre 108, 126
boys 36, 63, 136, 148
burden 102, 108, 139, 162
Bustān al-karaz (The Cherry Orchard) (Kilani) 64, 67–9,73
Butler, Judith 3, 134, 160

characterisation 57–8, 73, 80
Cherry Orchard, The (Bustān al-karaz) (Kilani) 64, 67–9,73
childlessness 117
class 110, 121, 138
Connell, R W 3–5, 24, 26, 41–2, 103,105,110, 128–9, 134, 144, 149, 159–160
cooke, miriam 108
cooking 131, 146, 148
cross writing 96, 100
Cyclones in the Levant (A'āṣīr fī bilād al-shām)(Khust) 128, 130, 134–5, 140, 143, 148

Damascus (Dimashq yā basmat al-ḥuzn) (al-Idlibi) 1,54, 56, 73, 81, 83, 92, 93, 111
Darwish, Usayma 45, 85
al-Dawwāma (The Whirlwind)(Kilani) 59, 60, 64, 67, 70, 71
Days with Him (Ayyām ma'ahu) (Khury) 19, 24–9, 42, 46–7
Diaries of a Divorcing Woman (Yawmiyyāt muṭalliqa)(Bitar) 32, 129, 139, 143
Dimashq yā basmat al-ḥuzn (Damascus) (al-Idlibi) 1,54, 56, 73, 81, 83, 92, 93, 111
division of labour 152
divorce 30, 117, 129, 139
dream masculinity 19

Elsadda, Hoda 2, 59, 61
Eriksson, Helena 25–26, 30
Euphrates (Furāt)(al-Rahbi) 76, 79, 82, 84, 88, 90, 93, 118

family 10, 143–4, 149, 163
father figure 37, 80–6, 143, 164
fatherhood 81, 85, 113, 118
Faysal, Atifa 16–17, 75, 164
al-Faysal, Samar 6, 11,12

fictional society 6
Firat, Alexa 13, 15
Fjelkestam, Kristina 8
focalisation 3,22,54–5, 80, 96, 99, 129
focalisor 54, 96–7, 129
Frantz, Sarah 3, 42
Furāt (Euphrates)(al-Rahbi) 76, 79, 82, 84, 88, 90, 93, 118

Gallagher, Sally 29, 111, 138
gaze, male 43, 96–9
gender
  boundaries 49
  roles 61
gendered bodies 129
Ghannam, Farah 7, 92, 111, 135, 140
Gikandi, Simon 100
Gilmore, David 143
girls 29, 35–6, 43, 120

al-Haffar al-Kuzbari, Salma 13, 15, 19, 21
Halberstam, Judith 132–3
Hanna, Kifah 17, 95
Harwala fawqa ṣaqīʿ tūlīdū (Hurrying over the Frost of Toledo)(Rashu) 79, 87, 90
hegemonic femininity 41
ḥikāyat jaddī (My Grandfather's Tale) (al-Idlibi) 78
Hill, Helena 8
Homeland in a Pair of Eyes, The (al-Waṭan fī al-ʿaynayn) (Na'na') 12, 53, 56, 59,60, 63,66, 68
homosexuality 103–5
Horlacher, Stefan 6, 7, 136
Ḥubb fī bilād al-shām (Love in the Levant) (Khust) 78
al-ḥubb wa al-waḥl (Love and Mud) (al-Musalima) 21,23, 26–7, 31–6, 43, 46, 161
Hurrying over the Frost of Toledo (Harwala fawqa ṣaqīʿ tūlīdū)(Rashu) 79, 87, 90
husband 20, 24–5, 30,35, 147, 157, 172

al-'Id, Yumna 10
ideology 51
al-Idlibi, Ulfat 81, 111, 116
Imra'a fī dā'irat al-khawf (Woman in a Circle of Fear)(Qasabji) 77, 85, 91
Inhorn, Marcia 105, 113

Jacob, Wilson Chacko 58
Jarrah, Amal 21, 31, 38
Joubin, Rebecca 85
al-Jurf, Maysun 2, 9, 37, 76, 92

Kandiyoti, Deniz 28, 62, 136
Kawābīs Bayrūt (Beirut Nightmares) (al-Samman) 12, 42, 53–4, 57, 64
al-Khani, Malaha 78, 124, 128, 135
Khaṭawāt fī al-ḍabāb (Steps in the Fog) (al-Khani) 83, 110, 128, 130, 133, 138–40, 143–6
Khury, Colette 12–13, 15, 19, 23
al-Khush, Umayma 76, 80
Khust, Nadya 9,12,45, 59, 77–8, 128, 149
Kilani, Qamar 12, 16, 53–54, 58, 60, 73
Kimmel, Michael 3, 7, 105, 107

labour division 146
Lanser, Susan 4,32
laws
  impact of 8, 139
Layla wāḥida (One Night) (Khury) 20, 29–31, 36, 40–1
Longing (al-Tawq)(al-Khush) 79, 86, 90
Love and Mud (al-Ḥubb wa al-waḥl) (al-Musalima) 21,23, 26–7, 31–6, 43, 46, 161
Love in the Levant (Ḥubb fī bilād al-shām) (Khust) 78

male femininity 132
Man yajru' 'alā al-shawq (Who Dares to Long) (Na'na') 12, 53, 55, 59, 63
man
  political 65, 161
  new 59–61, 66
  revolutionary 73
marginalisation 105–6, 111, 153
marginalised 95, 105, 150, 161, 164
marriage 24, 29–30, 41, 46, 66, 88
Martyrs and Lovers in the Levant (Shuhadā' wa 'ushshāq fī bilād al-shām)(Khust) 45, 78
Marxism 13

masculinity
female 132
hegemonic 8, 24–6, 34–5, 39, 46–7, 58, 61, 70–2, 78, 80, 89, 93, 98, 103–9, 111, 114, 118, 124,133, 149, 153–5, 159
ideal 59, 107
studies, 107, 136, 160, 163
subordinate 103–6, 109, 139, 161–2, 5, 95
unstable 77, 108–9
Massad, Joseph 104–5
mother 1,7,20–1, 28, 68, 79, 90
Mulvey, Laura 97
Murphy, Peter 6
Musalima, Im'am 21,23, 99
My Grandfather's Tale (Ḥikāyat jaddī) (al-Idlibi) 78

al-Na'na' al-barrī (Wild Mint) (Abbud) 77, 157, 86, 91, 107, 110, 114, 130, 150
Naked Back, The (al-Ẓahr al-'ārī)(Abbudi) 96, 101,129,132, 147, 151
Na'na', Hamida 12, 16, 53, 56, 59, 60, 67
narratology 4,22
Nasr bi-janāḥ waḥīd (A One-Winged Eagle)(Bitar) 96, 103, 106, 109, 112, 119–21
Nilsson, Bo 125, 137
Nordberg, Marie 7, 132
novel, Syrian 13, 15, 17, 76, 165
Nuwaylati, Hiam 13, 22

One Night (Layla wāḥida) (Khury) 20, 29–31, 36, 40–1

patriarchal
bargain 28
dividend 28, 83, 93–4, 173 n
perspective, female 54
problematic masculinity 17, 74, 77, 90–1, 95, 107, 123, 160–1
protection 38, 70, 86, 91, 93, 161
provision 9, 26, 36, 63, 83, 115, 118, 121, 126, 158

Qabbani, Ghalia 12, 76, 79, 99
Qabw al-'abbāsīn (The Abbaseen Basement) (Bitar) 79, 85, 87, 90, 91, 116, 118
al-Qadi, Iman 14, 16, 51, 76
Qasabji, Diya 77, 91

al-Rahbi, Mayya 79, 139
Rashu, Mari 78–9, 87
regime
Ba'th 11, 22
gender 2, 7, 138, 145, 154 - 5, 160, 162
Rennhak, Katharina 3, 42
rites of passage 136
al-Riwāya al-mal'ūna (The Cursed Novel) (Jarrah) 21,26,31, 38, 46, 48
al-Riwāya al-mustaḥīla (The Impossible Novel) (al-Samman) 99, 128, 129, 131, 134, 136, 139, 142
rujula 26 – 7

Ṣabāḥ Imra'a (A Woman's Morning) (Qabbani) 12, 76, 79, 87, 99
Sakakini, Widad 15, 19
al-Samman, Ghada 12, 16, 42, 53, 57, 59, 84, 95, 99,128
al-Samman, Hanadi 78
Schoene-Harwood, Berthold 100
Sevillan Eyes ('Aynān min ishbīliya) (al-Haffar al-Kuzbari) 21, 26–7, 37, 41
Shajarat al-ḥubb - ghābat al-aḥzān (Tree of Love – Forest of Sadness)(Darwish) 45, 87
Shams khalfa al-ḍabāb (A Sun behind the Fog) (Taqi al-Din) 88
Shuhadā' wa 'ushshāq fī bilād al-shām (Martyrs and Lovers in the Levant) (Khust) 45, 78
Sidewalks of Tedium (Arṣifat al-sa'm) (Nuwaylati, Umm 'Isam) 22–3, 27, 31, 33, 42, 46–7
Small Joys, Final Joys (Afrāḥ ṣaghīra afrāḥ akhīra)(Bitar) 79, 87, 89, 113
Snow under the Sun (Thulūj taḥta al-shams) (al-Yafi) 12, 20, 26–7,37,49, 125
social critique 34, 47, 52, 75, 77, 82, 95, 97, 155
social realism 6,11,13, 15, 165
socialism 10, 13, 165, 172n
society 32, 162–3

son 131, 136–7, 143
Steps in the Fog (Khaṭawāt fī al-ḍabāb) (al-Khani) 83, 110, 128, 130, 133, 138–40, 143–6
Sulayman, Nabil 13
Sun behind the Fog, A (Shams khalfa al-ḍabāb)(Taqi al-Din) 88

Taqi al Din, Nawal 88
Tarabishi, Jurj 5
al-Tawq (Longing) (al-Khush) 79, 86, 90
The Cursed Novel (al-Riwāya al-mal'ūna) (Jarrah) 21,26,31, 38, 46, 48
The Girls of our Neighbourhood (Banāt ḥāratina)(al-Khani) 122, 135, 136, 142
The Impossible Novel (al-Riwāya al-mustaḥīla)(al-Samman) 99, 128, 129, 131, 134, 136, 139, 142
Thulūj taḥta al-shams (Snow under the Sun) (al-Yafi) 12, 20, 26–7,37, 49, 125
Tjeder, David 8
Tree of Love – Forest of Sadness (Shajarat al-ḥubb - ghābat al-aḥzān) (Darwish) 45, 87

violence 90, 109, 122–5, 162
virility 60, 92, 98, 104–5, 113–14, 116–7, 140

Warhol, Robyn 4
al-Waṭan fī al-'aynayn (The Homeland in a Pair of Eyes) (Na'na') 12, 53, 56, 59,60, 63,66, 68
Wedeen, Lisa 81, 164, 173
Weiss, Max 165, 185 n
Whirlwind, The (al-Dawwāma)(Kilani) 59, 60, 64, 67, 70, 71
Who Dares to Long (Man yajru' 'alā al-shawq)(Na'na') 12, 53, 55, 59, 63
Wild Mint (al-Na'na' al-barrī)(Abbud) 77, 157, 86, 91, 107, 110, 114, 130, 150
Woman in a Circle of Fear (Imra'a fī dā'irat al-khawf)(Qasabji) 77, 85, 91
Woman's Morning, A (Ṣabāḥ Imra'a) (Qabbani) 12, 76, 79, 87, 99

al-Yafi, Laila 12, 20, 37–38
Yawmiyyāt muṭalliqa (Diaries of a Divorcing Woman)(Bitar) 32, 129, 139, 143

al-Ẓahr al-'ārī (The Naked Back) (Abbudi) 96, 101,129,132, 147, 151

www.ingramcontent.com/pod-product-compliance
Lightning Source LLC
Chambersburg PA
CBHW062225300426
44115CB00012BA/2221
9780755637669